Shortcut Keys for the Mouse-Challenged

Task	Keyboard Shortcut	Task	Keyboard Shortcut
Add a new contact or group	Insert	Move the selected object to the front	Ctrl+F
Add a sales opportunity for the current contact	Ctrl+F11	Open a new file or database	Ctrl+N
Attach a file to a contact, group, activity, or e-mail message	Ctrl+I	Open an existing file or database	Ctrl+O
Check spelling in a note	Alt+F7	Paste the items or text last cut or copied	Ctrl+V
Clear an activity	Ctrl+D	Print formatted contact information or calendars	Ctrl+P
Clear a field when replacing the field contents by inserting a null value (<< >>) for a search	Ctrl+F5	Record or stop recording a macro	Alt+F5
		Return to the Contacts view	F11
Close a menu or dialog box	Esc	Run a query (Query window only)	Ctrl+R
Close the current file or database	Ctrl+W	Save the current file or database	Ctrl+S
Copy the selected items or text	Ctrl+C	Schedule a call	Ctrl+L
Create a copy of the database	F12	Schedule a meeting	Ctrl+M
Create a history	Ctrl+H	Schedule a to-do	Ctrl+T
Create a note	F9	Switch between open windows	Ctrl+F6
Cut the selected items or text	Ctrl+X	Switch between the timer and the current window	Alt+F6
Delete a contact	Ctrl+Delete	Switch to List view	F6
Delete the character to the left of the pointer	Backspace	Switch to the previous layout	F8
Delete the character to the right of the pointer	Delete	Undo the last action	Ctrl+Z
Display the timer	Shift+F4	View the Activities tab	Alt+F9
Edit the drop-down list of the current field	F2	View the Groups tab	Ctrl+F9
		View the Groups window	F10
Exit ACT!	Alt+F4	View the monthly calendar	F5
Help	F1	View the Notes/History tab	Shift+F9
Launch SideACT!	Ctrl+Q	View the Task list	F7
Mini calendars	F4	View the weekly calendar	F3
Move the selected object to the back	Ctrl+B		

ACT!® 6 For Dummies®

Selecting a Continuous List of Names in the Contact List

1. Click the first name in the list that you want to select.
2. Press and hold down the Shift key.
3. Click the last name in the list that you want to select.

Selecting Multiple Names in the Contact List

1. Click the first name that you want to select.
2. Press and hold down the Ctrl key.
3. Click the next name that you want to select.
4. Continue selecting names while holding down the Ctrl key.

A Handy Tool Palette

Whether you're designing a label (Chapter 9), report (Chapter 11), or layout (Chapter 15), here's a tool palette that you'll see often. Become familiar with its tools!

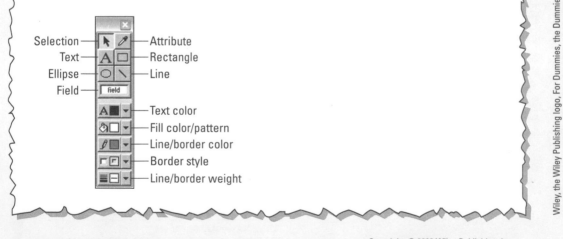

Selection — Attribute
Text — Rectangle
Ellipse — Line
Field —
— Text color
— Fill color/pattern
— Line/border color
— Border style
— Line/border weight

For Dummies: Bestselling Book Series for Beginners

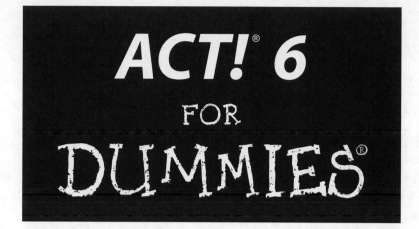

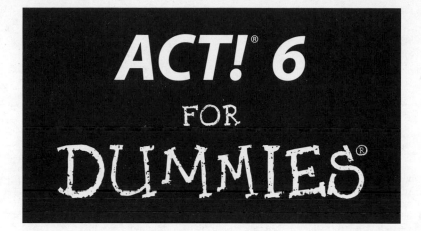

ACT!® 6 FOR DUMMIES®

by Karen S. Fredricks

ACT! Certified Consultant, ACT! Premier Trainer,
and Founder of the ACT! Users Group of South Florida

Wiley Publishing, Inc.

ACT!® 6 For Dummies®

Published by
Wiley Publishing, Inc.
909 Third Avenue
New York, NY 10022

www.wiley.com

 is a trademark of Wiley Publishing, Inc.

About the Author

Karen S. Fredricks began her life rather non-technically growing up in Kenya. She attended high school in Beirut, Lebanon — where she developed her sense of humor while dodging bombs. After traveling all over the world, Karen ended up at the University of Florida and has since been an ardent Gator fan. In addition to undergraduate studies in English and accounting, Karen has a Master's degree in psycholinguistics. Beginning her career teaching high school English and theatre, Karen switched to working with the PC at its inception in the early '80s — and has worked as a full-time computer consultant and trainer ever since.

Karen is an ACT! Certified Consultant, an ACT! Premier Trainer, and a QuickBooks Premier Certified Advisor. She is the author of many training manuals and a contributor to numerous newsletters. A true ACT! FanACTic, she founded the ACT! Users Group of South Florida and served as the official host for the ACT! 6 Launch Tour in Florida.

Karen resides in Boca Raton, Florida, with her long-suffering husband Gordon, over-achieving daughters Andrea and Alyssa, and her little white dog Carolina. Her company, Tech Benders, provides computer consulting, support, and training services. In her spare time, Karen loves to play tennis and write schlocky poetry. Feel free to send your comments about the book to Dummies@techbenders.com.

Dedication

In loving memory of Betsy Fredricks Levine (1959–2000).

I know you're still making friends out of strangers and asking questions along the way. We miss you!

Author's Acknowledgments

I have been blessed with so many wonderful people in my life that I hardly know where to begin.

The people at Wiley Publishing have been the greatest to work with and have made writing this book a true pleasure! Special thanks to my Acquisitions Editor, Terri Varveris, for discovering and having faith in me. Thanks for going that extra mile, Terri!

Nicole Sholly, my Project Editor, has a great eye for detail, wonderful insight, and a knack for pulling everything together. Her comments were always constructive, right on target, and presented in a truly supportive fashion. Nicole wore two hats and doubled as my Copy Editor, so I hope she got paid twice for this project!

My Technical Editor, Clifford Roberts, gives new meaning to the term *CliffsNotes*. It was wonderful working with someone who is a walking encyclopedia of ACT! and a technology buff extraordinaire. Cliff — thanks for taking time out of your overly busy schedule to help me!

Thanks also to the entire ACT! Certified Consultant community for their willingness to share and to Best, CRM for their continuing support. Susan Clark — you are one class ACT!; Lon Orenstein and Steve McCandlish — you are my idols among ACT! Certified Consultants!; Melissa and Ted — thanks for all your effort and hard work.

I'd like to also thank my marketing guru, Norma Wolpin, who qualifies as a true ACT! FanACTic — even if her coffee skills are no better than mine! Hugs go to Cecelia Alvarez, my wonderful assistant and ACT! Certified Consultant, for being my right hand — and for letting me steal her terrific layouts! Special greetings go out to my Wednesday, Saturday, and Sunday games at the Swim and Racquet Center of Boca Raton and to the CLAWS of Boca for your continuing support, love, and friendship. You guys rock!

When I grow up, I want to be just like my mom and dad! Mom is 87, has fewer senior moments than I do, volunteers at church several times a week, and has one of the most active social lives in South Florida. At 83, Papa Carl plays tennis, takes his boat out on Coast Guard patrols, and still does tax returns. You two are inspirational!

Words can't describe how special my daughters are to me. You have brought such joy to my life and are a constant source of pride and support. Love and thanks go out to "Dr." Andrea Fredricks and the very theatrical Alyssa Fredricks for putting up with my lack of presence over the last few months. Although we have all pursued very different paths in life, the three Fredricks women all share a single-minded devotion and dedication to the things — and people — we love!

And finally Gordon, my best friend, husband, and partner, deserves special recognition for being the #1 Dummy in my life — and I mean that in only the best of ways! He proofread, stapled, offered suggestions, and kept me supplied with red licorice as I typed away. He's also remained relatively sane despite living with his Type A wife for the past 27 years. T.B., I know you're now capable of writing *Grocery Shopping For Dummies*. I couldn't have done it without your help. I love you!

Publisher's Acknowledgments

We're proud of this book; please send us your comments through our online registration form located at www.dummies.com/register/.

Some of the people who helped bring this book to market include the following:

Acquisitions, Editorial, and Media Development

Associate Project Editor: Nicole Sholly

Acquisitions Editor: Terri Varveris

Copy Editor: Nicole Sholly

Technical Editor: Clifford Roberts

Editorial Manager: Kevin Kirschner

Media Development Manager: Laura VanWinkle

Media Development Supervisor: Richard Graves

Editorial Assistant: Amanda Foxworth

Cartoons: Rich Tennant (www.the5thwave.com)

Production

Project Coordinator: Dale White

Layout and Graphics: Carrie Foster, LeAndra Johnson, Stephanie D. Jumper, Michael Kruzil, Tiffany Muth, Janet Seib, Jeremey Unger

Proofreaders: John Tyler Connoley, John Greenough, Andy Hollandbeck

Indexer: TECHBOOKS Production Services

Publishing and Editorial for Technology Dummies

Richard Swadley, Vice President and Executive Group Publisher

Andy Cummings, Vice President and Publisher

Mary C. Corder, Editorial Director

Publishing for Consumer Dummies

Diane Graves Steele, Vice President and Publisher

Joyce Pepple, Acquisitions Director

Composition Services

Gerry Fahey, Vice President of Production Services

Debbie Stailey, Director of Composition Services

Contents at a Glance

Table of Contents

Introduction

• •

ACT! is the best-selling contact manager that's used by more than 4 million professionals and 11,000 corporations worldwide. For many of these users, ACT! represents their first foray into the area of contact relationship management (CRM). Contact management software is a little more complex to understand than other types of software. With a word processor, each document that you create is totally separate; if you make a mistake, you need only to delete your current document and start fresh. Contact management, however, builds its way into a final product; if you don't give a bit of thought as to what goal you wish to achieve, you could end up with a muddled mess.

I am a *fanACTic*. I'm not ashamed to admit it. I use ACT! at work. I use ACT! on the road. I use ACT! at home. I've even inspired my husband to use ACT!. I'm excited about the product and know that by the time you learn to unleash the power of ACT!, you'll be excited, too.

So what am I so excited about? I've seen firsthand how ACT! can save you time and help make you more efficient in the bargain. To me, accomplishing more in less time is an exciting thought — it allows more time for the fun things in life. Best of all, ACT! is a program that's very easy to master in a very short time. You'll be amazed not only at how quickly you can set up a database but also at how easily you can put that database to work.

Maybe by the time you finish this book, you, too, will have become a fanACTic!

About This Book

ACT! 6 For Dummies is a reference book. As such, each chapter can be read independently and in the order you want. Each chapter focuses on a specific topic, so you can dive right in, heading right for the chapter that interests you most. Having said that, however, I must say that I've tried to put the chapters into a logical sequence so that those of you who are new to ACT! can just follow the bouncing ball from chapter to chapter. More experienced users can use the Table of Contents and the index to simply navigate from topic to topic as needed.

Essentially, this book is a nuts-and-bolts how-to guide for accomplishing various tasks. In addition, drawing on many of my own experiences as a full-time ACT! consultant and trainer, I've included specific situations that should give you a feeling for the full power of ACT!.

Conventions Used in This Book

Like in most Windows-based software programs, you often have several different ways to accomplish a task in ACT!.

For the most part, I show you ways to perform a function by using the ACT! menus. When an instruction reads "Choose File⇨Open," you must access the File menu (located at the top of the ACT! screen) by clicking it with the left mouse button and then choosing the Open option from the subsequent menu that appears. In most cases, you can access these commands from anywhere within ACT!, although I generally advise new ACT! users to always start a task from the Contacts view. If you must be in a particular area to complete a task otherwise, I'll be sure to tell you where.

I'll also present you with shortcuts here and there. Generally, ACT! shortcuts are triggered by simultaneously pressing the Ctrl key and another key on the keyboard. For instance, the shortcut for deleting a contact is Ctrl+Delete. See the Cheat Sheet for a listing of these shortcuts.

At times, you'll need to access one of ACT!'s hidden menus, which you do by clicking an appropriate area of the screen with the right mouse button and then choosing from the menu that appears. In these instances, I simply say "right-click" when you need to right-click.

What You Should Read

Of course I'm hoping that you're going to sit down and read this entire book from cover to cover. But then again, this isn't the Great American Novel. And, come to think of it, the whole reason why you bought this book in the first place is because you want to get your ACT! together (no groans, please!) as quickly as possible because you're probably finding yourself with too much to do and too little time to do it in.

For the time being, I'm going to let you get away with just reading the parts that interest you most. I'll let you read the last chapter first and the first chapter last if you'd like because this book is designed to allow you to read each chapter independently. However, when you find yourself floating in a swimming pool, soaking up the sun and wondering what to do with all your spare time, you might want to go back and read some of those chapters you skipped. You just might discover something!

What You Don't Have to Read

This book is intended for both new and existing ACT! users. Most of the instructions apply to both groups of readers. Once in a while, I include some information that might be of special interest to more advanced readers. Newbies, feel free to skip these sections! Also, any information tagged with a Technical Stuff icon is there for the truly technically inclined. Everyone else can just skip this info.

Foolish Assumptions

One of my least favorite words in the English language is the word *assume*, but I've got to admit that I've made a few foolish — albeit necessary — assumptions when writing this book. First of all, I've assumed that you own a computer and that ACT! has been installed on it. Secondly, I assume that you have a basic knowledge of how to use your computer, keyboard, and mouse, and that ACT! isn't the very first application that you're trying to master.

I've also assumed that you have a genuine desire to organize your life and/or business and have determined that ACT! is the way to go.

Finally (and I feel quite comfortable with this assumption), I assume that you'll grow to love ACT! as much as I do.

How This Book Is Organized

I've organized this book into six parts. Each part contains several chapters covering related topics. Following is a brief description of each part, with chapter references directing you where to go for particular information:

Part I: The Opening ACT!

In Part I, you get an introduction to the concept of a database and why ACT! has become such a popular choice of database users (Chapter 1). In this part, you'll read about what to expect the first time you fire up ACT! (Chapter 2) and how to set the main preferences in ACT! (Chapter 3).

Part II: Putting the ACT! Database to Work

Part II focuses on putting your contacts into ACT! (Chapter 4) and, more importantly, how to find them again (Chapters 5 and 6). I show you how to view all the details about one contact, how to pull up a list of all your contacts, and even how to create an easy list report.

After you've mastered organizing your contact information, Part II helps you organize your day. ACT! makes it easy to take notes (Chapter 7) and to schedule appointments, calls, and to-dos — all while keeping you informed about the important events in your life. Part II also gives you a peek at the daily, weekly, and monthly calendars (Chapter 8).

Part III: Sharing Your Information with Others

Corporate America lives for reports, and ACT! is up to the challenge. Whether you want to print labels or telephone directories on commercially printed forms (Chapter 9) or prefer to utilize the ACT! built-in reports (Chapter 10), Part III shows you how. I even tell you about building your own reports from scratch (Chapter 11).

One of the best features of ACT! is the ability to communicate easily with the outside world (Chapter 12). Part III shows you how to work with templates to automate routine documents as well as how to send out mass mail merges — whether by snail mail, fax, or e-mail (Chapter 13).

Part IV: Advanced ACT!ing

Another great thing about ACT! is that you can customize it. ACT! is just an over-the-counter piece of software, but by adding fields (Chapter 14) and placing them on customized layouts (Chapter 15), you can make it perform as well as an expensive piece of proprietary software.

The old adage, "If it ain't broke, don't fix it!" does not apply to ACT!. So in this part, I show you how to maintain your database to achieve optimal performance (Chapter 16) and prepare you for when disaster strikes (Chapter 17).

Part V: Commonly Overlooked ACT! Features

Part V focuses on four of the most overlooked ACT! features:

- ✔ **The built-in Internet browser:** I show you how to integrate the Internet with ACT! (Chapter 18).
- ✔ **Sales Opportunities:** Track your prospective sales, prioritize them, and analyze what you did right — or wrong — in making the sale (Chapter 19).
- ✔ **The Group feature:** Group your contacts together to add a new dimension to your database (Chapter 20).
- ✔ **The Library tab:** This is an exciting new feature of ACT! 6. The Library tab enables you to view and edit files that were created in other applications (Chapter 21).

Part VI: The Part of Tens

With apologies to David Letterman, you'll have three of my favorite ACT! lists. First, in Chapter 22, I list the top ten best new features in ACT! 6 (for anyone who has used previous versions of ACT!). In Chapter 23, I give you ten of my favorite ways to customize your layouts. Finally, Chapter 24 supplies you with the names of ten ACT! add-on products that I particularly like. These add-ons can help you to further increase your productivity level.

Icons Used in This Book

The Tip icon indicates a special timesaving tip or a related thought that might help you use ACT! to its full advantage. Try it; you might like it!

The Warning icon alerts you to the danger of proceeding without caution. *Do not* attempt to try doing anything that you are warned *not* to do!

The Remember icon alerts you to important pieces of information that you won't want to forget.

The Technical Stuff icon indicates tidbits of advanced knowledge that might be of interest to IT specialists but might just bore the heck out of the average reader. Skip these at will.

Where to Go from Here

For those of you who are ACT! old-timers, you might want to at least skim the entire contents of this book before hunkering down to read the sections that seem the most relevant to you. My experience is that the average ACT! user is probably only using a portion of the program and might not even be aware of some of the really cool features of ACT!. You might be surprised to discover all that ACT! has to offer!

For the ACT! newbie, I recommend heading straight for Part I, where you can acquaint yourself with ACT! before moving on to other parts of the book and of the ACT! program.

Part I
The Opening ACT!

The 5th Wave
By Rich Tennant

"We can monitor our entire operation from one central location. We know what the 'Wax Lips' people are doing; we know what the 'Whoopee Cushion' people are doing; we know what the 'Fly-in-the-Ice Cube' people are doing. But we don't know what the 'Plastic Vomit' people are doing. We don't want to know what the 'Plastic Vomit' people are doing."

In this part . . .

You're excited about all the possibilities that ACT! has to offer and want to dive into the program as soon as possible. Here's where you'll find an overview of some of the cool features that you'll find in ACT!. You'll also become familiar with the many faces of ACT!; after all, you wouldn't want to get lost along the way. But first you have to do a bit of homework and whip ACT! into shape by fiddling with a few preference settings to ensure that ACT! will produce the type of results that you're looking for.

Chapter 1

An Overview of ACT!

So what is ACT!, anyway? I find that one of the hardest things that I have to do with ACT! is to explain exactly what it is. I like to initially explain ACT! by using very politically correct terminology. For example, ACT! 6.0

✔ Is a Customer Relationship Management (CRM) Software Package

✔ Provides users and organizations with powerful tools to manage their business relationships

✔ Is a packaged software product that can be customized based on your company's requirements

✔ Is the world's leading CRM software

Feel free to use these points to impress your friends. If, after telling all this to your friends and they look at you rather blankly, at least you know that your knowledge of computing is equal to — if not greater than — theirs. At that point, you might want to list some of the wonderful features of ACT!, which I do in the first section of this chapter. I also describe the typical ACT! user and give you a brief primer on some pertinent ACT! terminology. Finally, I end the chapter with a few ground rules that I've established over the years. I've watched new users wrestle with certain aspects of using ACT!, and I want to save you the trouble.

And then there was ACT!

Once upon a time, before the advent of the personal computer, busy people everywhere were forced to rely on such archaic tools as Day Timers and yellow sticky notes to keep themselves organized. You could easily spot busy people; they could be identified by the various bits of paper that trailed after them when they rushed frantically from appointment to appointment. You would also notice that these busy people were generally late to their appointments. You would often see busy people crying and/or mumbling to themselves. Busy people, you see, often scheduled conflicting appointments because they had failed to compare the schedule hanging on the refrigerator at home with the one that they carried in their somewhat disorganized briefcase. Divorce rates were high because busy people missed anniversaries and soccer games!

Pat Sullivan was a busy person. Sullivan, a salesman, came to the conclusion that it was actually more fun to play than it was to work. And, if he could organize his work life, he'd have more time for his personal one. He began to manually track his prospects, customers, and all the related data. Then, in 1985, Pat Sullivan created the first electronic contact manager: ACT!. What began as a side project quickly blossomed into a full-fledged business with over 3.2 million users.

What Does ACT! Do?

Using ACT! allows me to have more free time — which means that I have more playtime. Because I want you to enjoy the benefits of using ACT!, I've put together a little shopping list of features so that you can see all that ACT! can do for you, too. In parentheses after each item, I've included a chapter reference where you can find more information about a particular feature (if you're so inclined).

ACT! is a multifaceted personal management tool that

- Stores complete contact information, including name, company, phone numbers, mailing addresses, and e-mail addresses. (Chapter 4)

- Comes with 70 predefined fields for each contact that you add to your database. If you want to add new ones to meet your specific needs, go right ahead. (Chapter 14)

- Records an unlimited number of dated notes for each of your contacts so that you can easily keep track of important conversations and activities. This is particularly useful for those of us who, unlike our friend the elephant, do forget things on occasion. (Chapter 7)

✔ Keeps more than a boring old calendar. Your scheduled activities are cross-referenced with the appropriate contact so that you have a full record of all interactions that you have had — or will have — with that contact. In addition, you can set an alarm to remind you of the important stuff, and roll over the less important things until the next day. (Chapter 8)

✔ Prints out anything from simple phone lists, address books, or labels to detailed reports on activities, notes, leads, and sales opportunities. You can print reports of your reports if you feel so inclined. (Chapters 9, 10, and 11)

✔ Enables you to attach a Web page to any contact that can be referenced again later, even if the Web page has been changed or removed from the Internet. (Chapter 18)

✔ Creates mailing labels and envelopes. Or, if you prefer, perform broadcast faxes and e-mails with ACT!. (Chapters 9 and 12)

✔ Manages your sales pipeline with built-in forecasting tools. If you're so inclined, print a few sales reports — or create a graph showing your open, won, or lost sales. (Chapter 19)

✔ Synchronizes with virtually any handheld device so that you can enter — or view — information from either your personal digital assistant (PDA) or from ACT!. (Chapter 24)

✔ Integrates with QuickBooks and other accounting software to avoid double entry between your accounting and database software programs. (Chapter 24)

The Typical ACT! User

So just who is the typical ACT! user? Well, with more than 3.2 million users and 11,000 businesses currently using ACT!, you are safe to assume that nearly every industry is represented among its user base. Although ACT! started as primarily a tool for salespeople wanting to follow up on their prospects and customers, ACT! has evolved into a tool used by any individual or business trying to organize the chaos of daily life.

I think it's only fair to warn you about one of the possible side effects that you might develop if you use ACT!. If you're anything like me, you'll become addicted to ACT! and eventually use it to manage all facets of your busy existence. You might just become a fanACTic. Quite simply, a *fanACTic* is an ACT! user who has become addicted to using ACT!.

So just who is using ACT!? Everyone.

- ✔ The CEO uses ACT! because he wants to know what his salespeople are doing and how his customers are being treated.

- ✔ The administrative assistant is using it to automate routine tasks and to keep a schedule of various tasks and activities.

- ✔ A salesperson is using ACT! to make sure that she's following up on all her prospects.

- ✔ The disorganized person finds that using ACT! will help him to become more organized.

- ✔ The smart person uses ACT! because she knows that she'll have more time to play by working more efficiently.

- ✔ The lazy person uses ACT! because he knows it's more fun to play than to work.

So what kinds of businesses use ACT!? All kinds.

- ✔ Large businesses that want to improve communication among their employees

- ✔ Small businesses that have to rely on a small staff to complete a multitude of tasks

- ✔ Businesses of all sizes that are looking for software that will automate their businesses and make them more productive in less time

So who's *not* using ACT!? Okay, I just said that simply *everyone* is using ACT!, but a few stubborn folks remain out there who aren't looking to organize their lives, such as

- ✔ Workaholics who live to spend every waking moment at work

- ✔ People who don't use even a paper address book to keep track of their contacts

- ✔ Hermits who don't need to schedule any appointments or remember to make follow-up phone calls

- ✔ Individuals with photographic memories who retain all information and never need to take a note

- ✔ Companies that require no paperwork

- ✔ Businesses that do no marketing or that have no interest in expanding their customer base

Terms You Need to Know

Nobody likes technical jargon, but while I show you how to use ACT!, I'll be using a handful of somewhat technical terms; it just can't be avoided. It might be less painful in the long run to just become familiar with them now.

ACT! is a database program. A *database* is a collection of information organized in such a way that the user of the database can quickly find desired pieces of information. You might want to think of a database as an electronic filing system. Although most ACT! users create a database of contacts, some users develop ACT! databases to collect information about things other than contacts. For example, you might create an ACT! database to catalog all the CDs and DVDs in your collection.

Traditional databases are organized by *fields*, *records*, and *files*.

A *field* is a single piece of information. In databases, fields are the smallest units of information. A tax form, for example, contains a number of fields: one for your name, one for your Social Security number, one for your income, and so on. In ACT!, you start with 70 separate fields for each individual contact. You'll find out more than you ever wanted to know about fields in Chapter 4. In Chapter 14, I show you how to change the attributes of these fields and how to add new ones if you're the database administrator.

A *record* is one complete set of fields. In ACT!, all the information that you collect that pertains to one individual contact is a *contact record*.

A *file* is the entire collection of data or information. Each database that you create in ACT! will be given a unique filename; creating more than one file or database in ACT! is possible — head to Chapter 3 to find out how.

The Basic ACT! Ground Rules

Sometimes you just need to learn things the hard way. After all, experience is the best teacher. Luckily for you, however, I've compiled a list of Do's and Don'ts based on a few of the mistakes that I've seen other ACT! users commit. You're not going to find these rules written down anywhere else. And they might not even make a whole lot of sense to you at the moment. But as you become more and more familiar with ACT!, these rules will make all the sense in the world. You might even want to refer to them from time to time.

Karen's Three Rules of Never:

- ✔ Never use the drop-down arrow next to the Company field to try to find another contact.
- ✔ Never change a field or drop-down list without first consulting mutual users of your database.
- ✔ Never change your synchronization settings if your database is set to synchronize with another database.

Karen's Three Rules of Always:

- ✔ Always log in to ACT! as yourself.
- ✔ Always strive for standardization in your database.
- ✔ Always compress and reindex and perform a backup of your database at least once a week!

Chapter 2

The Various Faces of ACT!

After getting the hang of maneuvering in ACT!, you'll find that's it's an amazingly easy program to master. The key is to learn a little bit about the lay of the land *before* you start building your contact database. By doing so, you avoid playing hide-and-seek *later*. To that end, I show you how to log into and open an ACT! database. Although initially getting around in ACT! is pretty easy, you might become lost in the maze of views and tabs that ACT! is divided into. I help you navigate through that maze by taking you on a tour of ACT! so that you can become familiar with the various ACT! screens. Finally, you'll discover the places that you can turn to if you need additional help.

Locating the Correct Database

When you open ACT!, by default ACT! opens up the database that was last open on your computer. Easy enough, huh? If, however, you stumble into the incorrect database by mistake, you'll need to know how to find the correct one. If you're lucky enough to have inherited a database that someone else developed (someone who maybe even placed that database on your computer for you), be sure to ask where that database is located — before that person walks out of your life.

In Chapter 3, I show you how to change the *default database location*; that's the place on your computer that ACT! uses to store any new databases that you create and look in to open any existing database. If, by chance, your database isn't in the default location, you have to change the default location (as I discuss in Chapter 3), move your database to the correct location, or browse to the location of your database.

The first screen that you see when opening ACT! *each and every time* is the Contacts view. If you click around and end up in any of the other ACT! screens before choosing File⇨Open from the Contacts view (see Step 1, following), don't panic. One of the nice things about ACT! is that you're able to execute most commands from any ACT! screen (unless I tell you otherwise).

To open a database, make sure that ACT! is open and then follow these steps:

1. **Choose File⇨Open from the ACT! Contacts view.**

   The Open dialog box appears (see Figure 2-1).

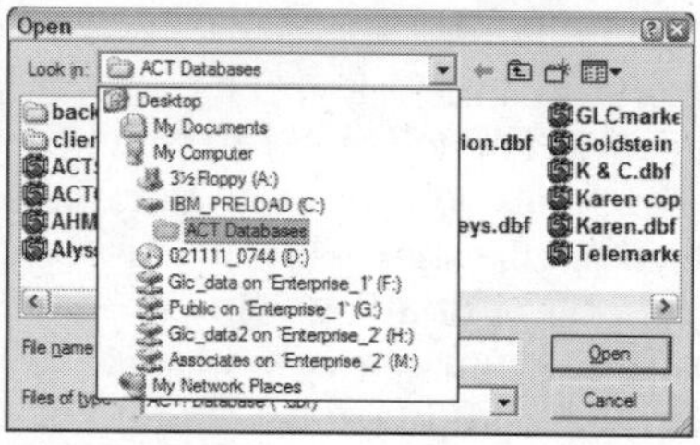

Figure 2-1:
Opening
an ACT!
database.

2. **Click the triangle to the right of the Look In box.**

3. **Double-click to expand the folder that contains your database.**

4. **Select the name of your database and then click Open.**

   If you prefer, double-click the name of the database that you want to open.

   The name of the currently opened database appears in the ACT! title bar (see Figure 2-2).

Although the ACT! database consists of over 20 files, all databases share the same file extensions. The most commonly known of these extensions is .dbf. If you're having trouble locating your database, search for all .dbf files by typing ***.dbf** as your search criteria in Windows. Make a note of the location for future reference so that you'll always know the exact location of your database.

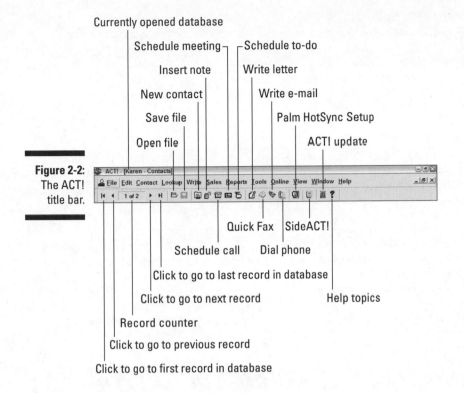

Currently opened database

Schedule meeting ⌐ ⌐Schedule to-do

Insert note   Write letter

New contact   Write e-mail

Save file   Palm HotSync Setup

Open file   ACT! update

Figure 2-2:
The ACT!
title bar.

Quick Fax   SideACT!

Schedule call   Dial phone

Click to go to last record in database

Click to go to next record   Help topics

Record counter

Click to go to previous record

Click to go to first record in database

The ACT! Login Screen

If more than one person is sharing your ACT! database, ACT! presents you with a login screen each time that you attempt to open your database. Essentially, the login screen, shown in Figure 2-3, is there just to ask you for your login name and your password. Although these logins and passwords are not case sensitive (that is, you can enter your login information by typing either lower- or uppercase letters), you must enter the information correctly. For example, if my login name includes my middle initial with a period, I must type that middle initial — including the period — to access my database.

Generally, your password is determined by the administrator of your database. The *database administrator* is the person who is responsible for making major changes to the database and for performing routine database maintenance. Although several users may all have access to an ACT! database, ACT! doesn't require that each user have a password. So if the database administrator didn't assign you a password, you can just leave the password area blank.

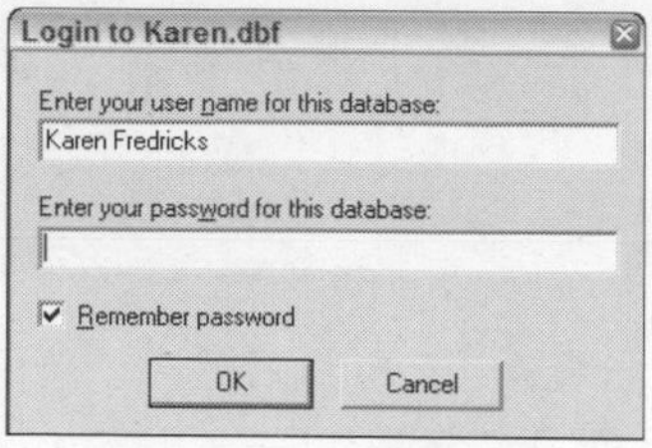

Figure 2-3:
Logging in
to ACT!.

Login to Karen.dbf

Enter your user name for this database:

Karen Fredricks

Enter your password for this database:

☑ Remember password

OK   Cancel

If you were assigned a password, notice that asterisks appear while you type it in. That's normal. Just like when you type your ATM card PIN, your ACT! database password is hidden while you type it to prevent any lurking spies who might be watching from learning your password. You're able to change your own password; see Chapter 3 to find out how.

Notice in Figure 2-3 that ACT! gives you the option of saving your password (an option automatically selected by default). Although this will make it easy for you to log in to your database in the future, you may want to rethink this decision. First of all, what good is a password if it always magically appears anytime that you attempt to access your database? Secondly, by having ACT! remember your password, you may eventually forget it yourself!

The Importance of Being My Record

The first contact that you should see when opening an ACT! database is your own — that's your *My Record*. My Record is nothing more than a contact record that has been associated with a user of the database. Your My Record stores all your own information, which automatically appears in some of the preset templates that come with ACT!. For example, a fax cover sheet will include *your* telephone and fax numbers; a report will have *your* name at the top; and letters will have *your* name at the bottom. If, for some reason, someone else's information appears as the first contact record that you see when you open your database, explore these three possibilities:

- Did you log in as yourself? If not, do so. Then, when you open ACT! again — logged in as yourself — your My Record should appear.

- Did you inadvertently change your own contact information? If that's the case, change it back.

- If you're 100 percent certain that you logged in as yourself and haven't changed your contact information, your database is likely corrupted. I'm not trying to scare you, but I recommend that you turn to Chapter 17, where I show you how to perform a little CPR on your database.

Taking the time to enter in all your own contact information is very important. If you don't, you may find that you're missing key information when you start to work with templates and reports. For example, if you never enter your own fax number, your fax number doesn't appear on the Fax Cover Sheet template, which means you'd have to fill it in every time that you send a fax. Save yourself the trouble and fill in your My Record right off the bat.

Your My Record also allows you to use a few other important ACT! features:

✔ Every time that you enter a new contact, your name appears as the creator of that contact (Chapter 4).

✔ When you delete a contact, a history of that deletion appears in the Notes/History area of your My Record (Chapter 4).

✔ Every time that you add a note to a contact record, your name appears as the Record Manager of that note (Chapter 7).

✔ When you schedule an activity, your name is automatically attached to that activity (Chapter 8).

✔ On a network, the ACT! database administrator is able to identify all users that are currently logged into the database (Chapter 16).

Finding Your Way around in ACT!

The purpose of this book is to serve as a reference book for both new and existing ACT! users. I certainly don't want to lose anyone along the way. Navigating through ACT! is fairly easy. However, to make the navigating even easier, I highlight throughout this section a number of pitfalls that you'll want to avoid.

The record counter

ACT! supplies you with a record counter in the top-left corner of the Contacts view (refer to Figure 2-2). The first number indicates the number of your record as it relates alphabetically to all the other members of your database. This number changes when you add or remove contacts. The second number supplies you with the total number of contacts in either your entire database or your current lookup. (A *lookup* refers to the contacts in your database that you're currently working with. You can find out everything that you'd ever want to know about a lookup in Chapter 6.)

I recommend getting into the habit of checking the total number of contacts in your database each time that you open ACT!. If the total number of contacts changes radically from one day to the next, you just might be in the wrong database. Worse yet, a dramatic change in the number of contacts may indicate corruption in your database.

To the left and right of the record counter is a set of left- and right-pointing triangles. You can click these triangles to navigate through the contact records. For instance, to go to the previous record, you simply click the left-pointing triangle. Refer to Figure 2-2, which shows how to use these triangles.

The layout

One of the largest sources of confusion to the new ACT! user is the use of layouts. The *layout* refers to the order in which fields appear on the ACT! screens as well as the colors, fonts, and graphics that you see. You can specify the colors, fonts, and graphics in the layout as well as the position and order of fields. If the database administrator created new fields for the database, these fields must then be added to a layout.

You can modify contact and group layouts and create your own layouts to suit your needs. (There's no right or wrong layout — only the layout that you prefer.) For example, the Sales Department may need to see certain fields, but the Customer Service Department may only need to see fields specific to its department. You can also remove fields that you don't use and add your own tabs to the bottom of a layout. Renaming and reordering the tabs to your liking helps you organize your fields. For example, you might want to keep all the personal information about a customer on one tab and the products that he's interested in on another tab.

The name of the layout that you're using appears in the lower-right corner of the ACT! screen, as shown in Figure 2-4. If you inadvertently switch layouts, you might not be able to see all the information in your database, or you might see your information arranged in a different order. At this point, panic often sets in. Don't worry — your data is most probably alive and well and viewable with the help of the correct layout. To switch layouts, click the name of the layout that you're currently using to access a list of all layouts; from that list, choose a different layout. In Chapter 15, I explain how you can create your own customized layouts.

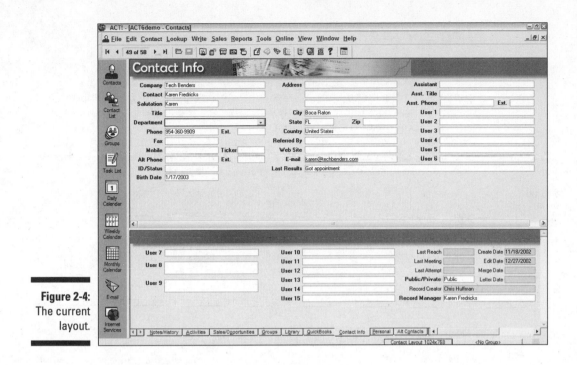

Figure 2-4:
The current
layout.

The menu bar

Like most software programs, ACT! comes equipped with a *menu bar* that
appears at the top of every ACT! screen. These menus include all the options
that are available for the current view. Unlike most other software programs,
however, ACT!'s menu options are dependent on the view that you are currently in. If you are in Contacts view, the Replace option appears in the Edit
menu; if you're in the Contact List view, however, the Replace option is not
available.

The menus also contain items that are relevant to the current view that you're
in. For example, when you're in the Groups view, a Group menu item will magically appear.

You're able to customize all menus to fit your needs; check out Chapter 3 for
the details.

The toolbar

ACT! also features a *toolbar* at the top of each window. The toolbar includes the most commonly used tasks of the current view. Toolbars work in much the same way as the menu bars. You can customize each toolbar to include the tasks that you use most frequently. And, like the menu bars, toolbars vary depending on the current view that you're looking at. For example, the toolbars that you see in the calendar views include a filter icon to change the view settings on your calendar, and the toolbar that you see in the Groups view include icons for creating groups and subgroups.

The View bar

The *View bar* allows you to move quickly between the various views in which you might want to view ACT!. For example, maybe you want to view all the information about one particular contact by clicking the Contacts icon, or maybe you want to see a list of all your contacts by clicking the Contact List icon (see Figure 2-5). The View bar allows you to access your daily, weekly, or monthly calendars and your task list — all by simply clicking a particular icon. When you click one of the View bar icons, a new separate window opens. If you'd like to view several aspects of ACT! simultaneously, you can resize and tile these windows.

By default, the View bar is located along the left edge of your screen. If you'd prefer, you can make the icons smaller (simply right-click the View bar and choose Small Icons from the menu that appears). You can also move the View bar location to the bottom-right corner of your screen by right-clicking the View bar and then choosing Mini View Bar.

The Contacts view

The Contacts view (see Figure 2-6) allows you to see all the information about one specific contact. You'll probably use the Contacts view to enter, modify, and view information about your contacts. Each contact record is displayed as a single page. The tabs at the bottom provide additional fields for contact information. I show you how to add contact information into your database in Chapter 4.

The top half of the screen is used extensively in the templates (that is, letters, fax cover sheets, and memos) that ACT! has already set up for you. The bottom half of the screen can — and should — be customized to better serve the needs of your business. You can scroll through the page tabs on the bottom of the screen to get an idea of some of the fields suggested by ACT!.

Figure 2-5:
The View
bar.

The ACT! tabs

Because ACT! comes with approximately 70 predefined fields, and because your database administrator might add another 50 or so customized fields, it is important to place those fields where they can be seen clearly. Plunking 100 fields on one half of your screen gives you a jumbled mess. I suppose that you could lay out those fields by using a smaller font, but the result — although neat — would be impossible to read!

ACT! solves this dilemma in a rather unique fashion. The top half of the Contacts view displays the most basic fields that are fairly generic to all contacts. In this portion of the screen, the fields include places for the name, address, and phone numbers as well as a few miscellaneous fields. The bottom half of the ACT! screen displays additional information about your contact that's divided into categories, which you access by clicking tabs. The first five of those tabs — Notes/History, Activities, Sales/Opportunities, Groups, and Library — are the same for any layout that you use. In fact, you cannot change the number or order of those first five tabs, nor can you delete any of them.

These first five tabs are actually *tables*; they don't hold single fields with a single piece of information in each one. Rather, you can add an unlimited number of like items to the same tab. For example, you can add multiple notes about your contact using the Notes/History tab, or you might have numerous sales opportunities that involve your currently displayed contact.

Depending on the layout that you're using, you'll probably see three additional tabs after the Library tab. These tabs generally display *more* but *less frequently used* information about your contact. For example, the Alt Contacts tab displays information about an assistant or a second or third contact related to the primary contact. The Home tab reveals your contact's home address and phone number as well as the spouse's name.

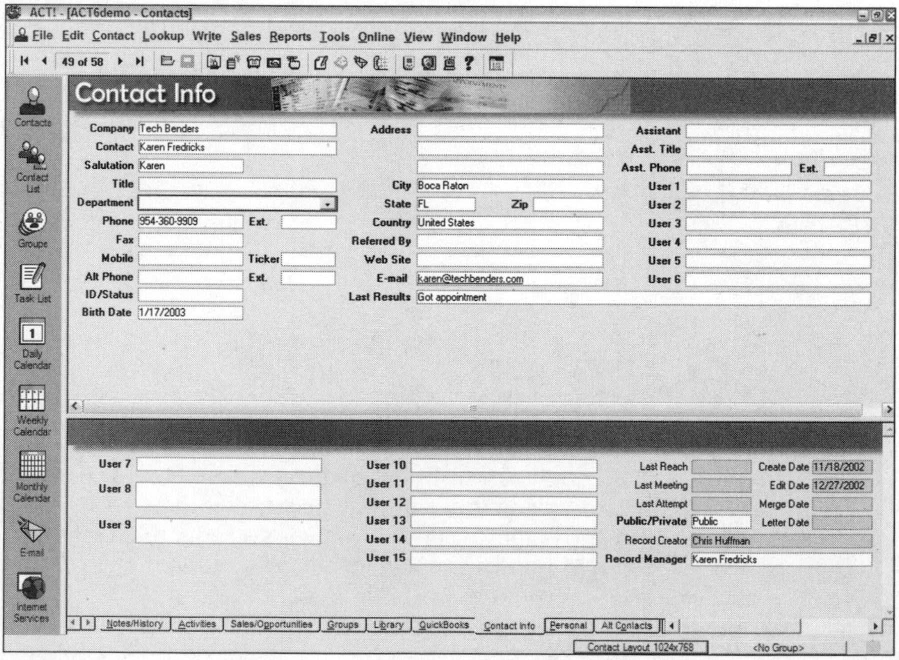

Figure 2-6:
The ACT!
Contacts
view.

With the exception of the first five tabs, all other tabs are dependent on the layout that you're currently using. If you switch layouts, your tabs will change as well.

Some of the ACT! add-on products add new tabs to your ACT! screen. For example, the ACT! QuickBooks link draws information from QuickBooks and plops it into a brand new tab called QuickBooks.

The Contact List view

When you click the Contact List icon on the View bar, you'll be able to view a list of *all* your contacts together on one screen. You'll probably want to use this view to sort your contacts or to compare information about your various contacts. The Contact List is extremely customizable, as you'll see in Chapter 5. For a preview of a Contact List, take a peek at Figure 2-7.

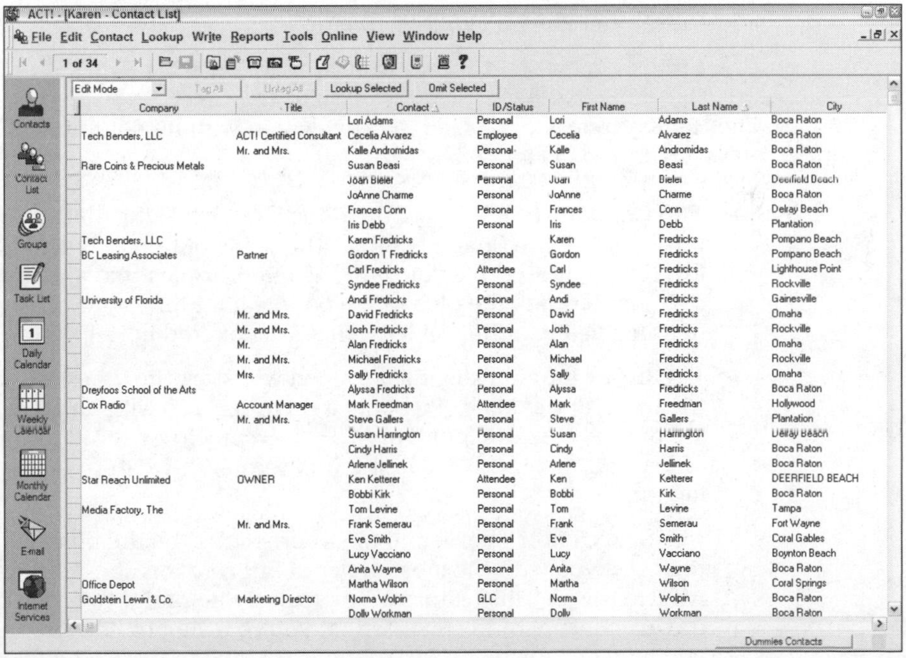

Figure 2-7:
The Contact List.

Finding ACT! Help

In addition to the information that I provide in this book, you have a number of places to turn to for help with ACT! 6. The Users Guide that you received with your purchase of ACT! provides directions to the most basic functions of ACT!. You'll also find a very good — and quite extensive — online Help system that supplies step-by-step instructions for just about any ACT! feature that you might want to explore. New to ACT! 6 is the ability to link directly to the ACT! Web site (www.act.com). From there, you'll be able to access both a Knowledge Base of topics and a list of certified consultants who are willing and able to help you in your hour of need.

Using the online Help system

You can access the ACT! online Help system in one of two ways:

> ✔ Press the F1 key on your keyboard.
>
> ✔ Choose Help⇨Help Topics from any ACT! main menu.

The Help system is organized to provide you with help in three different ways, as shown in Figure 2-8.

> ✔ **The Contents tab:** Clicking the Book icon will bring up the Contents tab. Think of the Contents tab as the Table of Contents in a book. The Contents tab presents you with the major topics that are covered in ACT!. If you click the plus sign next to each topic, you will find a more detailed listing of the subjects that are covered in Help.
>
> ✔ **The Index tab:** Clicking the key icon will start the Index tab, which is like the index at the back of a book. It provides you with an alphabetical listing of every feature found in ACT!. You can either scroll through the list of features or type in the first few letters of the feature that you are looking for.
>
> ✔ **The Search tab:** The Search tab, represented by the binoculars icon, provides you with the most in-depth information about the various ACT! features. This feature is particularly helpful if you aren't sure of the exact name of the feature that you're trying to find. For example, you may be looking for instructions on how to force a field to display only capital letters. A search of the Index tab won't help you (the feature is actually called *Initial Capitalization*), but you will be able to find the information by typing **capital** in the Search tab.

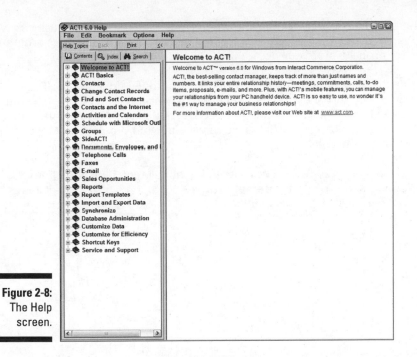

Figure 2-8:
The Help
screen.

Occasionally, the Help topic that you're reading might suggest related topics. You can find these suggestions at the bottom of the Help topic in the How Do I...? and Related Topics areas.

Help on the Internet

New to ACT! 6 is the ability to access Internet-based help directly from ACT!. Clicking the Online menu in ACT! will provide you with a link to the Technical Support Web site. This site provides you both with information about the technical support options provided by Best, CRM (the makers of ACT!), as well as an extensive Knowledge Base of common support issues. You'll also be able to learn about various special events and ACT! User Groups meetings that might be scheduled in your area.

ACT! Certified Consultants

Most of you know a brother, buddy, or colleague that "knows" ACT!. As the old saying goes, a little knowledge is a dangerous thing. In reality, these well-intentioned folks probably know ACT! as it pertains to their business . . . not yours. Unless they are earning a living by consulting in the ACT! program, they are probably not your best source for accurate information.

Your best source of help for ACT! is the ACT! Certified Consultants. These consultants, or ACCs, earn their livelihood by working with people like you. They can help you with anything from converting to ACT! from another program and customizing your database to training your employees. Most ACCs even make house calls.

For a complete list of ACCs, click the ACT! Online menu item and choose ACT! User Community. The ACT! Internet browser will open a page that displays a list of all certified ACT! consultants.

Chapter 3

Getting Your ACT! Together

- -

In This Chapter

▶ Creating a new database

▶ Adding new users to your database

▶ Changing the ACT! preferences

▶ Customizing your toolbars and menus

- -

I could easily have titled this chapter "Have It Your Way" because here's where I show you how to set up a new database and add a couple of users to it. You'll discover some of the preference settings that you can change in ACT!, especially if you're sharing your database across a network. Finally, if you're a real power user, you'll be excited to know how to change your menus and toolbars.

Creating a New ACT! Database with the QuickStart Wizard

If your initial meeting with ACT! entailed looking at the *ACT6Demo* database that comes with ACT!, you know that it's a great database to use for learning purposes *before* actually starting to work on your own database. After playing with the demo for only a short time, you'll probably be eager to start working on your very own database. The easiest way to create your first database is by using the QuickStart Wizard. In addition to setting you up with a new database, the wizard helps you set a few of the most basic preferences needed for ACT! to work correctly.

Follow these instructions to set up your new ACT! database with the QuickStart Wizard:

1. **From any ACT! screen, choose Help⇨QuickStart Wizard.**

   The QuickStart Wizard–Introduction screen appears, as shown in Figure 3-1.

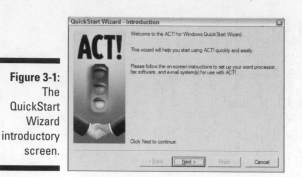

Figure 3-1:
The
QuickStart
Wizard
introductory
screen.

At this point, feel free to put your feet up on the desk, answer a few questions, and let ACT! do the grunt work for you.

2. **On the wizard's introductory screen, click Next to get started.**

   The QuickStart Wizard - Check for Updates screen appears. Despite a *beta-testing process* — in which testers try to find what works and (more importantly) what doesn't work in new software before it's sold to consumers — a few bugs can still end up in the finished product. You can update ACT! 6 with *release patches* (software fixes that corrects the bugs that might cause the program to do strange things) that the QuickStart Wizard - Check for Updates automatically looks for and finds. These update patches are free and result in better performance.

   If you don't have an Internet connection, you won't be able to update your software. Also, if you're using America Online (AOL), this process works better if you sign on to AOL *first*.

3. **Click Connect to look for updates and then follow the onscreen instructions to ensure that your copy of ACT! is up to date.**

   If you don't want to update ACT! at this particular moment of your life, click Next and bypass this step. If you choose to continue with the update process, ACT! will find the latest update and prompt you to continue with installing the update. If no new updates are found, you'll be directed to the next wizard screen.

4. **After you finish installing updates, click Next to continue with the wizard.**

   Quick as a flash, the QuickStart Wizard - Word Processor and Fax Software screen appears. Here's where you get to choose your word processor. It's an either/or proposition; you have only two choices (see the next step).

5. **Choose Microsoft Word (if Word is installed on your computer); otherwise, choose the ACT! word processor. Click Next.**

   If you've installed WinFax on your computer, be sure to communicate that to ACT!.

The next screen you see is the QuickStart Wizard–E-mail Setup screen, where you tell ACT! which e-mail client you'll be using with ACT!. (For information on determining which e-mail client you should be using, scurry over to Chapter 13.)

6. **Select the e-mail program of your choice and then click Next.**

   By now, I'm sure you've realized that running a wizard means clicking the Next button a lot. Smart reader! The QuickStart Wizard–Create a Database screen appears next, asking whether you'd like the QuickStart Wizard to set up an ACT! database for you now or to skip the database setup.

7. **Select Set Up Database Now and then click Next.**

   The QuickStart Wizard–Name Your Database screen appears, requesting a name for your new database. Being an unimaginative sort, the wizard suggests the name *Contacts*.

8. **Name your database and then click Next.**

   You might want to give the database a really cool moniker, such as the name of your company so that you can easily identify it later. By default, the database is saved to the default database folder. Unless you've changed that preference, the path is `c:\My Documents\Act\Database`.

   The QuickStart Wizard–Finish screen appears, recapping all the important decisions that you've just made about your new database. If you've made a mistake or simply changed your mind, now's the time to fix things!

9. **Double-check your answers carefully, make the appropriate changes (if any), and then click Next.**

   If you have an Outlook database, the wizard now asks whether you want to import it into ACT!.

10. **If you have an Outlook database to import, click Next and follow the subsequent onscreen instructions; otherwise, click Finish to complete the wizard.**

    If you need to create another database, simply repeat the wizard or check out the next section, where I show you how to make a copy of an existing database. When you're ready to add contacts to the database, head to Chapter 4.

Alternatively, if you are an ACT! veteran and have already set your preferences and just need a new, blank database, here's a little shortcut:

1. **Choose File⇨New from the ACT! Contacts view.**

   The New dialog box appears.

2. **Select ACT! Database and click OK.**

3. **Assign a name to the database and click Save.**

   The database is automatically saved to the default folder that you set for your ACT! databases. If you want to save the new database to a different location, browse to the new folder.

Copying an Existing Database

After you've been using ACT! for a while, you might want to create a new database without running the QuickStart Wizard. Or maybe you want to make a copy of an existing database. This is no problem for ACT! — just be sure to read the warning before following the steps.

If you make an exact copy of your database, you must be careful how you use it. If you merely want to place a database on another computer for reference, making an exact copy by following these steps is fine. Be aware, however, that you will not be able to make changes on the cloned database and then synchronize them back to the original database. If you're creating a copy of a database for backup purposes, check out Chapter 16, where I show you how to create an ACT! backup.

1. **Choose File➪Save Copy As from the Contacts view.**

   The Save Copy As dialog box opens (see Figure 3-2), where you decide what type of database you'd like to create.

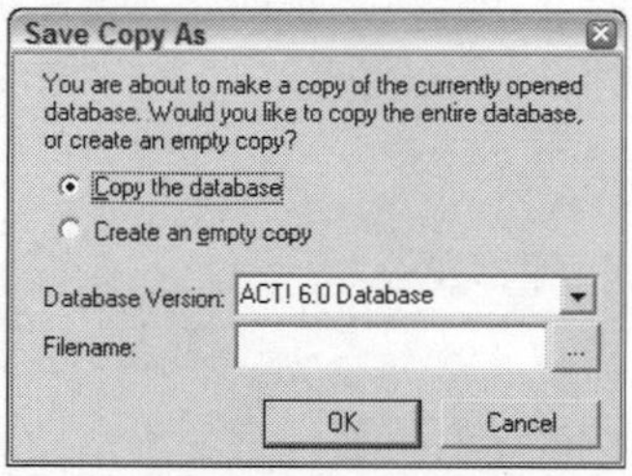

Figure 3-2:
Creating a copy of a database.

Although creating a copy of your existing database is easy, you must understand the consequence of your decision at this point. Consider your choices:

- **Copy the Database:** This creates an *exact replica* of your currently opened database. After you create a new ACT! database and customize it by adding many new fields, you may want to duplicate it for use by other offices or for other businesses that you might own.

The new database copies the field structure of your existing database as well as all the actual contact records within the database.

- **Create an Empty Copy:** This creates a blank database that will contain all the customized fields that you create in your existing database, but it will *not* contain any of the contact records from your original database.

2. **In the Filename text box (refer to Figure 3-2), type a filename for the copy of the database.**

Do not make the mistake of assigning the same name to the new database that you have already used for your existing database. Even if you save the copy database to an entirely new location, doing so will surely create problems in distinguishing between the two. By default, whenever you open ACT!, it opens the last database that you used, telling you the *name* of the currently opened database but not its *path*. If two databases have the same filename, you might end up working in the incorrect database — without even realizing it.

3. **Click OK.**

The Enter "My Record" Information dialog box appears. The *My Record* is the contact record for the creator of the database.

- If the My Record information is correct, click Yes.

- If the My Record information is incorrect and you know that the contact record for the new user is in the currently opened database, click Select, select the name of the user, and then click OK.

- If necessary, enter the My Record information, click OK, and then click Yes.

You are now ready to start entering contact records into your new database. Chapter 4 contains the details about adding contact records to a database.

Adding Multiple Users to a Database

If several people will be entering data into your ACT! database, I highly recommend setting up each person as an individual user. That way, because ACT! automatically enters several key pieces of information based on the way that you log into the database, each person is identified as a unique user of the database.

If you and Jane are both set up as individual users of the database, you're recognized as the *record creator* when you enter a new contact into the database. Likewise, if Jane enters a note, that note is associated with Jane. If you generate a document from one of ACT!'s templates, your name — not Jane's — appears as the generator of that document. Most importantly, your name will become associated with any meetings, calls, or to-do's that you schedule in ACT!. Having unique, identifiable users in a database allows you to view your own activities on a calendar. Otherwise, you might find yourself driving to Podunk to visit Jane's mom on her birthday!

Only the database administrator has permission to add new users to the ACT! database.

To add a new user to your database, follow these steps:

1. **From any of the ACT! screens, choose File⇨Administration⇨Define Users.**

   The Define Users dialog box opens, as shown in Figure 3-3.

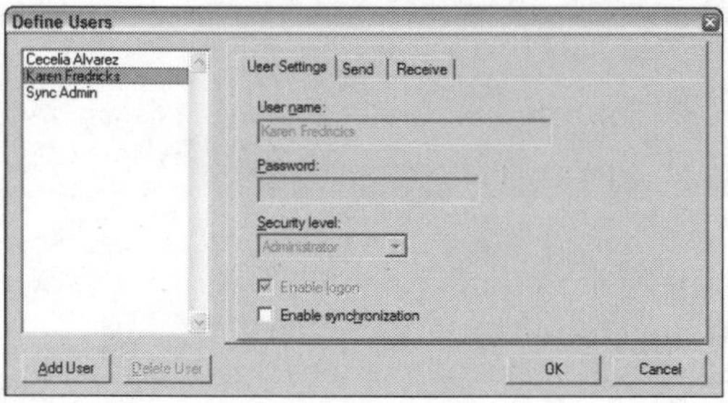

Figure 3-3:
Adding a
new user.

2. **Click the Add User button.**

   User 1 now appears in the User Name box.

3. **Change User 1 to the name of the user who you're adding.**

4. **Select the appropriate security level from the Security Level drop-down list.**

   Choose between three security levels:

   - A *browse* user is able to view any information that's stored in the database — but can't add, modify, or delete records.

   - A *standard* user is able to see the records in a database; add, delete, and modify records; and synchronize data. What a standard user cannot do is add new users to the database, perform database maintenance, back up the database, or modify database fields.

   - An *administrator* is able to perform any database function. The administrator is the chief, the head honcho, the Big Guy — the person everyone blames if something goes wrong with the database.

Be sure to note which users have been given the administrator user level. These users are the only ones who can add users, create a backup, and perform routine maintenance on the database.

Assigning two users as administrators of the database is always a good idea. Not only does this make two people feel extra special, it can save your little rear end. If you're the sole administrator and your My Record becomes corrupted, you might not be able to access the database. And because no one would then be able to perform routine maintenance, add users, or make field changes, you might find yourself looking for a new job. Equally troubling is the former database administrator who leaves and takes his password with him. No password, no entry!

5. Select the Enable Logon check box.

This will enable the new user to access your database. If, for some reason, you do not want a user to have access to your database, feel free to clear this check box. I show you how to delete and disable (but hopefully not maim!) your database users later in this chapter.

6. Click OK.

You now see the rather ominous message shown in Figure 3-4. Relax. This is ACT!'s not-too-subtle way of asking you to create a *My Record* (a contact record that contains the database user's contact information, which appears later in various reports and templates that the user creates) for the new user. In Chapter 2, I describe the importance of seeing your own My Record every time that you log into the database.

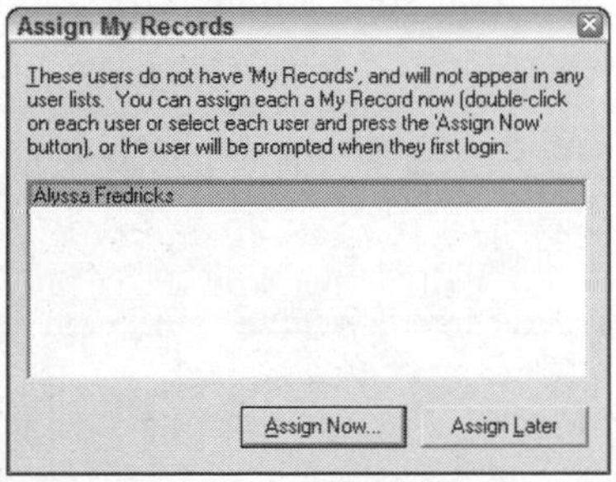

Figure 3-4:
Assigning
My Record
information.

Assign My Records

These users do not have 'My Records', and will not appear in any user lists. You can assign each a My Record now (double-click on each user or select each user and press the 'Assign Now' button), or the user will be prompted when they first login.

Alyssa Fredricks

Assign Now...   Assign Later

7. In the Assign My Records dialog box, click either the Assign Now or the Assign Later button.

- Assign Now enables you to, well, to assign the user information now.

- Assign Later gives you time to scurry around the office collecting all the vital information about the new user.

If you don't assign the contact information to the newly created My Record, that user will be prompted to provide the information the next time that she attempts to log into the database. Without providing her contact information, she will not be able to log in.

8. **If you selected Assign Now in Step 7, fill out the My Record information dialog box (see Figure 3-5).**

   ACT! is smart, but it's not brilliant. ACT! assumes that the new user is you. Unless you have a clone, you'll need to type in the information for the new user.

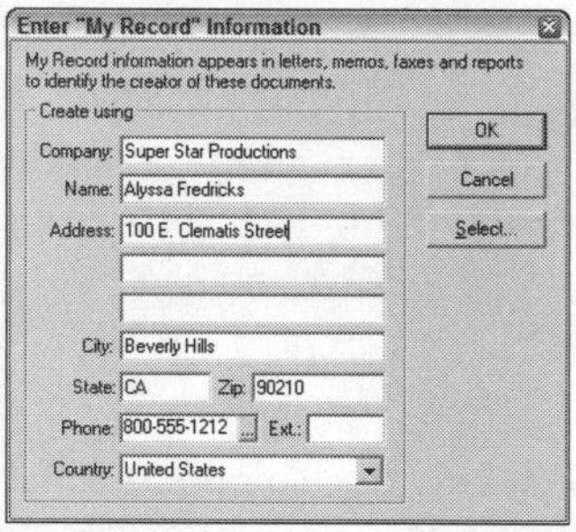

Figure 3-5:
Assigning
My Record.

If the user already has a record in the database, click the Select button and then choose the appropriate record from the list. If you don't select the user's existing record, you may end up having multiple records for the same user, which could cause great confusion later.

9. **Click OK.**

   The newly created user is now ready to log into the database and start using ACT!.

Setting up shared resources as an ACT! user

A user of your database doesn't necessarily have to be human. I know the jury is still out on the boss, but you might find it helpful to create a user for some resources that more than one person in your office is sharing. For example, one of your users could be *Conference Room* and another *Overpriced LCD Projector*. By scheduling appointments that include these resources, other people in your office are able to view a schedule to check the availability on these resources — *before* double-booking the conference room!

Deleting Login Users

After you master adding new users to your database, you'll need to know how to delete users when they leave. Easy come, easy go. The first thing that you need to do is to determine whether you're going to actually delete the user or just deny him or her access to the database. There is a slight difference.

If you are the database administrator and you simply want to stop someone from accessing the database, you can do so without having to actually delete that person as a user. You can simply shut off her login privileges (a very simple process):

1. **Choose File⇨Administration⇨Define Users.**

2. **In the Define Users dialog box that appears (refer to Figure 3-3), select the name of the user and then remove the check mark from the Enable Logon check box.**

3. **Click OK.**

One of the reasons why you add users to the database is so that they can perform various functions, such as scheduling appointments and creating notes. The user's name is also associated with any contact that he might have created. Opting to shut off a user's login privileges, rather than delete that user entirely, eliminates the possibility of losing this information.

Suppose that you decide to delete a particular user — call this user *Jon*. However, you're now faced with a situation in which Jon's name is no longer associated with various notes, histories, and contacts. But ACT!, being the smart program that you've grown to know and love, allows you to delete Jon while preserving the contact records (and notes, histories, and so on) associated with him by reassigning his contact records to another user:

1. **Choose File⇨Administration⇨Define Users.**

   The Define Users dialog box appears (refer to Figure 3-3).

2. **Select the name of the user who you want removed from your database and then click the Delete User button.**

   The Delete User dialog box appears, where ACT! gives you the opportunity to reassign your contact records (and all related notes, histories, and so on) to another user, as shown in Figure 3-6.

Figure 3-6:
Reassigning
a user.

3. **To delete a user and reassign the contact records to another user, select the Reassign to Another User radio button, select a name from the Select from Existing Users box, and then click OK.**

ACT! searches through your database and reassigns every record, note, and contact one at a time. This might be a good time to perfect the art of thumb-twiddling; the larger your database, the longer this will take.

After you've reassigned contact records to a new user, you can't reverse the process. From here on, the notes, histories, and contacts that the deleted user created appear to have been created by the new user. However, if you simply delete a user without reassigning his records, you risk losing a lot of contact information. If you don't want that to happen, I recommend simply removing the former user's log on privileges, as I describe previously.

Rather than deleting a user of your database, you might also consider changing the Record Manager field for all contacts that are now associated with the new user. Skip over to Chapter 16 to find out how you can change the field data for a whole bunch of contacts at once.

Working with Passwords

If you're the only user using your ACT! database, or if your clients love you and would chop their arms off at the wrist before turning to one of your competitors, security might not be an important issue for you. But if you're like most people, you'd probably prefer not to share every tidbit of information in your database with anyone who wanders into your office. Whether you want to prevent certain personnel from changing the basic field structure of your database or adapt a "look but don't touch" attitude with the unfortunate computer-challenged among your employees, ACT! has two security methods that will help you accomplish your security goals. You can either

 ✔ **Assign a specific security level to each user.** See Step 4 in the earlier section, "Adding Multiple Users to a Database."

 ✔ **Password-protect your database.** I discuss this option throughout the rest of this section.

Unless a contact record is marked as *private*, ACT! has no way of allowing someone access to only a portion of the contacts in a database. If you want to limit the contacts a particular user sees, you have a couple of choices. You can supply that user with his own database and synchronize just those contacts that he has access to from the main database or use the online version of ACT!. You can read about ACT for Web in Chapter 18.

Setting a password

Both the database administrator and the individual database user can set a password for the user. The theory for this is that the individual is able to pick a password that has some meaning to him — and so, hopefully, he won't forget it. (If a user does forget his password, however, the administrator can reset it.)

If you have access to a database and are afraid that some nasty person might use your name to gain access illegally, I recommend assigning a password to yourself, which is ridiculously easy. Here's what you do:

1. **From any of the ACT! screens, choose File➪Administration➪Password.**

2. **In the Set Password dialog box that appears, enter the password in the New Password text box.**

3. **Retype the password in the Retype New Password text box.**

4. **Click OK.**

Resetting a password

You might not know your password because you don't have one, so before tracking down your administrator to change a password for you, try leaving the password field blank. (I frequently get phone calls and e-mails from ACT! users who have no idea what password was assigned to them. Guess what? They often don't have one!)

But if you've tried every password that you can think of — and even have tried using no password at all — and still can't gain access to the database, you might have to bribe the database administrator into resetting your password. I find that chocolate chip cookies work the best, but feel free to pick the bribe of your choice. Then, make sure the administrator follows these steps:

1. **From any ACT! screen, choose File⇨Administration⇨Define Users.**

2. **On the User Settings tab of the Define Users dialog box (refer to Figure 3-3), select the name of the user whose password is being changed.**

3. **Delete the entry in the Password text box and type the new password.**

4. **Click OK.**

Changing a password

From time to time, you might want to change your password. Perhaps you feel that your security has been compromised by a former employee, or maybe you've just been watching too many James Bond movies. Whatever the case, remember the new, improved password, or you may be forced to chase the database administrator around with another batch of cookies!

1. **Choose File⇨Administration⇨Password.**

   If you've been going through this chapter section by section, you already know that you can do this from within any of the ACT! screens. I don't mean to sound like a broken record here; I just want you to get used to the idea.

2. **Enter the current password in the Old Password text box.**

3. **Enter the new password in the New Password text box.**

4. **Enter the new password in the Retype New Password text box.**

5. **Click OK.**

Giving ACT! the Preferential Treatment

After you install ACT! on your computer, becoming familiar with various preferences is a good practice. If you're the sole user of the database, these settings will likely save your sanity. If you share the database with other users, these settings will probably save you a lot of head scratching.

If you created your original database by using the QuickStart Wizard, some of your preferences have already been set. However, it never hurts to review your work! Your preference settings are the place to turn to if you're the kind of person who likes to have things your own way. You might routinely store all your documents in a specific location and want ACT! to follow that same example. Or you might have a fondness for fuchsia and orange and want to have your ACT! screens coordinate with this color scheme.

Here's how to change several of the most basic preference settings. Feel free to flip through the various preference tabs to get an idea about additional preference settings that you might also want to tweak.

1. **Choose Edit⇨Preferences.**

   The ACT! Preferences dialog box opens (see Figure 3-7).

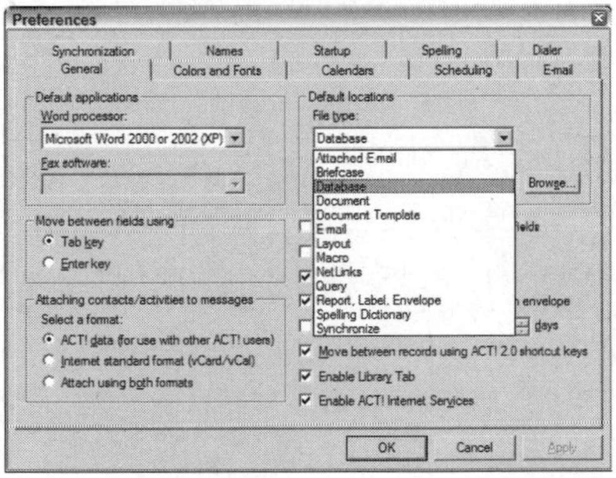

Figure 3-7:
Indicate the
location of
the various
file types
in ACT!'s
Preferences
dialog box.

If you're sharing your database over a network, you must set up the following folders on the network to house the various files shared by all of your ACT! users:

- Database
- Document templates
- Layouts
- Report, label, envelope

When first installed, ACT! makes the assumption that you are a single, solitary user and therefore want to store all your information on your hard drive. If you're sharing your database, however, the database needs to be located on a network drive. In addition, many network administrators overlook the importance of placing other key files on the network as well. For example, your users may want to share a snazzy fax coversheet, the layout that has been customized for the company, and various ACT! reports.

2. **On the General Tab, choose Microsoft Word from the Word Processor drop-down list (if you're a current Word user).**

   In Chapter 12, I introduce you to the exciting world of template creation. If you don't change your word processor preference, all those templates will be created in ACT!'s own word processor, limiting your customization choices when you create new templates: The ACT! word processor isn't as robust as Word, and templates created using Word can't be viewed using the ACT! word processor (and vice versa). This can lead to confusion when other users don't change the preference and find that they can't use your templates. You might spend hours creating new templates only to find that you have to re-create them in Word.

3. **Choose each of the categories from the File Type drop-down list and navigate to the corresponding location.**

   For example, if the file type is database and you've created a folder on the network called F:\ACT\DATABASE, navigate to that folder. You will need to repeat these preference settings on the computer of each of your ACT! users. Figure 3-7 shows ACT!'s Preferences screen and the various file type settings that you need to redirect.

4. **If you want ACT! to configure your personal preferences, choose from the various options on the Names, Colors and Fonts, Calendars, and Scheduling tabs.**

   These options are not necessary for ACT! to function properly. But if you want to set your ACT! screens to fuchsia, here's where you do it.

5. **Click OK.**

Setting Reminders

I like to tell people that before I started using ACT!, I had lists of my lists. For many of you, ACT!'s strength lies in its ability to keep you organized. In addition to the reminders that you can set for your meetings, calls, and to-do's, you can also have ACT! remind you to perform various housekeeping tasks. Each time that you open your database, ACT! then reminds you of the various chores that you need to do. You can set reminders for the following ACT! tasks:

✔ Backing up a database

✔ Performing database maintenance

✔ Updating your ACT! and Outlook calendars

✔ Running group membership rules

✔ Synchronizing data

✔ Rolling activities from a previous date to today's calendar

You can set different reminders for different databases. For example, you might set a reminder to back up a personal database every day but have no reminder set for another database that you know is being backed up by your network administrator.

To set an ACT! reminder, here's what you need to do:

1. **Log on as the database user who will receive the reminder.**

   Reminders are associated with specific users of the database. If the responsibility to perform routine database maintenance belongs to the database administrator, then he or she needs to set the reminders — or you need to log on as the administrator.

2. **Choose File⇨Set Reminders from the ACT! Contacts view.**

3. **Select the reminder that you want to set.**

4. **Indicate how often the reminder should appear.**

5. **Click OK.**

   The next time that the user opens ACT!, a reminder appears (if it is time to perform a certain action). Based on the time intervals that you've set, a list of all the necessary housekeeping chores appears. Figure 3-8 shows an example of the ACT! Reminders window.

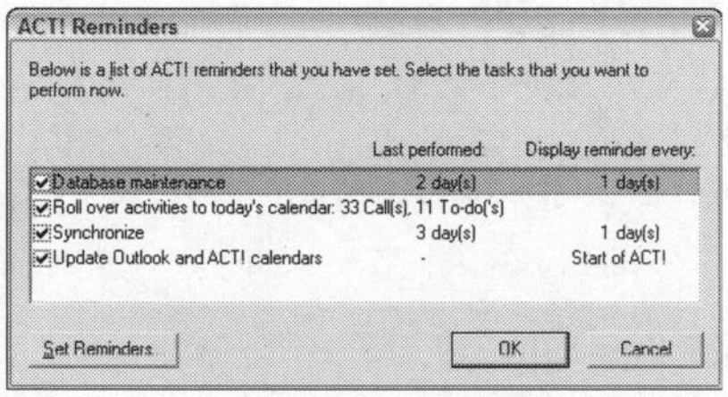

Figure 3-8:
The ACT!
Reminders
window.

You now need to follow through on those reminders.

6. **Select the activities that you want to perform.**

   You can leave all items checked depending on the time of day and the number of users currently accessing your database. For example, if you're the first one opening ACT! in the morning, you might want to routinely perform database maintenance. However, because various tasks (including database maintenance, backups, and synchronizations) require that no other users be logged on to your database, you may need to postpone these tasks until a later time.

7. **Choose one of the following options:**

   • Click OK to perform the selected task(s).

   • Click the Cancel button to postpone running all the selected tasks.

If you decide to cancel the Reminder warning, make sure that you know who is performing the tasks and how often they are being done. All too often ACT! users click Cancel when prompted to perform database maintenance — without realizing just how important that routine maintenance is!

• Click the Set Reminders button to add a new reminder or to change the frequency of a reminder. To turn off the reminder, select the Don't Remind Me Again option.

If you're working on a shared database and, each time you open the database, you're nagged to perform administrative tasks that are not part of your job description, you might want to select each action listed in the ACT! Reminders window and then select Don't Remind Me Again.

Modifying Menus and Toolbars

Customizing the various ACT! menus and toolbars to include functions that you use on a regular basis improves its efficiency.

Adding menu commands

In subsequent chapters, you find out how to create lookups (Chapter 6), document templates (Chapter 12), and new reports (Chapter 11). You can add these new items to the Lookup, Write, and Report menus, respectively. Here's all you need to do:

1. **Click Modify Menu from the Lookup, Write, or Reports menu.**

   The Modify Menu dialog box opens, as shown in Figure 3-9.

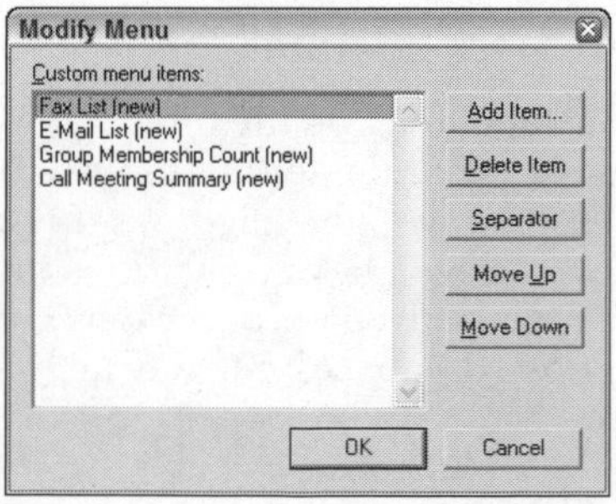

Modify Menu

Custom menu items:

Fax List (new)
E-Mail List (new)
Group Membership Count (new)
Call Meeting Summary (new)

Add Item...
Delete Item
Separator
Move Up
Move Down

OK   Cancel

Figure 3-9:
The Modify
Menu dialog
box.

2. **Click the Add Item button.**

3. **Click the Browse button to the right of the Filename and Location field.**

4. **Browse to the query file, template, or report that you want to add to the menu.**

   ACT! makes this step easy for you because the Browse button automatically takes you to the default folder. For example, when you create a new document template, ACT! saves it to your default template folder. If you decide to add that template to your Write menu, ACT! looks in that default folder.

5. **Click Open.**

6. **Enter the text that you want to appear in the menu in the Command Name to Display in Menu field.**

   ACT! displays the complete filename for any new items that you add to a menu. For example, if the name of your document template is `newfile.adt`, that's exactly what will appear in the menu.

7. **Click Move Up or Move Down to rearrange the order of the commands in the menus.**

8. **Click OK.**

Adding toolbar icons

The ACT! toolbars are a little bit tricky because they vary depending on your current view. For example, the toolbar that you see when you're in the Contacts view is not the same toolbar you see in the Contact List. At least customizing them is fairly easy. This is all you need to do:

1. **Display the window containing the toolbar that you want to customize.**

2. **Jot down the menu that contains the action that you're adding to the toolbar.**

   Trust me on this one — jotting down this info is going to come in handy. If you want to add a Synchronize icon to the toolbar, make sure that you know that to perform a synchronization you must choose File➪Synchronize.

3. **Choose Tools➪Customize.**

   The Customize ACT! Contacts Window dialog box opens, as shown in Figure 3-10.

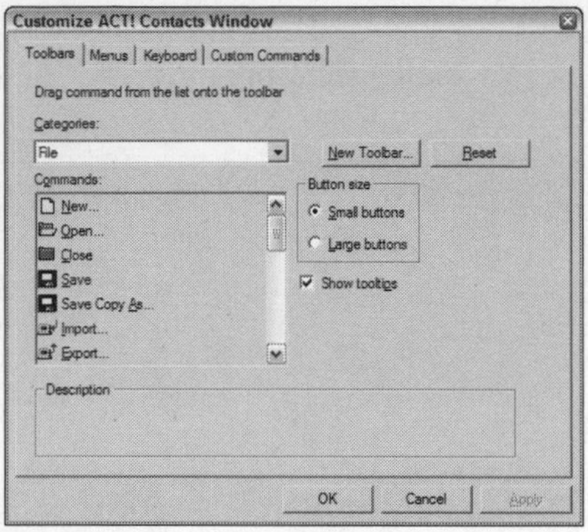

Figure 3-10:
Customize
ACT!
toolbars
here.

4. **Drag an icon up and away from the toolbar to remove it from the toolbar.**

   If you want to rid your toolbar of unwanted icons, now's your chance. While the Customize ACT! Contacts Window dialog box is open, you can remove icons that you don't use from the toolbar by dragging them up and off of the toolbar. After you close this dialog box, you'll no longer be able to do this.

5. **Drag an icon to a new location in the toolbar if desired.**

   What the heck — live it up. Feel free to drag the icons to your heart's content.

6. **On the Toolbars tab, select the category of tool that you want to add from the Categories list.**

   This is where your homework is going to come in handy. Remember those steps you jotted down in Step 2? This will help you find the icon. If you're looking for a command that's in the File menu, choose File as your category.

7. **In the Commands list, click and drag the command icon onto the toolbar.**

   When you drag the icon up onto the toolbar, overlap it slightly with the preceding icon. If you attempt to drag an icon to the end of the toolbar without having it overlap another icon, it won't remain on the toolbar.

8. **Continue adding commands from other categories as needed.**

9. **When finished, click OK.**

   You're now the proud owner of a customized ACT! toolbar!

Part II
Putting the ACT! Database to Work

The 5th Wave — By Rich Tennant

OK, one of you will stay in the field, but the other one will handle clients over the Internet.

But which one?! Brad or Igor?! Brad or Igor?!

In this part . . .

Okay, you've whipped ACT! into shape; now it's time to get your life back in order. ACT! is a contact manager, which, as the name implies, makes it a great place to manage your contacts. First you must add new contacts to your database, and then you need to know how to find them again. After you locate your contacts, you can schedule an activity with any one of them, set a reminder, and maybe add some notes for good measure. Sure beats the heck out of a yellow sticky note!

Chapter 4

Making Contact(s)

A database is only as good as the contacts that it contains. In ACT!, adding, deleting, and editing the contacts in your database is easy to do. In this chapter, I show you how to do all three of these tasks to maintain an organized, working database. Adding new contacts is only half the fun; being able to find them again is the point of having the database in the first place. Inputting contacts in a consistent manner ensures that all your contacts are easy to find. After you've added a new contact, you may need to change that contact's information or even delete the contact entirely. I demonstrate how to change contact information if necessary and even how to "unchange" changes that you might have made by mistake!

Adding New Contacts

On the very simplest level, the main purpose of ACT! is to serve as a place to store all the contacts that you interact with on a daily basis. Although you can add contacts from either the Contacts view or Contact List, most users find it more convenient to add contacts from the Contacts view because it focuses on all the information that pertains to one particular record and will allow you to see all your contact fields.

Note: Every time that you add a new contact, ACT! automatically fills in information in two fields: Record Creator and Create Date. If you click the very last tab of your layout, generally called either Status or Record Info, you'll notice the Record Creator and Create Date fields. When you add a new contact, ACT! inserts your User Name into the Record Creator field and the current date into the Create Date field. This enables you to search for all the new contacts that you created within a given date range. These fields serve as a permanent record and cannot be changed.

You probably have many contacts to enter into the database, so what are you waiting for? Jump right in and follow these steps:

1. **If you aren't already in the Contacts view, go there by clicking the Contact icon on ACT!'s View bar.**

   Don't know about the View bar? Check out Chapter 2, where you'll find out all you need to know about the View bar and then some.

2. **In the Contacts view, choose from one of three ways to add a new contact to your database:**

   • Choose Contact⇨New Contact.

   • Click the New Contact icon on the toolbar.

   • Press the Insert key on the keyboard.

   Initiating any of the preceding commands results in a blank contact record. You're now ready to enter the new contact's information.

3. **Begin entering information by clicking in the Contact Name field (depending on the layout that you're using, the fields appear in either the top half of the Contact screen or on one of the tabs along the bottom) and typing the contact's name.**

   ACT! doesn't distinguish between actual contacts and blank contacts. Failure to enter information or repeatedly pressing the Insert key results in numerous blank contact records, which are of no use and only serve to clog up the database. So, although you are free to leave any of the ACT! fields blank, you do have to enter something — at the very least, I recommend the key pieces of information — so you might as well begin with the contact's name.

   You can always go back to a record later and add, change, or delete (see the later sections "The Contacts, They Are A'Changin'" and "Deleting Contact Records") any information in any field.

4. **Click in the next field where you want to enter information and start typing.**

   You can also use the Tab key to advance to the next field. If, in your initial excitement to start entering all your existing contacts, you inadvertently press the Tab key once too often, you may find that you've advanced one too many fields and have ended up in the wrong field. But don't fret: Press and hold down the Shift key and then press Tab to move your cursor in the reverse direction.

5. **Continue filling in fields.**

   As I mention in Chapter 2, ACT! comes with approximately 70 pre-programmed fields that reflect the needs of most users. Many of the fields are fairly self explanatory (and reflect the type of information that you'd probably expect to find in an address book): contact name, company name, phone, city, state, and Zip code. These are conveniently located in the top half of the Contacts view; see Figure 4-1. A few of the fields are a little less obvious:

- **Address:** If you assume that the three fields ACT! provides for the address is meant to store three *alternative* addresses, you're wrong! The second and third address fields are meant for really long addresses. This is a good place to include a building name if it is an integral part of the address.

5160-style labels, popularly used for mass mailings, generally print four lines of information: company, contact, street address, city/state/Zip code (all on the fourth line). If you need to use the second and third address fields, you'll need larger labels.

- **ID/Status:** The ID/Status field is essentially the category field, and it files each of your contacts into categories. By using the ID/Status field, you won't have to manually set up a variety of databases: one for your friends, one for your clients, one for your vendors, and so on. The ID/Status field comes preset with 12 of the most commonly used categories, including friends, customers, vendors, and competitors, making it easy to search for each of these categories in a flash.

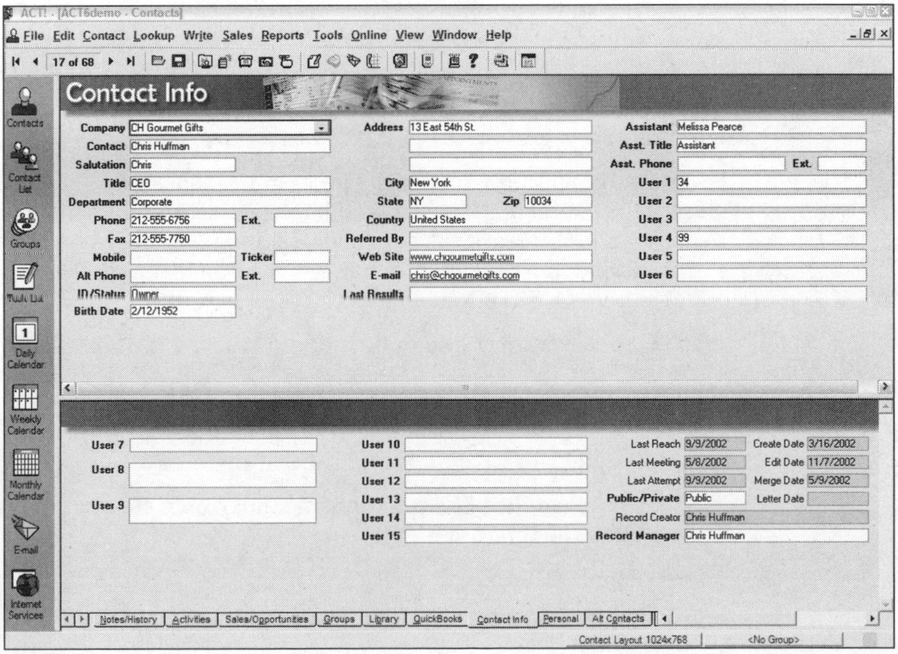

Figure 4-1: The Contacts view.

• **Salutation:** This field refers to the name that comes after the word *Dear* in a letter, which is used in your letter templates. By default, ACT!, being the friendly type, uses the first name. Feel free to change the salutation to a more formal one.

• **User:** Notice that there are several User fields in the bottom half of the Contacts view (refer to Figure 4-1). These fields hold information that's specific to your business. In Chapter 14, I explain how you can change these field names to better reflect their contents. For example, you might rename *User 1* to *Social Security number*.

I recommend leaving these particular fields blank until you've renamed them. If you don't, you might end up with various kinds of data entered into one field.

You can always go back and add, change, or delete field data at any time! (See the sections "Deleting Contact Records" and "The Contacts, They Are A'Changin'" later in this chapter.)

6. **Don't be alarmed when ACT! automatically formats some of your field data when you enter information.**

   See the later section, "Letting ACT! do the work for you: Automatic formatting," for the lowdown on what ACT! will and won't do for you.

7. **Add your data as uniformly as possible.**

   Check out the later section, "Getting the most out of ACT!: Using the drop-down lists," to find out how to easily keep your data uniform and yourself sane.

8. **If necessary, add multiple entries to a field.**

   Generally, limiting yourself to one item per field is the best practice. From time to time, however, you'll find a situation in which a contact falls into two categories. For example, Joe Blow might be both a friend and a client. If this is your situation, you can force ACT! to let you enter more than one item into a field.

   To select several criteria to be included in a single field, follow these steps:

   a. **Place your cursor in the field.**

   b. **Press F2 to bring up the Edit List dialog box.**

   c. **From the Edit List dialog box, hold down the Ctrl key while you click the desired entries.**

   d. **Click OK.**

      The two entries appear in the field, separated by a comma (Figure 4-2).

Multiple entries in the ID/Status field

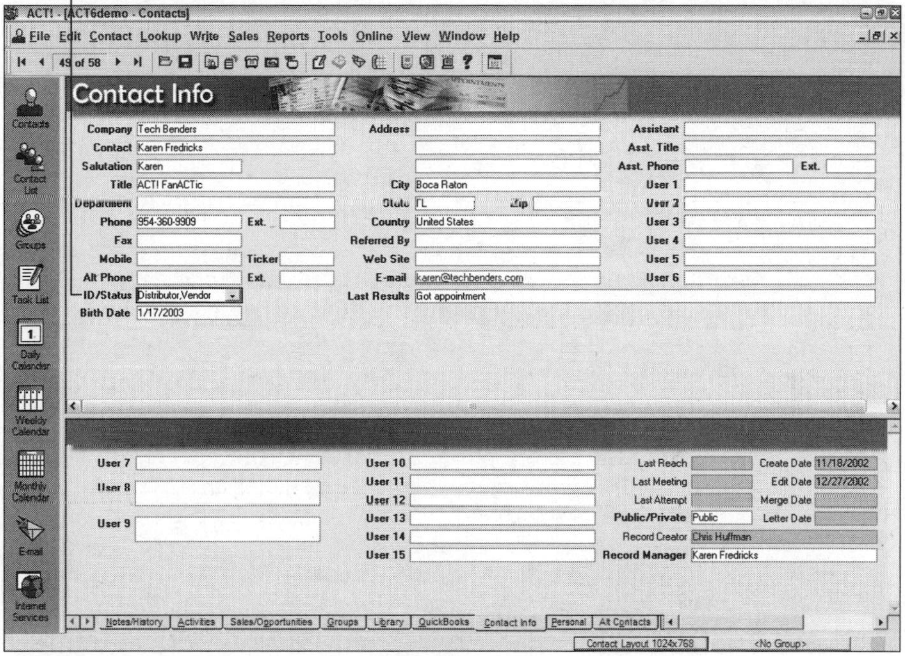

Figure 4-2:
Multiple
entries in a
field.

9. **When you fill in the information for each new contact, don't forget to click the various tabs at the bottom of your layout.**

   You'll find additional fields lurking on these tabs. Depending on the layout that you're using, you'll find fields for a spouse's name and home phone number on the Home tab and a place to enter a referral source on the Alt Contacts tab.

   Different layouts display different tabs. If you change your current layout, you'll probably be looking at a different set of tabs. Confused? Check out Chapter 2 for a quick refresher.

   If you forget to click those tabs along the bottom of the Contacts view, you just might overlook some of the fields that you needed to fill in with important information. So be sure to click those tabs!

10. **Save the new contact by clicking the Save button (represented by the small floppy disk icon on the toolbar).**

    The Save button is grayed out after the contact record is saved.

    The new contact is also automatically saved to your database:

- After you execute any other ACT! command, which includes anything from adding a note or sales opportunity to scheduling an appointment

- When you move on to another record in the database

Letting ACT! do the work for you: Automatic formatting

Entering a new contact into the ACT! database is so easy that you may overlook some of the magical things that happen when you begin to input contact information. ACT! is here to help by automatically formatting some of the contact information that you input, including

✔ **Automatic phone number formatting:** A great example of ACT!'s magic is found in the telephone field. When you type in a phone number, notice how ACT! automatically inserts the necessary hyphens. ACT! automatically inserts the dialing format for the United States each time that you enter a new phone number. Have relatives living in Turkmenistan? Have no fear: If you click the ellipsis button (the two little dots) to the right of the phone field, ACT! gives you a list of the telephone formats for just about any country that you can think of, including Turkmenistan (see Figure 4-3). After you click OK, the correct telephone country code and format is applied to the telephone number.

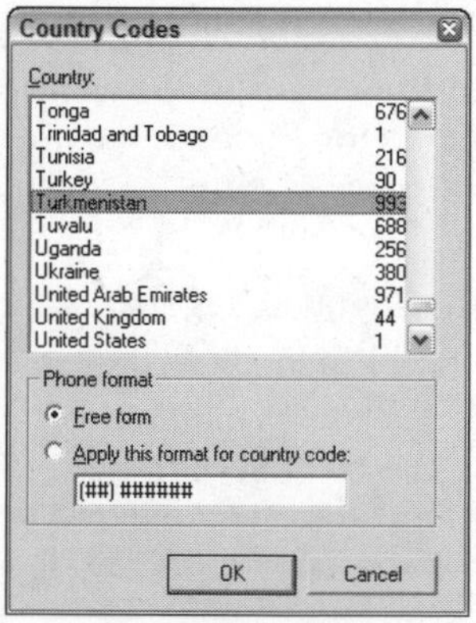

Figure 4-3:
Automatic
telephone
formatting.

Make sure that your My Record contains your own telephone number. Failure to do so results in the country code appearing next to all phone numbers in your database, even if you set the preferences not to show them! Chapter 3 walks you through adding additional users and their corresponding My Records to your database.

✓ **Automatic name formatting:** Another field that ACT! automatically provides you with is the salutation field. The salutation field is the field that appears after the word *Dear* in a letter. If you enter Mary Ellen Van der Snob as the contact name, Mary Ellen magically appears as the salutation. Of course, if you prefer to address your contacts in a more formal manner, feel free to change Mary Ellen to Ms. Van der Snob. When you enter a contact name into the database, ACT! automatically divides it into a first name and a last name. Again, if you click the ellipsis to the right of the contact field, ACT! shows you how it plans to divide the contact's name. This allows you to sort your database alphabetically by last name or to look up a contact by first name. If you attempt to enter a rather large, unique name, ACT! automatically opens this dialog box, shown in Figure 4-4, and asks you how you'd like to divide the name.

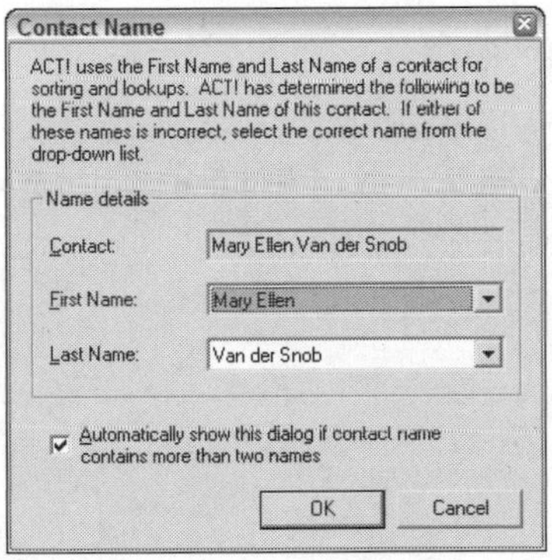

Figure 4-4:
The Contact
Name
dialog box.

Getting the most out of ACT!: Using the drop-down lists

One sure-fire way to sabotage your database is to develop new and creative ways to say the same thing. In Florida, users often vacillate between *Fort, Ft,* and *Ft.* Lauderdale, resulting in a bad sunburn and the inability to correctly find all their contacts. You'll notice that several of the ACT! fields contain drop-down lists. In these fields, you can select an item in the list, or you can type the first few letters of an item, and the field automatically fills with the item that matches what you typed or clicked. When you type an entry that isn't in the drop-down list for the Title, Department, City, and Country fields, the item is automatically added to the list so that you can then select it for other contacts.

You have two ways of using the drop-down lists to enter information:

✔ Type the first few letters of an entry that already appears in the drop-down list, and ACT! completes the word for you. For example, if you type **Ch** in the City field, *Chicago* magically appears.

✔ Access the drop-down list by clicking its arrow and then choosing an item from the list.

Using these drop-down lists whenever possible helps ensure consistency throughout your database. In Chapter 14, I explain how to add additional drop-down fields to your database and control how you use them.

If you'd like to change the content of the drop-down lists that come with ACT!, follow these steps:

1. **Click in a field that has a drop-down list.**

2. **Click the drop-down arrow in the field.**

3. **When the drop-down list appears, scroll to the bottom of the list and choose Edit List.**

   The Edit List dialog box appears, as shown in Figure 4-5.

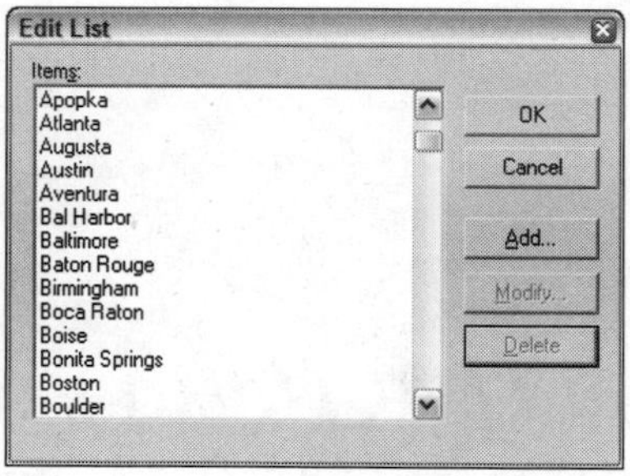

Figure 4-5:
Editing the drop-down list.

4. **In the Edit List dialog box, do one of the following:**

   • Click the Add button to add an item to the list. The Add dialog box appears. In the Item field, enter the text that you want to appear in the list and then click OK.

   • Click the Delete button to remove an item from the list. Click Yes when ACT! asks you to confirm the deletion.

   • Click the Modify button to edit an existing item in the list. Change the Item Name or Description and then click OK.

5. **Click OK when you've finished editing your list.**

And that's all there is to it. What an easy way to ensure consistency, huh?

Duplicating Your Contacts

As you can see from the "Adding New Contacts" section, entering a new contact into ACT! involves quite a few things. Thankfully, ACT! makes it very easy to duplicate a previously saved record.

Suppose that you've just entered Jane Jones' contact information, and now you find yourself looking at a pile of business cards from Jane's co-workers. All of them have the same company name and address; the only variables are the contact name and phone number. ACT! gives you two options for duplicating contacts. You can either copy the *primary* information or *all* the information. The primary fields are Company, Address 1, Address 2, Address 3, City, State (County, Land, or Province), Zip (Postcode), Country, Phone, and Fax. When you copy all fields, every field is copied into the new contact record except the Contact and E-mail Address fields.

To duplicate contact information without extra typing, follow these steps:

1. **Open the record that you want to duplicate.**

2. **Choose Contact⇨Duplicate Contact.**

   The Duplicate Contact dialog box appears, shown in Figure 4-6.

Figure 4-6: Duplicating contact information.

3. **Select either the Duplicate Data from Primary Fields or Duplicate Data from All Fields radio button and then click OK.**

   A new contact record appears, filled in with the copied information from the original contact record.

4. **Continue creating the contact record by filling in the variable information and proceeding as you would with an entirely new contact.**

Deleting Contact Records

What do you do if you find that a contact has been duplicated in your database? Or that you're no longer doing business with one of your contacts? For whatever reason that you decide that a name no longer needs to be a part of your database, you can just delete that contact record.

ACT! allows you to either delete one contact record or a lookup of contact records. (A *lookup* is the group of contacts that is displayed after a database search. Peruse Chapter 6 for more information about lookups.) Just realize that you will be deleting either the current contact that you're viewing or the current group of contacts that you just created a query for. When you're on the contact that you want to delete, do one of the following:

✔ **Choose Contact⇨Delete.**

✔ **Press Ctrl+Delete.**

✔ **Right-click the contact record and choose Delete Contact.**

Any one of these choices brings up the warning shown in Figure 4-7.

Figure 4-7:
Ominous
warning
when
deleting a
contact.

If you click the Delete Contact button, you'll delete the current contact that you're viewing. If you click the Delete Lookup button, you'll delete the current contact lookup.

Thinking before deleting a contact

Although the procedure is rather simple, you may want to rethink the issue of deleting contacts. When you delete a contact, you are also deleting all the associated notes and histories that are tied to that contact. For example, suppose that State College is using ACT! to keep track of all prospective students that it has contacted — or has been contacted by. State College admissions personnel may receive thousands of inquiries a month and fear that the database will become too large to manage . . . and subsequently think that deleting all prospects that they haven't had contact with in over a year is the best course of action. However, some of those prospects might be attending different schools that they aren't happy with and may want to enter State College as transfer students. Other prospects may transfer in after completing two years at a community college, and still others might consider attending State College as graduate students.

What to do in such a situation? I'd consider moving the contacts that you no longer need into another archival database. That way, should the need ever arise, you can still find all the original information on a contact without having to start again from scratch. How nice to be able to rekindle a relationship by asking, "So tell me, how did you find the accounting department at Podunk University?" Although the setup of an archival database is beyond the scope of this book, an ACT! Certified Consultant can assist you with this matter.

Four warnings before deleting a contact

Losing contacts in your database is a very scary thought. You will undoubtedly rely very heavily on your ACT! database; losing that data can be potentially devastating to your business. Worst of all, if you realize that you have just accidentally removed several — or even hundreds of — contacts from the database, panic may set in!

Divert this panic by following these tips *before* you attempt to delete any of your contacts:

- ✔ Know the difference between deleting a *contact* and deleting a *lookup* so that you don't delete numerous contacts when you only wanted to delete a single record.

    The *current contact* is the single record that you view from the Contacts view. A *lookup* is the group of contacts that's displayed after a database search.

- ✔ Read the warning and make note of the number of contacts that you're about to delete. Don't be afraid to click Cancel if a large number of contacts start to disappear.

- ✔ ACTDiag also enables you to restore your deleted contacts — *if* you haven't compressed and reindexed! Turn to Chapter 17 for further details about undeleting a previously deleted contact.

- ✔ Remember the three rules of computing: backup, backup, backup! Chapter 16 provides you with instructions on how to create a backup. Although undeleting your deleted records is sometimes possible, a backup provides the easiest method to restore all your information after it has been accidentally deleted.

The Contacts, They Are A'Changin'

Companies relocate and change their names, people move, and your fingers sometimes slip on the keyboard. People change e-mail addresses. You might want to add additional contact information for one of your contacts. All these predicaments require the editing of contact fields. Not to worry; changing the information that you've stored in ACT! is as easy as entering it in the first place.

ACT! gives you two ways of replacing contact information:

✔ Click in the field that you want to change and then press the Delete or Backspace key to remove the existing field information. Then simply type in the new information.

✔ Click in the field *above* the one that you want to change. When you press the Tab key, you'll move into the desired field — and all the information will be highlighted for you. By typing in the new information, the old information is automatically replaced.

If you've overwritten information in a single ACT! field, press Ctrl+Z to undo the changes that you just made to that field — *before* you move your cursor to another ACT! field. For those who are keyboard challenged, an alternative is to choose Edit⇨Undo from the Main menu. After you've moved on to another field, neither of these options is available to you.

To undo multiple changes that you've made to an ACT! record, choose Edit⇨Undo Changes to Contact *before* you move on to the next record. Remember, after you execute another ACT! command or move on to another record, ACT! automatically saves the record so that you then can't undo your changes.

Chapter 5

The Contact List

*T*he basic *Contacts* view shows you a majority of the fields in your database as they pertain to a single contact. Conversely, the *Contact List* view allows you to see all your contacts together in one list. In the Contact List, you can find contacts, sort your list of contacts, create lookups of contacts, or enter contact information. Best of all, after you arrange the Contact List just the way that you like it, you can print out the information exactly as it appears onscreen.

Understanding the Contact List

The Contact List is a good way to view your contacts if you're working with large numbers of contacts at one time. Changing the columns that appear in the Contact List provides you with a way of comparing information between your various contacts. For example, you may want to see how many of your contacts purchased one product and also another product.

The road to the Contact List is simple to follow — just click the Contact List icon on the ACT! View bar. A list of your contacts displayed in columns appears, as shown in Figure 5-1.

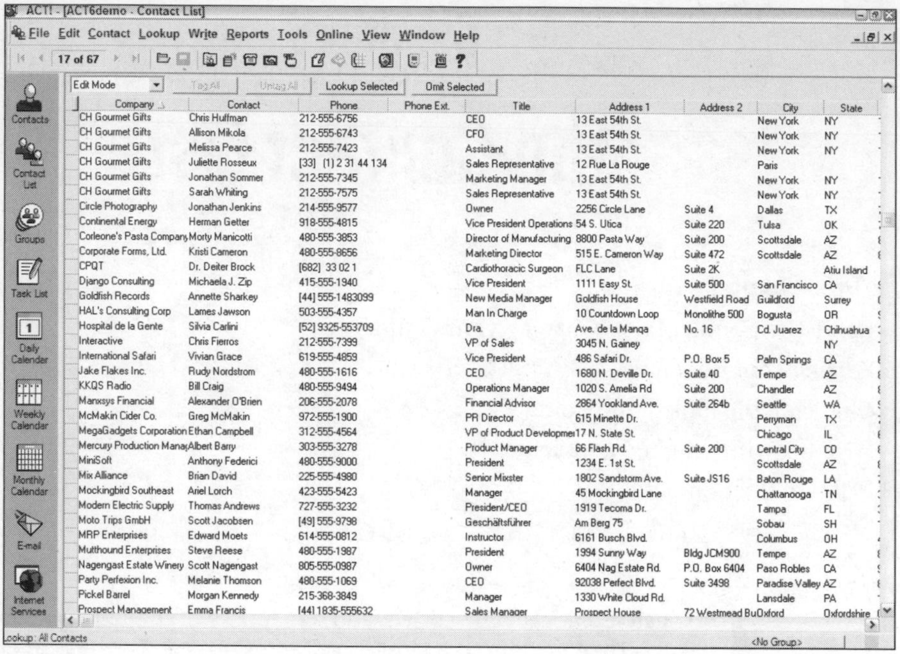

Figure 5-1:
The ACT!
Contact List.

Sorting your contacts

By default, your contacts are sorted alphabetically by the Company field. You know this for two reasons:

- The small triangle that appears after the Company column heading.

- You remember your alphabet from grammar school, and you notice that companies starting with the letter B appear directly below those starting with the letter A.

Click the column heading that you want to use to sort the list. For example, to sort by the contact's last name, click the Contact column heading.

To reverse the sort order, click the column heading again. An up arrow in the column heading indicates that the contacts are listed in ascending order (in alphabetical, A-to-Z order). If the list is sorted in ascending order, contacts that have no information in the selected column appear first in the list. In descending order, they appear last in the list.

Sorting your contacts is so simple that you may decide to get really adventurous and sort based on another criterion. Go ahead — I dare you! Click any column heading to re-sort the Contact List by the field of your choice.

Why aren't my contacts sorting correctly?

At times, it may appear that your contacts just aren't alphabetizing correctly. Possible reasons for this are

- ✔ A stray mark or a blank space in front of the field name; *'Zinger & Co.* will appear alphabetically in front of *Gadgets R Us*.

- ✔ Numbers appear alphabetically in front of letters. *1st Financial Savings & Loan* will

appear alphabetically in front of *AAA Best Bank*.

- ✔ ACT! may be a little confused about the first and last name of a contact; a quick trip to the Contacts view is worth your time. Click the ellipsis button next to the Contact's name and then double-check that the correct first and last names appear in the appropriate spots.

Although the Contact List provides you with a quick-as-a-bunny way to sort your contacts, it is creating the sort based on the contents of a *single* field. If you want to sort your contacts based on multiple criteria, here's how you do it:

1. **From the Contact List, choose Edit➪Sort.**

2. **In the Sort Contacts dialog box that appears (see Figure 5-2), choose an option from the Sort Contacts By list to specify the first-level sort criterion.**

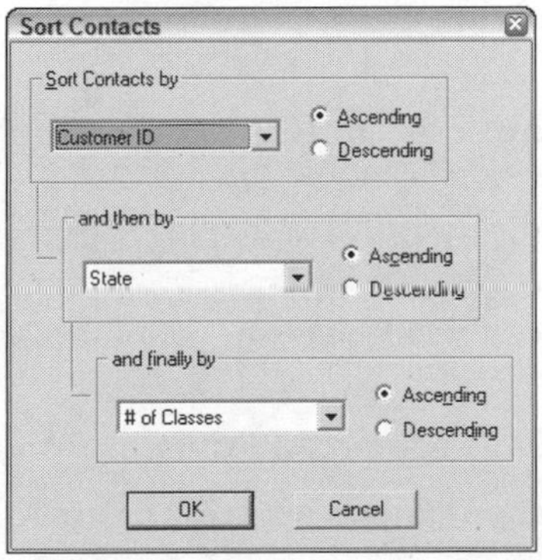

Figure 5-2:
The Sort
Contacts
dialog box.

3. **Select the sorting order (Ascending or Descending).**

   Ascending sort order means from A to Z or from the smallest number to the largest number. Records with no information in the field used for the sort appear first. *Descending* means from Z to A or from the largest number to the smallest number. Records with no information in the field used for the sort appear last.

4. **Choose a second field option from the And Then By list and specify Ascending or Descending.**

5. **If you'd like a third level of sorting, choose a field from the And Finally By list and specify Ascending or Descending.**

6. **Click OK.**

Finding a contact in the contact list

In Chapter 6, I show you how to create a lookup to find contacts that meet your specific criteria. The Contact List also allows you to go to a specific contact record in the blink of an eye. Here's what you need to do:

1. **Click the column heading to select that column.**

   For example, if you want to find a contact by last name, click the Contact column heading.

2. **Start typing the first few letters of the contact information that you want to find.**

   If you sorted the Contact List alphabetically by company name, type in the first few letters of the company that you're looking for. If you sorted by Contact, start typing the first few letters of the contact's last name.

   Typically, when I show this feature to an ACT! user and say, "Start typing," the first response I get is, "Where?" My answer is, "Just start typing" — as long as you see the triangle indicating that your Contact List is sorted, you're good to go!

3. **As soon as you begin typing, the Look For text box appears above the column heading that you clicked.**

   ACT! scrolls down the Contact List to the closest match. For example, if you sorted the list by Contact and typed the letter **s**, you might land on Colonel Sanders' contact record. If you typed **sm**, you'll probably be looking at all your Smiths.

4. **Continue typing until you reach the contact for whom you were looking.**

5. **The Look For window closes when you press Enter or click elsewhere in the Contact List.**

Remodeling the Contact List

One of the reasons that you might find the Contact List to be particularly useful is the ease in which you can customize it. You can change the order of the columns, widen the columns, add or remove columns, and even *lock* columns so that they remain visible onscreen as you scroll the window right or left. For example, in the Contacts List, you can lock the Company and Contact columns so that they remain visible as you scroll through other columns.

Here's a few ways in which you can change the look of the Contact List:

✔ **Add columns to the Contact List:** Probably the first thing that you want to do to modify the Contact List is to add an additional column — or two or three!

    1. **Right-click in the Contact List window and choose Select Add Columns from the menu that appears.**

    2. **In the Add Columns dialog box that appears (see Figure 5-3), select the field that you want to add and drag it to the desired position on the Contact List.**

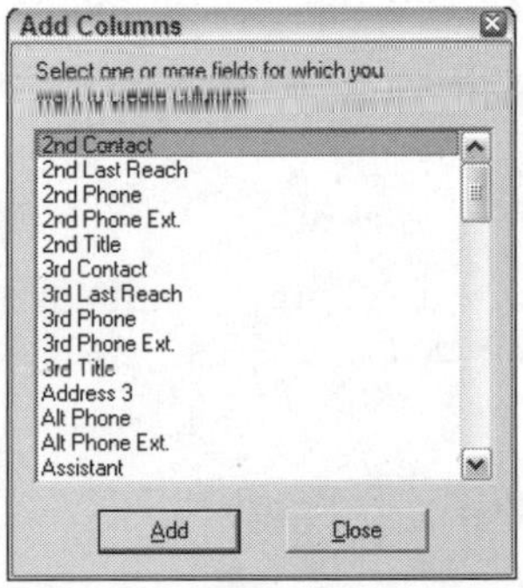

Figure 5-3:
Adding columns to the Contact List.

![Add Columns dialog box showing a list of fields: 2nd Contact, 2nd Last Reach, 2nd Phone, 2nd Phone Ext., 2nd Title, 3rd Contact, 3rd Last Reach, 3rd Phone, 3rd Phone Ext., 3rd Title, Address 3, Alt Phone, Alt Phone Ext., Assistant, with Add and Close buttons]

    3. **Click the Close button when you're done.**

    If you're tempted to click the Add button, refrain. Although this isn't a bad thing, it can be a pain in the patookie. (*Patookie* is an official computer term.) When you click the Add button, the new column is automatically added to the far right edge of the Contact List. If you have several columns in the Contact List, you're now forced to drag the column leftward so that it's more conveniently located near the Contact or Company columns.

✔ **Change the order of the column headings:** You can drag-and-drop the various column headings to change the order in which they appear on the Contact List. For example, if you want the Contact field to appear before the Company field, simply hold down your mouse on the Contact column heading while dragging it over to the left of the Company column heading.

✔ **Change the width of the columns:** If you move your mouse on the line between any two column headings, your cursor transforms into a double-headed arrow. When that arrow appears, hold down your left mouse button and drag to the left or right to narrow or widen a column. You'll change the size of the column to the left of your mouse.

✔ **Delete a column heading:** You can remove a column from the Contact List by simply dragging the column heading approximately one inch above its current location. A little garbage can appears, indicating that your column is about to join that great recycle bin in the sky. Let go of the mouse, and the column disappears. Before you start to reach for your antacid, rest assured that you have not permanently deleted the column — it's still alive and well in the Contacts view!

✔ **Lock the first column(s):** You can lock columns in a list view so that they remain visible onscreen while you scroll the Contact List to the right or left. For example, the first two columns of the Contact List might display the Company and Contact fields, and you want the next ten columns to display the various products that you sell. You find that when you scroll to the right to examine products 9 and 10, you lose track of the corresponding contact name. By locking the first two columns, you ensure that they always remain visible.

1. **Place your cursor on the column anchor.**

   The column anchor is the little vertical button immediately to the left of your first column heading. See Figure 5-4.

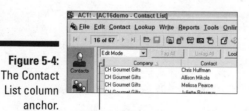

Figure 5-4:
The Contact List column anchor.

Column anchor

2. **Drag the column anchor to the right of the column(s) that you want to anchor.**

   A solid, vertical line appears to the right of the anchored column; see Figure 5-5. The anchored column and any columns to the left remain in place while you scroll the Contact List to the right or left.

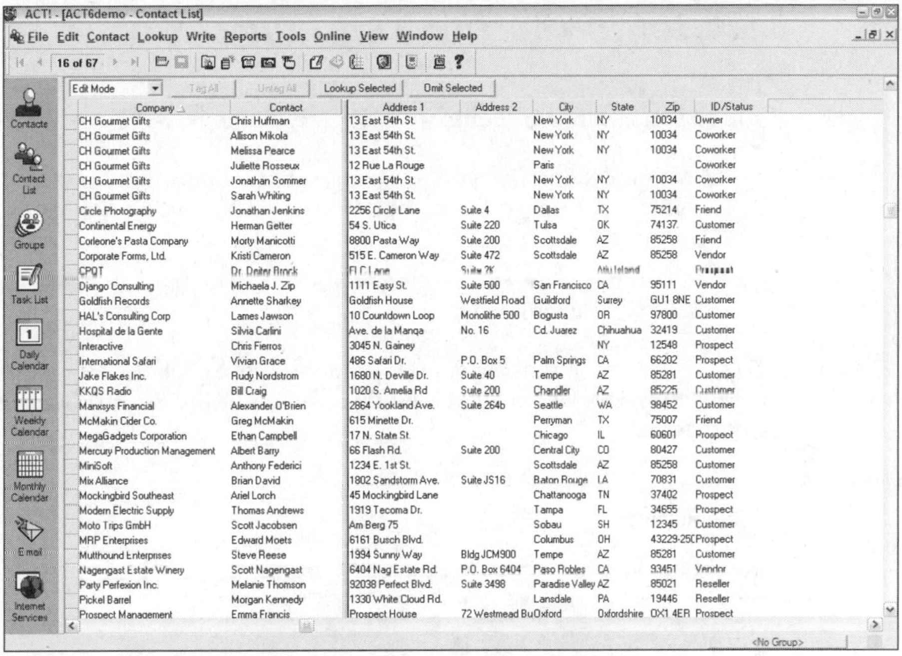

Figure 5-5:
Columns to
the left of
the vertical
gray bar are
locked.

Playing Tag with Your Contacts

One of ACT!'s best features is that it gives you the ability to perform a mail merge or to create labels or documents that are relevant to only certain members of your database. You can do this by using the ACT! lookup (which I discuss in more detail in Chapter 6). However, many users find it easier to accomplish the same goal by using the Contact List.

Using the Contact List, you can either select — or *tag* — contacts to manually create a lookup of your contacts. For example, say that you want to target some of your best clients for a special promotion; a general lookup probably wouldn't produce a list of those contacts because you don't have a field that includes special promotions. Instead, you can tag those contacts based on your own instincts.

Switching to the Tag mode

There are two viewing modes in the Contact List. Although similar, they allow you to work with your contacts in slightly different ways.

- ✓ **Edit mode:** Enables you to change contact information in any of the fields, add a new contact, or delete an existing one. You can also select contacts.

- ✓ **Tag mode:** Allows you to tag contacts to create lookups easily, but you can't edit any information.

To switch between the Tag and Edit modes, just click the Mode indicator (see Figure 5-6), which is located directly under the Record Counter in the Contact List.

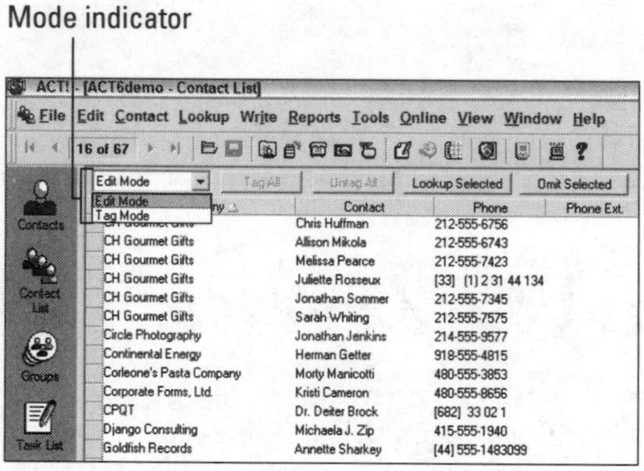

Mode indicator

Figure 5-6:
The Contact
List Mode
indicator.

Selecting contacts in the Contact List

The look of the Contact List changes slightly when you switch between the Tag and Edit modes. And the procedure for selecting contacts also differs slightly depending on which mode you're working in.

Selecting contacts in the Tag mode

In the Tag mode, the Selection button to the left of each contact is missing. Although you can't edit your contacts in the Tag mode, you can still easily select them:

- ✓ *To tag a single contact*, click anywhere on your contact to tag it; a plus sign appears to the left of the contact indicating that you have tagged it. Figure 5-7 shows tagged contacts.

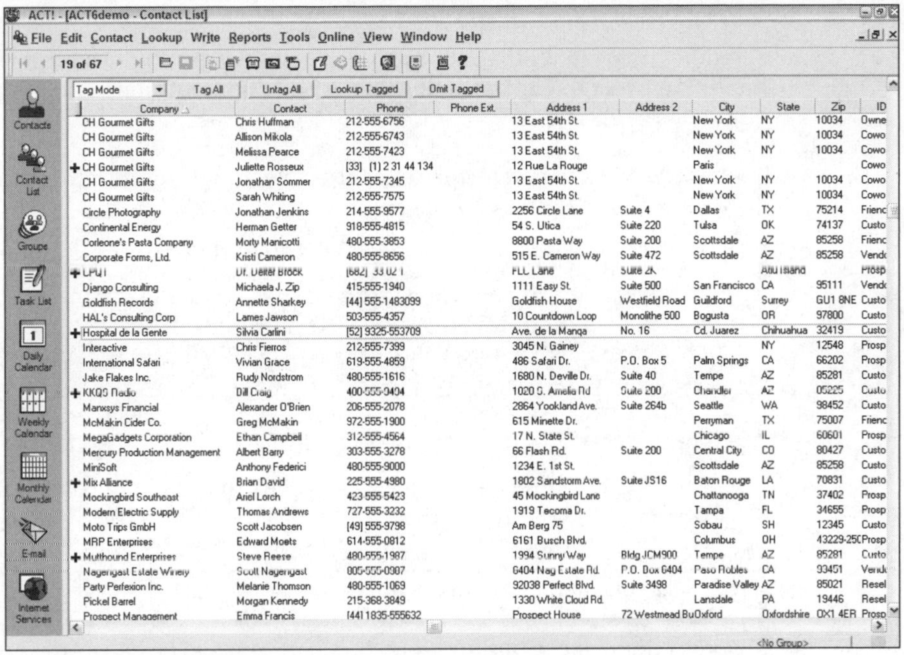

Figure 5-7:
Selected
contacts in
the Tag
mode.

✔ *To untag a contact*, click anywhere on a contact and the plus sign disappears.

✔ *To tag a continuous list of names*, click the first name in the list that you're selecting, and then press and hold down the Shift key while you click the last name in the list that you're selecting.

Notice the four buttons to the right of the Mode indicator (refer to Figure 5-7). After you tag the contacts that you want to work with or those that you want to omit temporarily, choose one of the following four options:

✔ **Tag All** allows you to create a lookup based on all the contacts currently showing in the Contact List.

✔ **Untag All** allows you to deselect any contacts that you've already selected.

✔ **Lookup Tagged** allows you to created a lookup based on the contacts that you have tagged.

✔ **Omit Tagged** allows you to remove the contacts that you selected from the Contact List.

Selecting contacts in the Edit mode

Selecting contacts in the Edit mode is very easy, but it does require a steady hand. You need to click directly on the Selection button to the left of each contact.

✔ *To select a contact record*, click the Selection button to the left of that record. The entire contact row becomes highlighted.

✔ *To deselect a record*, click the Selection button a second time.

Be careful not to click anywhere on the Contact List after you have selected your contacts, or you'll deselect all currently selected contacts! This can be extremely annoying, especially after you have just spent the last 15 minutes carefully selecting contacts that you want to work with. I strongly advise against consuming large quantities of caffeine if you're going to select a large number of contacts using the Edit mode.

✔ *To select a continuous list of names*, click the first name in the list that you want to select, and then press and hold down the Shift key while you click the last name in the list that you're selecting.

✔ *To select multiple names in the Contact List*, click the first name that you want to select, and then press and hold down the Ctrl key while clicking another name. Continue selecting names while holding down the Ctrl key.

Figure 5-8 shows an example of the Contact List containing records that have been selected in the Edit mode.

Selection button

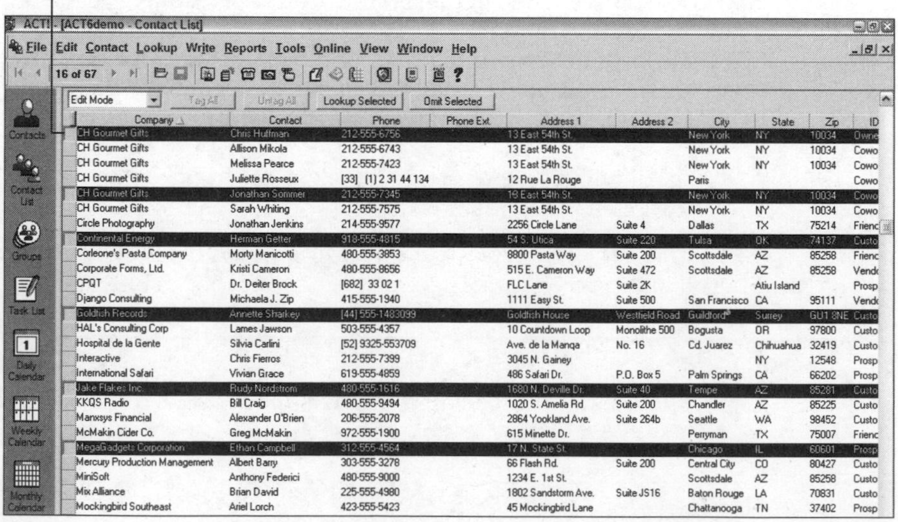

Figure 5-8:
Contacts that were selected in the Edit mode.

After you select your contacts using the Edit mode, choose one of the follow-ing choices (in Edit mode, you have only two choices):

- ✔ **Lookup Selected:** Allows you to create a lookup of your currently selected contacts.

- ✔ **Omit Selected:** Enables you to temporarily omit the selected contacts from the Contact List.

Switching back to the Contacts view

Although you can change data from the Contact List, you'll probably find it easier to return to the Contacts view when you come across a contact record that requires a bit of tweaking. There are two ways to accomplish this:

- ✔ In Edit mode, double-click the Selection button for a contact in the Contact List. The Selection button is located directly to the left of the first column in the Contact List (refer to Figure 5-8).

- ✔ In Tag mode, double-click anywhere on the contact.

The Contacts view appears with the selected contact's record. To return to the Contact List, click the Contact List icon on the View bar.

Printing the Contact List

You can use the Contact List as a way to create on-the-fly reports when you want to analyze one key field of information as it pertains to all or a selected group of your contacts. Printing the current contents of the Contact List pro-duces a hard copy of everything that you currently see in the Contact List.

Printing the Contact List is not meant as a replacement for using ACT!'s reports. The Contact List cannot be memorized. In order to re-create it, you would have to start again from scratch. If you need to produce the informa-tion from the Contact List on a continuing basis, save yourself some trouble by creating a new report. Check out Chapter 11 for details on ACT! reports.

Here's how you print out a copy of your current Contact List:

1. **Go to the Contact List by clicking the Contact List icon on the View bar.**

2. **Add, move, delete, or resize columns as necessary.**

3. **Create a lookup or, using either the Tag or Edit mode, select the con-tacts that you want to work with.**

4. **Choose File⇨Print Contact List.**

   The Print dialog box opens.

5. **Click OK to select your printer.**

   The Print List Window dialog box opens, as shown in Figure 5-9.

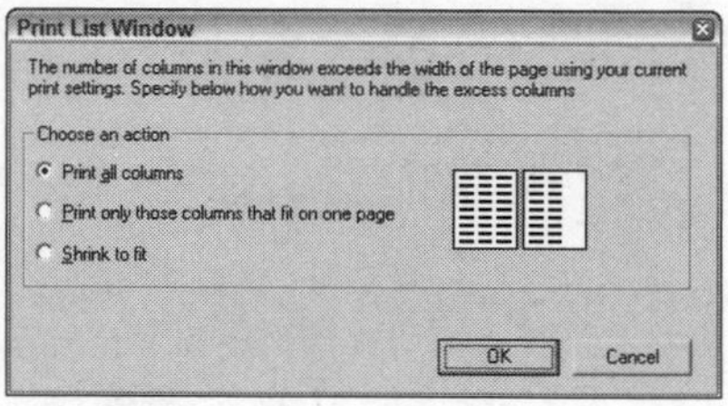

Figure 5-9:
Printing the
Contact List.

6. **Choose from one of the following three options:**

   • **Print All Columns:** If you have more columns than will fit on one page, all additional columns appear on a second sheet of paper.

   • **Print Only Those Columns That Fit on One Page:** Only those columns that are currently visible in the Contact List are printed. This is generally your best option.

   • **Shrink to Fit:** This prints all columns in your Contact List but squeezes them on to a single sheet of paper. Basically, if you have more than one or two columns that can't be seen in the Contact List, shrinking them makes them too small to be legible. Never use this option if you're over 40!

   If all columns are currently visible in the Contact List, this option doesn't appear.

Chapter 6

The ACT! Lookup: Searching for Your Contacts

. . . .

In This Chapter

▶ Understanding the basic ACT! lookup

▶ Searching by keyword

▶ Performing advanced queries

. . . .

*I*f all roads lead to Rome, then surely all processes in ACT! lead to the lookup. A *lookup* is a way of looking at only a portion of the contacts in your database, depending on your specifications. A good practice in ACT! is to perform a lookup *first* and then perform an action *second*. For example, you might perform a lookup and then print some labels. Or you might do a lookup and then perform a mail merge. Need a report? Do a lookup first! In this chapter, I show you how to perform lookups based on contact information, on notes and history information, and on advanced query information.

ACT! Is Looking Up

The theory behind the lookup is that you don't always need to work with all your contacts at one time. Not only is it easier to work with only a portion of your database, at times, it's absolutely necessary. If you're changing your mailing address, you probably want to send a notification to everyone in your database. If you're running a special sales promotion, you probably only notify your prospects and customers. If you're sending out overpriced holiday gift baskets, however, you probably want the names of only your very best customers.

Don't create an extra database — use the ACT! lookup instead

Some ACT! users originally create several databases, not realizing that one database can be used to store information about various different types of contacts. Although you might want to create two separate databases — for instance, one for customers and one for vendors — a better alternative is to include both your customers and vendors together in one database. To this one database you can then add a few miscellaneous contacts, including prospects who aren't yet customers or referral sources that might lead to new customers. Then when you want to see only vendors or only prospective customers, simply perform a lookup to work with that particular group of contacts.

In ACT!, you can focus on a portion of your contacts by

✔ Creating basic lookups based on the information in one of the ten most commonly used contact fields in ACT!. (See the later section "Performing Basic Lookups.")

✔ Conducting a query based on information stored in your Notes/Histories, Activities, Group, and Sales Opportunities. (See the later section "Performing Special ACT! Lookups.")

✔ Creating your own, more advanced queries based on the parameters of your own choosing by using logical operators. (See the later section "Creating Advanced Queries.")

Performing Basic Lookups

The easiest way to pose a query is to choose one of your main contact fields from a menu and then fill in the search criteria. This way is easy because the menus guide you, but it's also the least flexible way. The Lookup menu that ACT! provides is probably the best — and simplest — place to start when creating a lookup; just follow these steps:

1. **On the Contacts view menu, click Lookup.**

   Figure 6-1 shows you the Lookup menu that drops down and the criteria that you can use to perform your lookup.

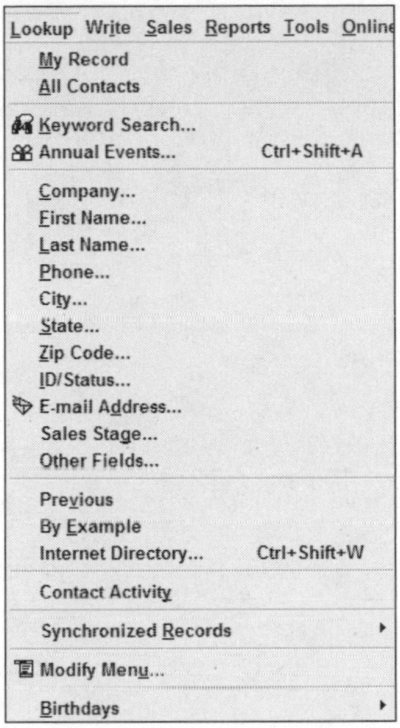

Lookup	Write	Sales	Reports	Tools	Online
My Record					
All Contacts					
Keyword Search...					
Annual Events...		Ctrl+Shift+A			
Company...					
First Name...					
Last Name...					
Phone...					
City...					
State...					
Zip Code...					
ID/Status...					
E-mail Address...					
Sales Stage...					
Other Fields...					
Previous					
By Example					
Internet Directory...		Ctrl+Shift+W			
Contact Activity					
Synchronized Records		▶			
Modify Menu...					
Birthdays		▶			

Figure 6-1:
The ACT!
Lookup
menu.

2. **Choose one of the criteria listed in Figure 6-1 to create a basic lookup.**

   The ACT! Lookup dialog box appears, as shown in Figure 6-2.

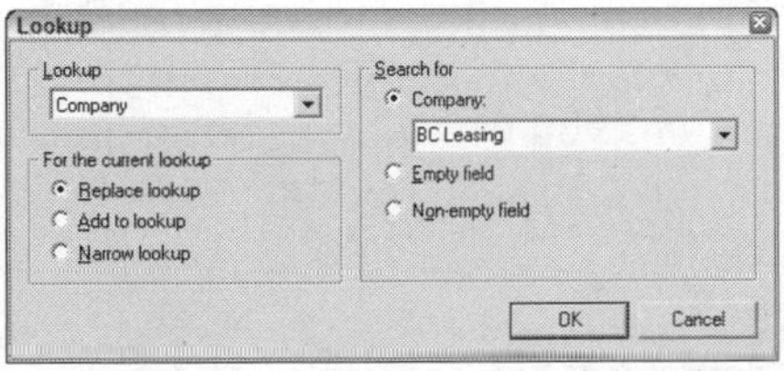

Figure 6-2:
The ACT!
Lookup
dialog box.

3. **If you're searching based on an Other Field, click the Lookup drop-down arrow and choose a field from the drop-down list.**

4. **In the For the Current Lookup area, select an option:**

   • **Replace Lookup:** Creates a brand-new lookup based on your criteria.

   • **Add to Lookup:** Adds the contacts based on your criteria to an existing lookup. For example, if you've created a lookup for your contacts based in Chicago, select this option to add your New York clients to the set of Chicago clients.

   • **Narrow Lookup:** Refines a lookup based on a second criterion. For example, if you've created a lookup of all your customers, select this option to narrow the lookup to only customers based in Philadelphia.

5. **In the Search For area, select an option:**

   - **Company:** Type the word to search for or select a word from the drop-down list if you're looking for contacts that match a specific criterion.

   - **Empty Field:** If you're looking for contacts that don't have any data in the given field — for example, people who don't have e-mail addresses — choose this option.

   - **Non-empty Field:** If you want to find only those contacts that have data in a given field — for example, everyone who *has* an e-mail address — choose this option.

6. **Click OK.**

   The Record Counter now reflects the number of contacts that matched your search criteria.

7. **Choose Lookup⇨All Contacts when you're ready to once again view all the contacts in your database.**

Performing Special ACT! Lookups

The ability to perform a simple lookup based on a single field criterion is an element common to most databases. But ACT! isn't your average database. All databases contain fields, but only special databases contain things such as notes and activities. And after creating a note to store a useful tidbit of information (which I show you how to do in Chapter 7), you'll want to find that information again. ACT! provides you with three *special* query options to find information that was entered into ACT! in a *special* way.

Searching by keyword

The *keyword search* can be an extremely useful way to find data about your contacts no matter where that information might be lurking. ACT!'s keyword search enables you to perform lookups for information in contact fields, Notes/Histories, Activities, Sales/Opportunities, and E-mail Addresses. For example, suppose that you're looking for someone to design a new logo for your business but you can't remember where you stored that information. Is *logo* part of the company's name, did you enter it into the ID/Status field, or did you stick it in a note somewhere? A keyword search searches throughout your database, checking all fields, until it finds the word *logo*.

Here's how to perform a keyword search:

1. **From the Contacts view, choose Lookup⇨Keyword Search.**

   The Keyword Search dialog box opens (see Figure 6-3).

2. **Enter the word or phrase that you want to find in the Search For text box.**

   The keyword search is a powerful searching tool, and so it does take a bit longer to run than other searching methods. When you perform a keyword search, ACT! sifts through every last bit of information in your database, hoping to find a match that fits your specifications. To speed up the process, limit the amount of elements that you're searching through.

3. **In the Search These Records area, choose an option:**

   • **All Records:** ACT! sifts through all records in your database.

   • **Current Record:** ACT! searches only the record that was onscreen when you opened the dialog box. Use this option if you know that somewhere in the deep, dark past, you entered a specific tidbit of information as a note.

   • **Current Lookup:** ACT! searches only the records that you've selected in a previous lookup.

   • **Selected Group:** ACT! combs through the specified group that you select from the accompanying drop-down list.

4. **In the Search In area, choose an option.**

   In addition to choosing what records to search, you can select which fields, tabs, or even groups you want to search.

   First you must choose between

   • **Contact Records:** Searches only in the contact records

   • **Group Records:** Searches only in the group records

Then you're free to choose as many of the following as you'd like:

- **Contact Fields:** Searches in the contact fields

- **Groups Fields:** Searches the group fields; you can search the Group fields only if you've decided to search through the Group records.

- **Sales/Opportunities:** Searches the information on the Sales/Opportunities tab.

- **Activities:** Searches in your activities.

- **Notes/History:** Searches in the notes and histories you've created.

- **E-mail Addresses:** Searches through your e-mail addresses

5. **After making all your choices, click the Find Now button.**

   ACT! responds with a list of records, similar to what's shown in Figure 6-4. The lookup results show the contact's name and company and the field in which ACT! found the matching data, as well as the data that it found. For example, if you searched for the word *ACT!*, your search would include such diverse words as *interactive* and *contractor* because the letters *act* appear in the middle of these words.

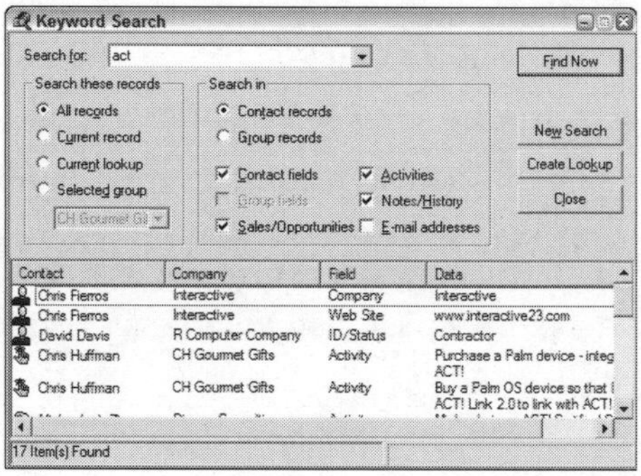

Figure 6-4: Results of a keyword search.

6. **Decide what you want to do with the results.**

   Like the old saying goes, be careful of what you search for because you just might find it! Okay, the saying doesn't go exactly like that, but now that you've found a number of records using the keyword search, you must decide which one(s) to focus on. Here are some of your options:

   - Click the Create Lookup button to see all the records in the Contacts view.

   - Double-click any part of a single record, and you land on that contact record. To get back to your search, double-click the Keyword Search tab that now appears in the bottom-left corner of the Contacts view, as shown in Figure 6-5.

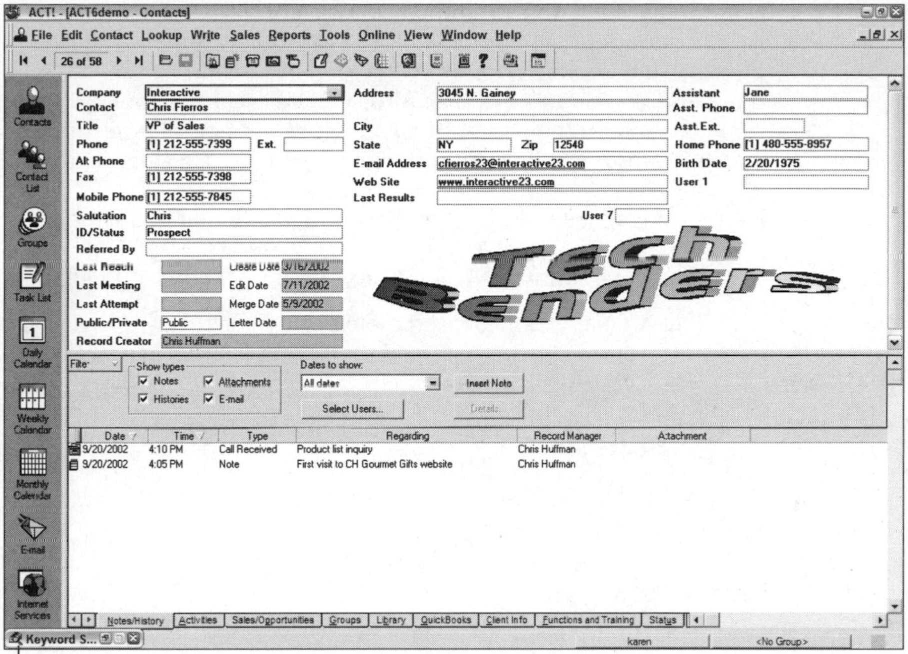

Figure 6-5:
The
Keyword
Search after
it has been
minimized.

Double-click to return to your search

- Select multiple adjacent records by clicking the first record, holding down the Shift key, and then clicking the last record. Right-click one of your selections and choose Lookup Selected Records. You now have a lookup that consists of only the contacts that you selected.

- Select records that aren't adjacent by clicking the first record, holding down the Ctrl key, and then clicking the other records that you want. Right-click one of your selections and choose Lookup Selected Records. You now have a lookup that consists of only the contacts that you selected.

Annual events

In Chapter 14, I show you how to create Annual Event fields. Annual events help automate the processes of tracking important dates, such as birthdays, anniversaries, or even policy renewals. When you enter a date in an annual event field, ACT! automatically tracks the event date from year to year. Because annual events don't appear on your calendar, you must perform an Annual Event lookup to display them. You can use the Annual Events lookup to generate a printed list to display events for the current week, the current month, or a specified date range.

Combining the power of Annual Events with an ACT! Mail Merge is a great way to save yourself lots of time. For example, suppose that your company offers yearly service contracts. You can easily find all the customers whose contracts are about to expire. After you've created a lookup of these customers, you can then send them all a renewal letter by performing a mail merge. (I show you how to perform a mail merge in Chapter 12.)

Here's all you need to do to create an Annual Events Lookup:

1. **From the Contacts view, choose Lookup⇨Annual Events.**

   The Annual Events Search dialog box opens, as shown in Figure 6-6.

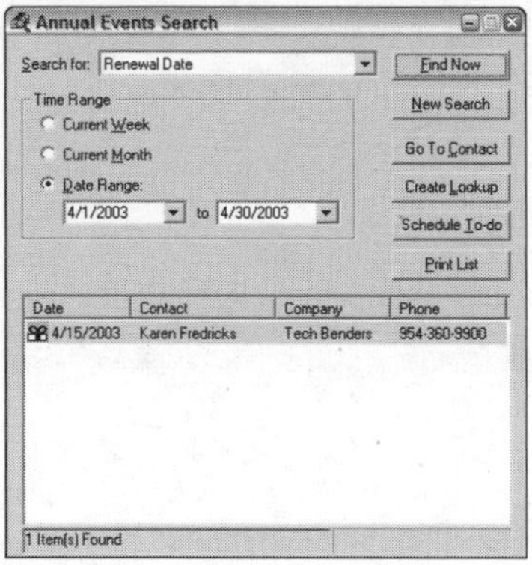

Figure 6-6:
The Annual
Events
Search
dialog box.

2. **Choose the Time Range in which you'd like to search.**

   Your options are the current week or month, or a selected date range.

3. **Click the Find Now button.**

   The results appear in the lower half of the Annual Events Search dialog box. Your results will vary depending on the number of contacts that meet your search criteria. If no contacts meet your search criteria, you receive a message nicely telling you so.

4. **Click one of the following option buttons:**

   • **Go To Contact:** To go to the Contact record of the selected contact.

   • **Create Lookup:** To create a lookup of all the contacts.

   • **Schedule To-Do:** To schedule an activity for the selected contacts. Unfortunately, you can schedule only one activity at a time.

   • **Print List:** To print a list of the contacts.

Searching by contact activity

I've often estimated that at least 20 percent of the average database consists of long, lost contact information. You can either ignore these forlorn contacts, or you might realize that there's gold in them there hills! What if you could find all the contacts that you haven't contacted in, say, the last two years? Chances are that many of those contacts will be glad to hear from you. Maybe they lost your contact information or chose a company other than yours that they weren't happy with. Suddenly those "lost" contacts have become a virtual treasure trove.

You can create a lookup of contacts based on the last time that you made any changes to their record or contacted them through a meeting, call, or to-do. You can look for the contacts that either have or have not been changed within a specified date range. You can also narrow the search according to activity or history type.

To create a lookup by contact activity:

1. **Choose Lookup⇨Contact Activity.**

   The Contact Activity dialog box opens, as shown in Figure 6-7.

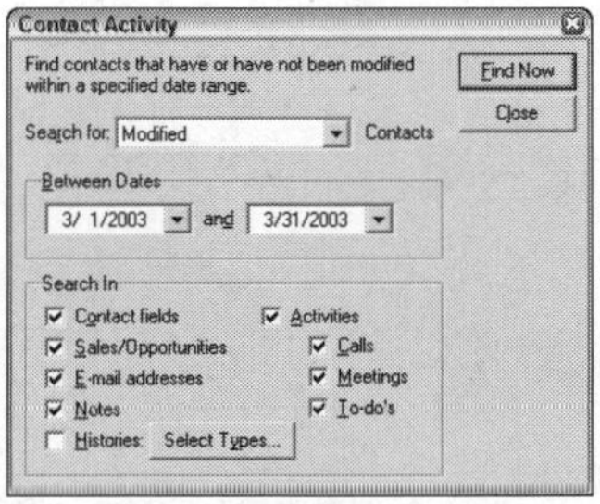

Figure 6-7:
The Contact
Activity
dialog box.

2. **Select either Modified or Not Modified from the Search for Contacts list.**

   The neat thing about using the Contact Activity Lookup is that you can look for "touched" or "untouched" contacts. In other words, you're able to search for all the contacts that you *contacted* last month or for all the contacts that you *didn't contact* last month.

3. **Select a date range to search.**

   If you select Not Modified in Step 2, the ending range date defaults to the current date, and you can't change it. Don't ask me why; that's just the way it is!

4. **Select options in the Search In area to narrow your search.**

   Typically, I recommend limiting your search to only one or two of the search options. Figure 6-8 shows you some of the history options that you have when searching your contact records based on their histories.

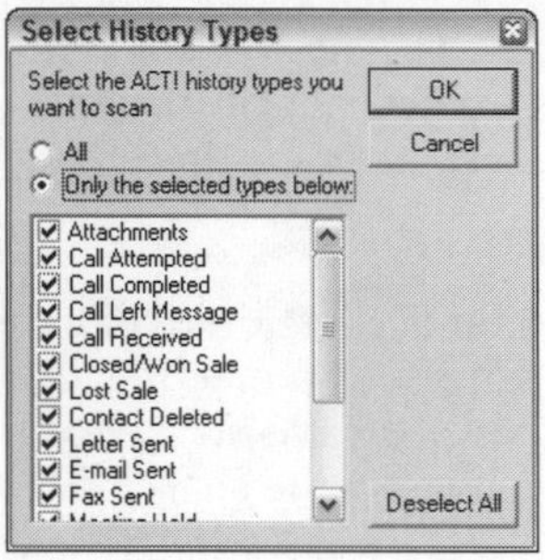

Figure 6-8:
Selecting
history
options for
the Contact
Activity
Lookup.

Select History Types

Select the ACT! history types you
want to scan

OK

Cancel

○ All
⦿ Only the selected types below:

☑ Attachments
☑ Call Attempted
☑ Call Completed
☑ Call Left Message
☑ Call Received
☑ Closed/Won Sale
☑ Lost Sale
☑ Contact Deleted
☑ Letter Sent
☑ E-mail Sent
☑ Fax Sent

Deselect All

5. **Click the Find Now button.**

   ACT! searches for the selected field or activity that was or was not modified within the specified date range. The Contact List appears and displays your selection.

   ACT! isn't searching just through all your contacts; it's also scouring all your notes, histories, activities, sales opportunities, and e-mail addresses, so it may take a moment or two to create your search results. Relax and practice a few deep breathing exercises while you wait.

Creating Advanced Queries

If you need to base your lookup on multiple criteria, you can perform a basic lookup and then use the Narrow Lookup option (refer to Figure 6-2) in the Lookup dialog box to create a more specific search. This works fine if you're willing to create several lookups until you've reached the desired results. A better alternative is to use a query to create a lookup. A *query* searches all the contacts in your database based on the multiple criteria that you specify and then creates a lookup of contacts that match those criteria.

ACT!'s other lookup functions require that you perform multiple lookups to add to or subtract from a set of contacts. By using an Advanced Query, you can find contacts based on criteria in multiple fields or based on multiple criteria in one field. You can enter values in any fields on any Groups window tab except the Notes/History, Activities, Sales/Opportunities, and Contacts tabs.

Looking up by example

When you create a Lookup by Example, ACT! responds by presenting you with a blank contact record and lets you specify the fields and values that define the query.

This is what you do:

1. **Choose Lookup⇨By Example.**

   The Query window opens. The Query window, shown in Figure 6-9, looks just like any other contact record with one major difference — all the fields are blank!

2. **Click in the field that you want to query.**

   You can create a query on virtually any field in your database. Don't forget to check out some of those neat fields that might be located on your various layout tabs. For example, the Status tab contains the Creation and Edit Date fields, which are common things to query on.

3. **Fill in any criteria on which you want to search.**

   Fill in as many criteria as you need. The whole purpose of doing an advanced lookup is that you're looking for contacts that fit more than one criterion. If you're looking for all customers who are located in San Diego, type **customer** in the ID/Status field and **San Diego** in the city field.

   If you're at all familiar with Boolean logic and programming, you'll find the rest of this chapter easy to understand; proceed to Step 4. If you aren't familiar with Boolean logic — or, for that matter, the whole notion of queries — bailing out now might not be a bad idea. Just click the green exclamation point at the top of the Query window. You're now good to go; your mission — and your query — has been accomplished, and you now have a lookup based on multiple field criteria.

4. **Choose Query⇨Show Query Helper to open the Query Helper if needed.**

   Many ACT! users, even long-time ACT! users, are often surprised when they discover a new, powerful ACT! feature. ACT! is deceptive because although mastering most features is relatively easy, a whole, untapped wealth of features is just waiting to be discovered by you. The Query Helper is one such tool.

   ACT!'s Query Helper aids you in performing even more complex searches: for example, if you want to find every contact record that was created during the month of April, or before January 1, 2000; or if you want to find all contacts residing in either one of two states, as in all customers in Florida *or* Georgia.

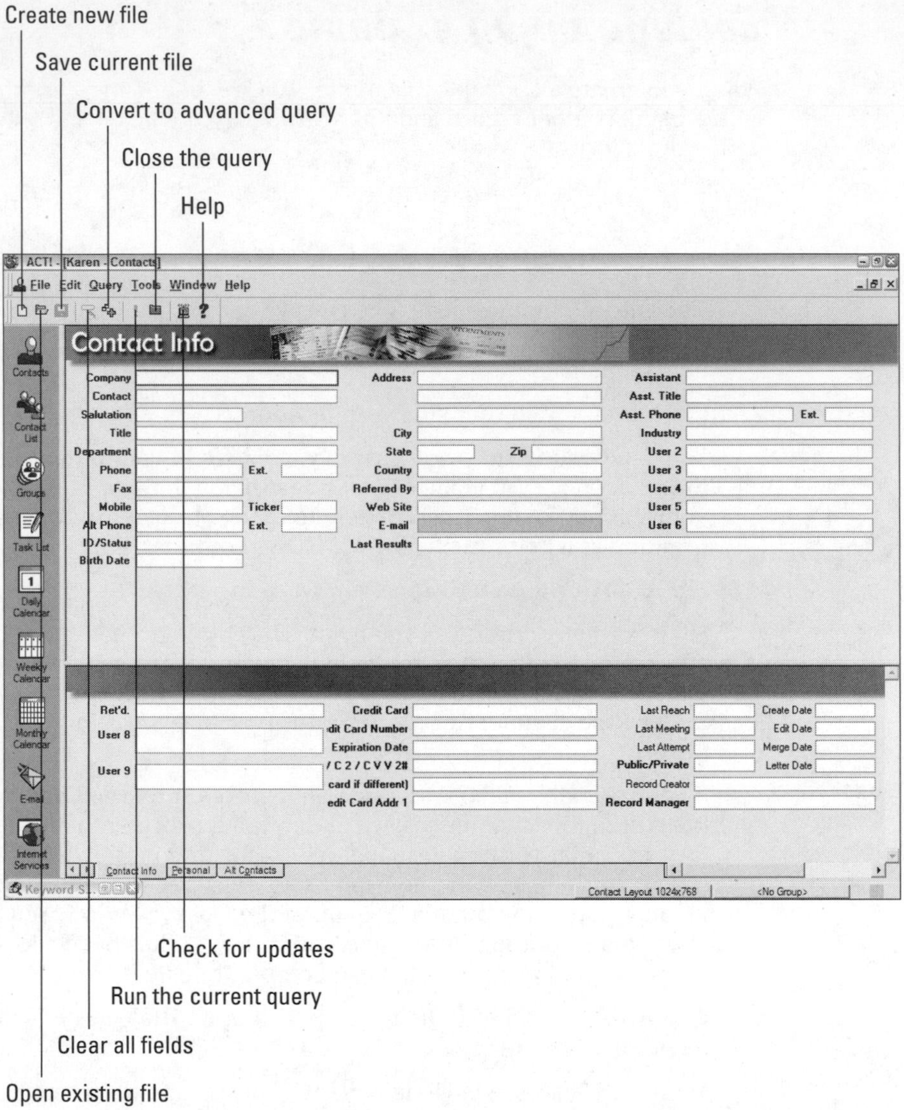

Create new file

Save current file

Convert to advanced query

Close the query

Help

Figure 6-9:
The Query
Window is
similar to a
contact
record, but
it's blank.

Check for updates

Run the current query

Clear all fields

Open existing file

5. Type in the beginning of the range for the Query in the selected field.

The Query Helper allows you to perform a lookup through the use of
ranges. When you query based on a *range*, you're asking ACT! to create a
lookup based on one or more defined parameters. For example, if you're
looking for customers in Florida or Georgia, type **FL** in the State field.

6. **Click the operator and then click the Insert button to insert a query operator.**

   The Query Helper (shown in Figure 6-10) contains 11 operators. These *operators* determine the relationship between the parameters (see Table 6-1). For example, you might want to find all contacts that were created from January 1 up to and including January 31. Or, you might want to find only contacts that were created after July 1 and not limit your search by including an ending point.

Figure 6-10:
The Query
Helper.

Table 6-1		Query Operators
Operator	*What It Does*	*Example of How Operator Is Used*
&& (and)	Matches *both* of the specified criteria	Customer&&Friend finds all contacts that have both Customer and Friend in the ID/Status field (It doesn't return customers who aren't friends or friends who aren't customers!)
|| (or)	Matches *one* of the specified criteria	Miami || West Palm Beach returns contacts in either Miami *or* West Palm Beach
= (equals)	Matches only the specified criteria	=Miami finds all your contacts in Miami; by default, when you don't specify an operator, ACT! assumes that you want to use the = parameter
<> (is not equal to)	Returns contacts that do *not* equal the specified value	<>Miami finds all contacts except those that are located in Miami
< (is less than)	Finds data that is less than the specified value	<02/01/02 finds all records that have a date prior to February 1, 2002

(continued)

Table 6-1 *(continued)*

Operator	What It Does	Example of How Operator Is Used
> (is greater than)	Finds data that is greater than the specified value	>02/01/02 finds all records that have a date after February 1, 2002
* (asterisk)	Contains data that begins or ends with the specified characters	*beach would find both Pompano Beach and Delray Beach; Los* would return both Los Angeles and Los Alamos
<= (less than or equal to)	Finds data that is less than or equal to the given value	<=33433 returns contacts in the 33433 Zip code as well as those that are in Zip codes smaller than 33433
>= (greater than or equal to)	Finds data that is greater than or equal to the given value	>=33433 returns contacts in the 33433 Zip code as well as those that are in Zip codes larger than 33433
<> (blank)	Returns contacts that have no data in the specified field	Use this to find contacts that are missing fax numbers or e-mail addresses
.. (range)	Contains data that falls within the specified range	01/01/02..12/31/02 returns contacts for the year 2002

 7. **Fill in the ending range for the query.**

    If you were looking for all customers in Florida or Georgia, your query would now look like Figure 6-11.

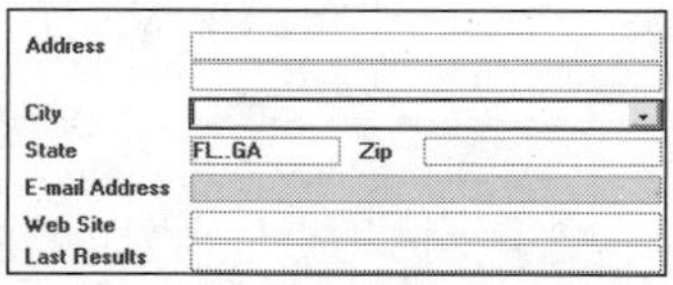

Figure 6-11:
A completed
query.

 8. **Click the green exclamation point on the Query window toolbar to find all the contacts that meet your selection criteria.**

Creating a really advanced query

Throughout this chapter, I show you how to create increasingly difficult queries. The final stop in the journey to Querydom involves creating an *advanced query*. Like many other database systems, ACT!'s advanced queries are requests for information in the form of a stylized query that's written in a special query language. This is the most difficult of the query methods because it forces you to learn the specialized language, but it's also the most powerful.

Two benefits of creating an advanced query are that

✔ Although the query helper (see preceding step list) enables you to query information *within* a given field, advanced queries enable you to query *between* fields.

✔ You can save and reuse a query. You can also add a command to the Lookup menu to run a saved query. You don't have this capability with other lookups.

To create an advanced query:

1. **From the Contacts view, choose Lookup⇨By Example.**

   A blank Contact or Groups window appears.

2. **Enter search criteria in the various fields of the By Example window.**

   Enter the values or criteria for which you want to search, adding operators as needed from the Query Helper (refer to Table 6-1).

   Although you might be anxious to dive into the exciting world of advanced queries, stifle the impulse. Unless you're extremely good at programming, I suggest cheating a little by filling in the basic parameters of your search before moving on to the Advanced Query.

3. **Choose Query⇨Convert to Advanced Query.**

   The query appears as a text screen, with an expanded version of the Query Helper (see Figure 6-12). The Query Helper now includes several advanced query operators. More importantly, it includes a list of all the fields of your database.

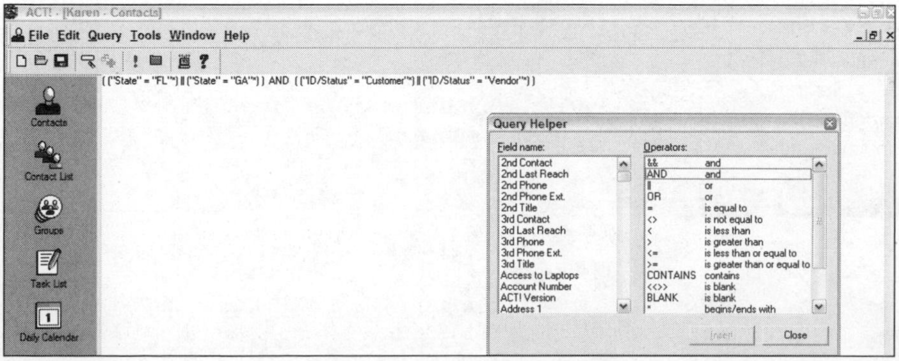

Figure 6-12:
An example
of an
Advanced
Query.

4. **Edit the existing query as needed by double-clicking a field or operator in the Query Helper to insert it into the Advanced Query.**

Although you can type your query directly in the window, selecting fields and operators from the Query Helper is much easier.

By default, the By Example query automatically connects the fields with the *and* operator; you may want to change this to the *or* operator. By using *and,* you're indicating that you want to find only those records that meet both criteria. Using "FL" and "GA" will return only those folks living in both states simultaneously; using "FL" or "GA" will find both Florida residents *and* Georgia residents.

Note: Operators are not case sensitive; feel free to type using all caps or no caps. I've included quote marks around FL and GA in the preceding paragraph because although quote marks should not be included as part of a lookup, you do need to use them when creating an advanced query.

5. **Choose Query⇨Check Query Syntax to check the query syntax.**

Nothing is more frustrating than to waste your time building an Advanced Query only to discover that you goofed somewhere along the line, and it just doesn't work. A simple click tells you whether you've been naughty or nice.

6. **Choose Query⇨Specify Query Sort.**

The Sort Contacts dialog box appears, as shown in Figure 6-13. Although you're able to sort results after you run a query, you may as well indicate the way you would like to have the final results sorted now. Kind of like a one-stop shopping trip . . . you'll save yourself a little time.

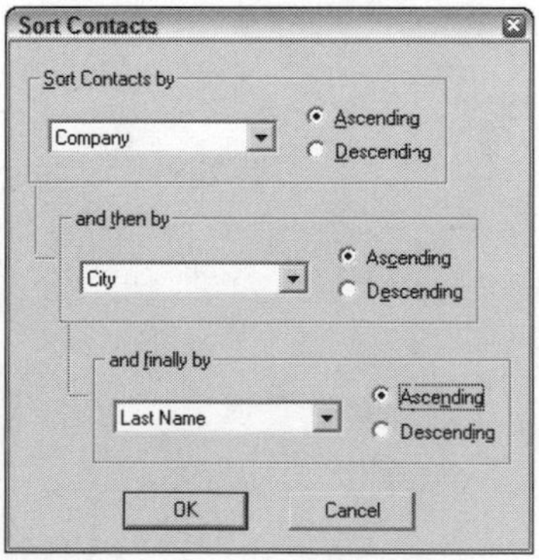

Figure 6-13:
Sorting
options for
an advanced
query.

7. **Specify the order in which you want contacts to appear after you run the query and then click OK.**

8. **Click the green exclamation point.**

9. **Click Yes to save the query.**

10. **In the Save As dialog box that appears, type a name for the query and then click OK.**

    Your query is saved with the .qry extension.

One of the things that I love most about computers is that I have to be brilliant only for a few seconds. I can then save my brilliance and use it again on an off day. If you're always brilliant and love to repeat your work, then don't save your query.

After you save the query, one of two things will happen. If the syntax of your query is correct, you can replace, narrow, or add to the current lookup. This means that you've created your query correctly and you get to proceed with your work. However, if you have an error in your query, ACT! sends you back to the drawing board. Clicking OK in the error message that appears takes you back to the Advanced Query window.

ACT! searches the open database and finds all contacts or groups that match your query specifications.

11. **In the dialog box that appears, specify whether you want to replace, narrow, or add to the current lookup with the query results and then click OK.**

    ACT! searches the open database and finds all contacts or groups that match the search specifications.

Chapter 7

Make a Note of That

*L*ook around your desk. If you have more than one sticky note attached to it, you need to use ACT! Look at your computer monitor; if it's decorated with sticky notes, you need to use ACT!. Are your file folders obscured by a wall of sticky notes? Do you panic when you can't find your pad of sticky notes? Do you have small sticky notes clinging to larger sticky notes? You need to use ACT!!

In this chapter, I show you how to make a note in ACT!. I also tell you all about the notes that ACT! creates for you automatically and give you a short course in reviewing your notes.

Getting to Know ACT! Notes

What if one of your best clients called requesting a price quote? You jot down some information on a piece of paper — only to have the paper disappear in the mountain of clutter that you call your desk.

Or imagine that one of your more high-maintenance customers calls you on March 1 in immediate need of an imported Italian widget. You check with your distributors and guarantee him one by March 15. On March 10, he calls you, totally irate that he hasn't yet received his widget.

Sound familiar? The ACT! note is one of the easiest features to master but one that too many of you overlook. A simple note in ACT! provides you with several benefits:

✔ Your entire office can now be operating on the same page by having access to the same client data.

   ✔ You can find all correspondence with your contacts in one neat location.

   ✔ You have a record, down to the date and time, of all communications that you have had with each of your contacts.

Adding a Note

Here's all you do to add a note to a contact record:

1. **Make sure that you're on the contact for which you're creating a note.**

2. **Click the Contacts icon on the View bar.**

3. **On the Notes/History tab (bottom of the screen), click the Insert Note button.**

   A blank note appears, date- and time-stamped with the current date and time.

4. **Start typing your note in the regarding column.**

   Your note can be as long or short as you want. While you type in additional information, the note scrolls to the next line. Figure 7-1 shows you a note in the Notes/History tab.

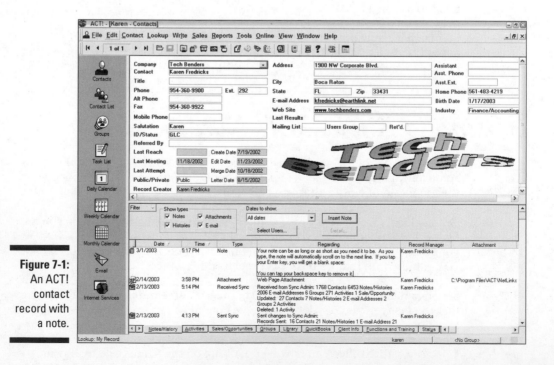

Figure 7-1:
An ACT!
contact
record with
a note.

That was almost too easy for you; move on to a few tricks that I have up my sleeve.

Working with Notes

After you create a note (see preceding section), here are more than a few things that you can do with notes to further enhance your ACT! experience:

- ✔ **Change the note information:** To edit a note, just click in the Regarding area of the note that you want to change and start typing exactly as you would with any word processor.

- ✔ **Change the date on a note:** No matter how much you depend on your computer, sometimes you still rely on good old-fashioned paper. Maybe you've jotted down a note after you turned off your computer for the day or made notes — both mental and on paper — at a trade show. When you start to input those notes into ACT!, they all have the current date, rather than the date when you actually created them. To change the date on a note, simply click the date of a note and from the drop-down menu that appears (see Figure 7-2), choose a new date.

As your list of notes becomes longer, various key notes might get lost in the shuffle. A real low-tech solution is to postdate the note by giving it a date several years into the future so that your note will always appear at the top of the Notes/History tab.

Now that you know how easy it is to change the date of a note, you might want to prevent other users of your database from changing note information. If you're the database administrator, you can do this by choosing Edit➪Define Fields, and then, on the Advanced tab, remove the check mark next to Allow History Editing.

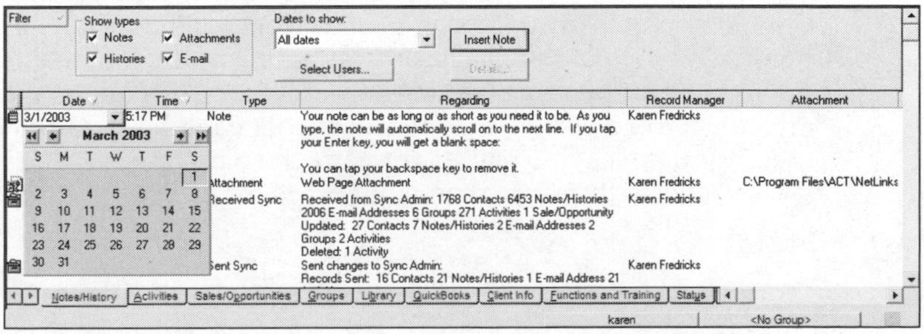

Figure 7-2:
Changing
the date in
an ACT!
note.

✔ **Delete a note:** To delete a note, you must first select it. Click the notepad icon to the left of the note and then press the Delete key; the note is gone. You can also right-click the selected note and choose Delete Selected from the ensuing menu. Either way, ACT! presents you with a warning before you remove the note permanently.

✔ **Delete several notes:** Eventually, you'll want to delete certain notes or even histories (see the later section "Discovering ACT! Histories"). To delete several notes in one fell swoop, just select the notes that you want to delete and then press the Delete key:

 • If you're selecting several continuous notes, click the first note, and then press and hold down the Shift key while clicking the last note that you want to delete.

  In the next section, you can read about *histories* (automatic notes that ACT! creates when you complete various tasks). Histories are categorized into types, such as E-mail Sent or Meeting Held. If several similar notes are grouped together by type, deleting them all at once is easy. Sort your notes by type by clicking the Type column heading on the Notes tab.

 • If the entries aren't continuous, press and hold down the Ctrl key while clicking each note individually.

✔ **Copy a note:** When you find duplicate contacts in your database, you probably want to delete them — but not any notes attached to them. Or, maybe you want a note from one contact record also attached to another record. Luckily, ACT! gives you the ability to copy notes from one contact to another contact with a simple copy-and-paste procedure:

 1. Highlight the notes that you want to copy and then press Ctrl+C.

 2. Find the contact where you want to insert the copied notes and, on the Notes/History tab, press Ctrl+V.

✔ **Attach files to a contact record:** In Chapter 21, I talk about adding files to the Library tab so that you can view and edit them right from the Contacts screen. In addition, you can attach a file to a note in a contact record. When you double-click the attachment, ACT! automatically opens the program that was used to create the file. You might want to attach a file of a certain type to a note that can't be added to the Library tab; for example, you may want to attach an architectural rendering that was created with software not supported by ACT!.

To attach a file to a note:

 1. Right-click the Notes/History tab and choose Attach File.

 2. Navigate to the file that you want to attach and click Open.

Figure 7-3 shows an example of a note attachment; the path to the attachment appears in the Attachment column on the Notes/History tab.

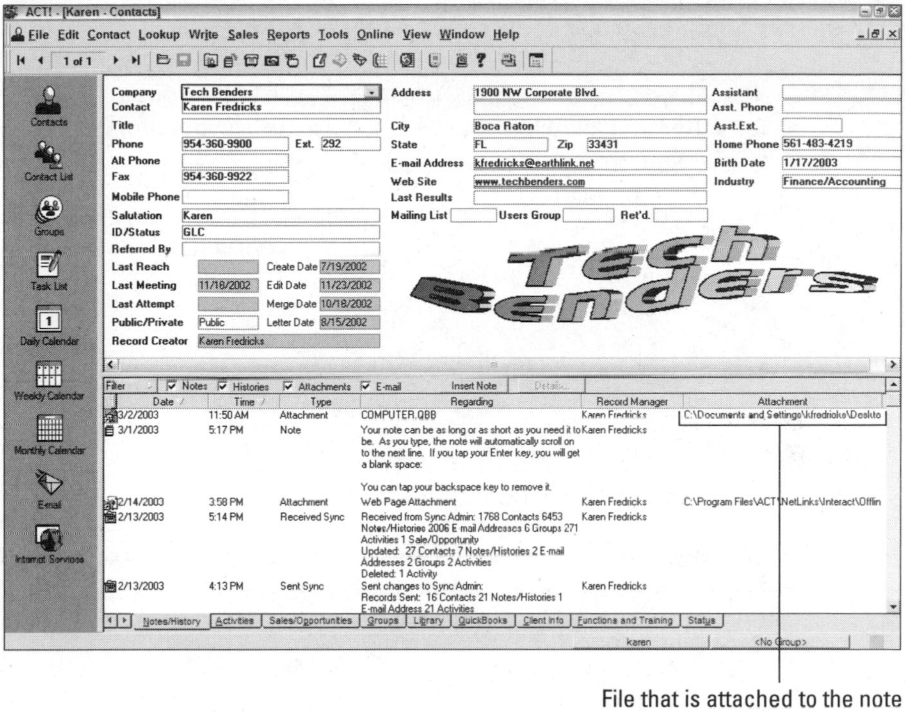

Figure 7-3:
A note that
contains an
attached
file.

File that is attached to the note

Remember these two things when attaching a file to a note:

- If the attached file is located on a local drive or on a private drive on your local network, other ACT! users will not be able to access the file (although they will see the path to the attached file).

- Attached files are not included as part of a synchronization. The users with whom you synchronize will see the path to the attached file, but they will not be able to access it.

✔ **Spell check a note:** If you're like me, you type notes while doing a hundred other things and end up with a lot of typos. Don't fret; rather, run a spell check. Simply click the Regarding portion of the note that you're spell checking and then choose Tools➪Spelling. ACT! opens the spell checker and locates any misspellings. Unfortunately, you can only check the spelling for one note at a time.

Discovering ACT! Histories

If you insist on doing things the hard way, feel free to skip this section. If you love the thought of having someone else doing your work for you, however, read on!

Maybe you've noticed that the Notes/History tab is called, well, the Notes/History tab. In the earlier sections of this chapter, I show you how to add and modify notes. ACT!'s history entries are items that magically appear on the Notes/History tab after you

- Delete a contact (Chapter 4)
- Complete a scheduled meeting, call, or to-do (Chapter 8)
- Write a letter, fax, or mail merge (Chapter 12)
- Change information in a field designated to create history (Chapter 14)

When you clear an activity, a history of the activity is recorded in the contact record of the person with whom you scheduled the activity. You can also edit or add activity details to the history, such as adding information about the decisions made during the meeting. View these histories again later or create reports based on activities with your contacts.

Creating field histories

By default, ACT! automatically creates a historical note when you change the information in either the ID/Status or Last Results field. When you enter information into either of these fields, it's automatically saved into the contact's Notes/History tab.

ACT! provides you with a very powerful tool when you combine the use of drop-down fields with the ability to create a note based on the changed information in the field. Suppose that you've created ten steps to coincide with the average progression of one of your prospects into a customer. These steps should be created by using ACT!'s Last Results field. As you progress through the sales cycle and change the content of the Last Results field, ACT! automatically creates a history indicating when the change took place. Figure 7-4 shows both the content of the Last Results field and the automatic histories that were created as the contact progressed through the sales stages.

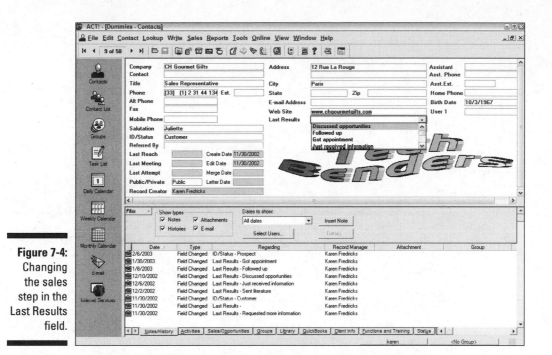

Figure 7-4:
Changing
the sales
step in the
Last Results
field.

By relying on the field's drop-down list to create new content information, you ensure that your information remains consistent. You can then create reports on the various sales stages by creating a lookup based on the notes and histories.

In Chapter 6, I show you everything there is to know about creating lookups — and then some! Chapter 10 explains the various ACT! reports and shows you how to filter them by date range.

Recording activity histories

In Chapter 8, I explain how to use ACT! to plan your busy schedule. After you hold or attend a meeting, place a call, or complete something on your to-do list, clearing the activity is important. Figure 7-5 shows you the ACT! dialog box that opens each time you clear an activity. Selecting the Add Details to History check box causes ACT! to automatically insert a history on the Notes/History tab.

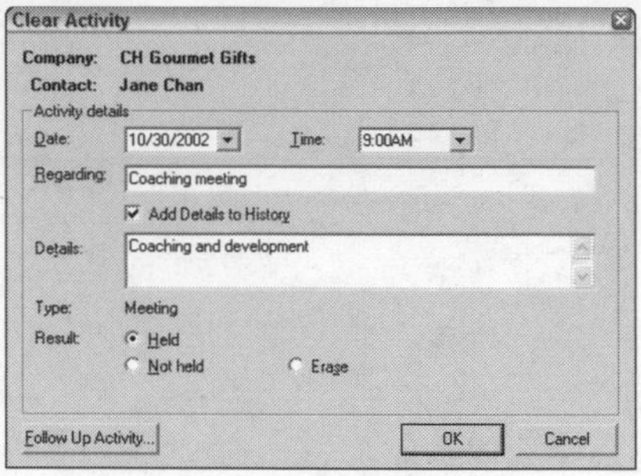

Figure 7-5:
Clearing an
activity.

ACT! provides you with the same option when you get in touch with a contact through a letter, e-mail, or fax. Figure 7-6 shows you an example of the dialog box that appears after you create a letter in ACT!. Of course, you can always choose not to include a history, but you'll probably find it more useful to record one. You can even add additional details in the regarding area.

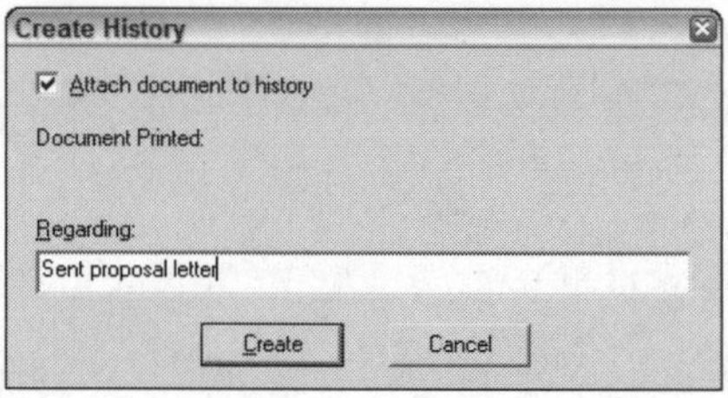

Figure 7-6:
Attaching a
history to a
letter.

Manually recording a history

Situations will arise when it just isn't possible to record a history of an event. You can create a history record for a contact without scheduling and clearing an activity for that person. You can even add a history for someone who isn't yet in your database. For example, you might have called a potential new client from your car and found it just a bit too daunting a task to juggle the steering wheel, your phone, and your lunch while typing on your laptop. But when you return to the office, you still need to record the calls that you made and the tasks that you completed.

You can also record one history for an entire group of people. For example, you might have attended a meeting at your local Chamber of Commerce and wanted to record a few details about the meeting for each of the attendees. Regardless of why you need to do it, here's how you create a history after the fact:

1. **Find the contact for whom you want to record a history.**

   If you're creating a history for an entire group of people, create a lookup of the contacts for whom you want to add a note and then:

   a. Switch to the Contact List.

   b. Switch to Tag mode and tag all contacts. (See Chapter 5 for the details on tagging.)

2. **Choose Contact⇨Record History.**

   The Record History dialog box opens, as shown in Figure 7-7.

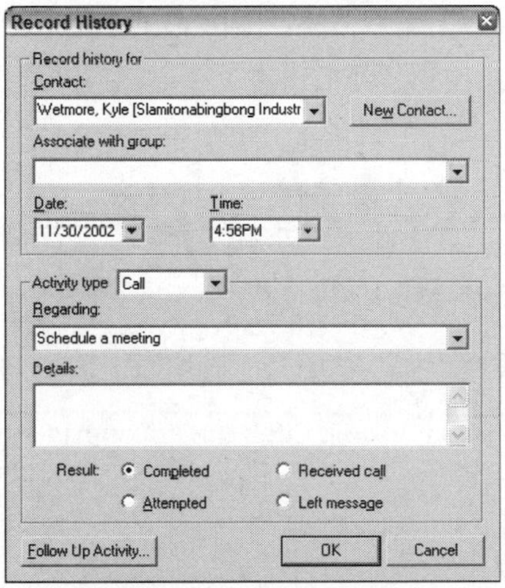

Figure 7-7:
The Record
History
dialog box.

3. **Select the group from the Associate with Group drop-down list to associate the history with a group.**

   If you associate the history with a group, the information appears in the Notes/History tab in the Group view.

4. **Select an activity type from the Activity Type list.**

   You don't have much choice here; all ACT! activities must be categorized as a Meeting, Call, or To-Do.

5. **Enter activity information in the Regarding field or select a description from the drop-down list.**

6. **Add additional information in the Details field.**

   The information that you enter is added to the Regarding field in the Notes/History tab.

7. **Select a Result option.**

8. **Click OK.**

   Your note has now been recorded in the contact's record. If you created a history for an entire group of contacts, the note appears in the contact record of each of the individuals in the group.

If you click the Follow Up Activity button instead of OK, you can schedule a new, follow-up activity in the same way that you scheduled your original activity. Talk about one-stop shopping! The result of your phone call might be that you left a message or that you attempted to make the call but couldn't get through. By scheduling a follow-up activity, you have the results of your original phone call — and a reminder to try to make contact again in the future. You can also schedule follow-up activities for the next step in your sales process.

Viewing Your Notes and Histories

You view your notes in ACT! in exactly the same way that you view any of the other ACT! lists. Following are some of the things that you can do to change the look of the Notes/History tab:

- ✔ **Sort by Date, Time, or Type columns:** Click the appropriate column headings.
- ✔ **Widen a column:** Move the column separator to the right of a column heading to the right.
- ✔ **Rearrange columns:** Drag the appropriate column heading to a new position.
- ✔ **Delete a column:** Drag the column heading off of the Notes/History tab.

Mind your filters!

When viewing the Notes/History tab, you must be aware of the effect that the filters have on what information you see — or don't see. In ACT!, you can choose to view or not to view the following items (essentially, you can choose to filter out this information or to include it):

- ✔ Notes
- ✔ Histories
- ✔ Attachments
- ✔ E-mail

In addition, you can specify the following two options:

- ✔ View the specified Date range of the notes and histories
- ✔ View notes and histories created by Selected Users

The tricky thing about setting the filters on the Notes/History tab is that you can't always see your current settings. Figure 7-8 shows you the Notes/History tab with the filter settings showing. Figure 7-9 shows you what happens when you click the filter button on the Notes/History tab: The filter options disappear. Although closing the filters allows you more space to see your notes, you can't see the current filter settings.

Click to hide filter settings.

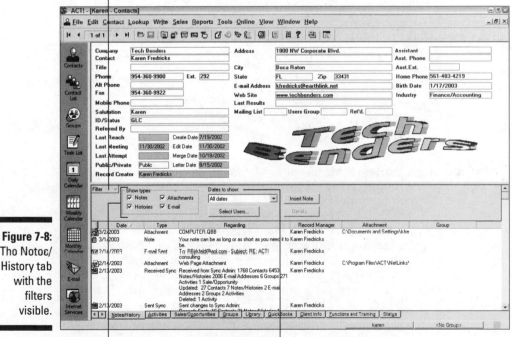

Figure 7-8:
Tho Notoc/
History tab
with the
filters
visible.

Filter settings   Dates to Show options

Click to show filter settings.

Figure 7-9:
The Notes/
History tab
with the
filters
closed.

The important thing to remember when viewing your notes in the
Notes/History tab is that your filters should be set to include all options.
There are a couple of reasons for this:

✔ As my good friend Liz Hendon, a wonderful ACT! Certified Consultant
hailing from Bethesda, Maryland, says: "When frustrated, check your filters!" If you accidentally set the Dates to Show option (refer to Figure 7-8)
to include only notes and histories for Future Dates, you might be left
wondering why no notes are showing on the Notes/History tab today!

✔ If you turn off any of the filters by deselecting their check boxes, ACT!
will seem to grind to a stop while you scroll between contact records
because ACT! is having to stop and filter out all the appropriate notes
and histories for each contact.

Switching the filter settings while you view the current record's data is
perfectly acceptable; just remember to change the filters when you're
done!

Setting preferences

If you're feeling somewhat artistic, in need of a change, or just plain having trouble with your forty-something eyesight, you might want to either add gridlines around your notes or change the color and/or font style. Or, you might just decide to walk on the wild side and change the whole ball of wax. Take a stroll down preference lane to accomplish this:

1. **Click the Notes/History tab in ACT!'s Contacts view.**

2. **Choose Edit⇨Preferences.**

   The Preferences dialog box opens, as shown in Figure 7-10.

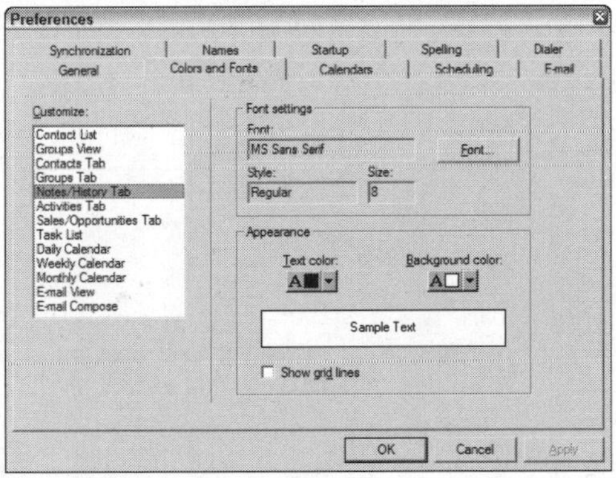

Figure 7-10: The Preferences dialog box.

3. **Click the Colors and Fonts tab.**

   The Notes/History Tab should be highlighted in the Customize area. If it's not, click it.

4. **Click the Font button to select a different font, style, or size.**

5. **Click OK to close the Font window.**

6. **Choose a Text Color and Background Color from the Appearance area.**

7. **Select the Show Grid Lines check box if you want gridlines to appear in the Notes/History tab.**

   The ACT! gridlines are just like the gridlines you see in Excel. If you change your preference to show gridlines, horizontal lines appear between each of your notes and vertical lines between columns.

8. **Click OK.**

   Your Notes/History tab will now be modified according to the preference settings that you selected.

Chapter 8

Organizing Your Daily Tasks

*I*n this chapter, I show you how to schedule activities with your contacts, how to view those activities and modify them if necessary, and even how to find out whether you've completed a scheduled activity. You'll also discover the intricacies of navigating through the various ACT! calendars, how to use your Task List to keep you on top of your activities, and the joy of sharing a list of your scheduled activities with others.

Scheduling Your Activities

One of the most useful of ACT!'s features is its ability to tie an activity to a contact. More basic calendaring programs allow you to view your appointments and tasks on your calendar, but they don't offer a way of cross-referencing an appointment to a contact. For example, if you schedule an appointment with me and forget when that appointment is, you have to flip through your calendar until you see my name. Plus, you can't easily see a list of all appointments that you've ever scheduled with me. But ACT! does offer these helpful features.

In ACT!, every activity is scheduled with a specific contact. If the contact doesn't exist in your database, add the person to your database — or schedule the appointment with yourself.

The three kinds of activities that you can schedule in ACT! are a *call*, a *meeting*, and a *to-do*. Seem like a limited number of choices? It isn't really. Calls and meetings are self explanatory, and a to-do is everything else. Need to fax something? It's a to-do. Need to order more brochures? It's a to-do.

Need to do anything other than make a call to a prospective client or attend a meeting with your boss? It's a to-do — and here's what you need to do to schedule one:

1. **Go to the contact with whom you're scheduling an activity.**

   Here's the drill. You create a lookup (I show you how in Chapter 6) to find a prospect's phone number. You call the guy, and afterward, you want to schedule a meeting. At this point, you're already on the contact record of the person with whom you're scheduling an activity.

2. **Schedule a call, meeting, or to-do in one of three ways:**

   • Click the Call, Meeting, or To-Do icon on the toolbar in the Contacts view or the Contact List.

   • Choose Contact⇨Schedule in the Contacts view or the Contact List view.

   • Double-click the appropriate time slot on any of the ACT! calendars.

   Using different methods to schedule different activities is a smart plan of action. For example, I recommend scheduling meetings through the calendars to make sure that you don't have a conflict for a specific time slot. When you're scheduling calls and to-dos, however, which are generally "timeless" activities, you can simply click the corresponding icon on the toolbar.

   In any case, all roads lead to the Schedule Activity dialog box that's shown in Figure 8-1.

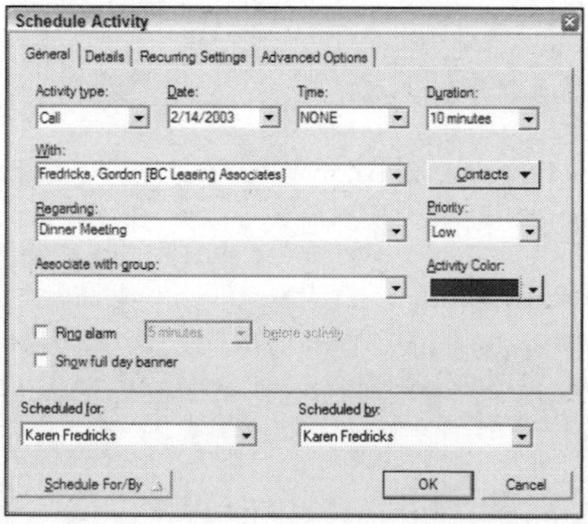

Figure 8-1:
Scheduling
an activity
in ACT!.

3. **On the General tab, fill in the various options.**

   If Options is your name, ACT! is your game! The Schedule Activity dialog box offers a myriad of scheduling options from which to pick, and ACT! has thoughtfully filled in many of these options based on your default scheduling preferences. (Chapter 3 walks you through changing some of these preferences.) You can leave the information in the following fields as is or override the default preferences:

- **Activity Type:** Choose Call, Meeting, or To-Do from the drop-down list.

- **Date:** Click the arrow to the right of the field to display the calendar and select a date.

- **Time:** Enter a time for the event. Choose Timeless if you're scheduling a call or to-do that doesn't need to occur at a specific time (and ACT! mysteriously enters None in the field).

- **Duration:** Click the arrow to the right of the field to choose a duration for the activity. You can also manually specify a time range; an hour-and-a-half-long meeting can be entered as either **90 m** or **1.5 h**.

- **With:** Select the contact with whom you're scheduling the activity. You can type the first few letters of a contact's last name to locate the contact in the list.

- **Contacts:** Click the Contacts button and then choose Select Contacts to select more than one contact, New Contact to schedule an activity with a contact not currently in your database, or My Record to schedule a personal appointment.

- **Priority:** Choose High, Medium, or Low.

- **Schedule For/By:** This is where you can assign a task to one of your co-workers (as if ACT! hasn't made life easy enough for you already!).

You might want to use these optional fields as well:

- **Regarding:** If you want to give a brief description of the activity, type it here or choose an item from the drop-down list.

- **Associate with Group:** If you want to associate the activity with a group as well as with a contact record, do it here.

- **Activity Color:** Click the arrow to the right of the field to display a color palette, and then click the color that you want to assign to the activity. Feel free to design your own system of color-coding your calendar.

- **Ring Alarm:** Sets an alarm to remind you of a scheduled activity.

- **Show Full Day Banner:** Lets you display a banner on the monthly calendar if an activity involves one or more full days.

4. **On the Details tab, add additional details and print the details (if you want).**

These are two relatively important tasks:

- **Details:** Add additional information regarding an activity. For example, you might want to add special instructions about the items that you need to bring to a meeting.

- **Print:** This is where you can print the activity details.

5. **On the Recurring Settings tab, designate the activity as recurring if that's the case; otherwise, go to Step 6.**

If the activity that you're scheduling will repeat on a regular basis, you can designate it as a *recurring* activity rather than setting up several separate activities. For example, if you're taking a class that meets once a week for the next 12 weeks, you can designate the class as a meeting with a weekly recurrence. Be sure to specify the date on which the activity will stop recurring.

Here are the recurring option settings:

- **Daily:** Select to schedule an activity that occurs daily and the date on which the activity will stop.

- **Weekly:** Select to schedule an activity that occurs weekly, on which day or days of the week the activity is scheduled, and the date on which the activity will stop.

- **Monthly:** Select to schedule an activity that occurs monthly, the weeks in the month when the activity is scheduled, the day of the week the activity is scheduled, and the date on which the activity will stop.

- **Yearly:** Select to schedule an activity that occurs every year, and the date on which the activity will stop.

- **Custom:** Select to schedule activities for specific days of the month.

The *Annual Event* field can eliminate the need to set reminders for activities, such as birthdays, anniversaries, and renewal dates. Find out how to set up Annual Event fields in Chapter 6.

6. **On the Advanced Options tab, prevent other users from editing your scheduled activity and/or send an e-mail to activity participants.**

These two options are rather useful:

- **Private Activity:** Prevents others from editing an activity when they log on to the database. Although they can see that you have an activity scheduled, they aren't able to see any of the activity details.

- **Send E-mail Message to Activity Participant:** Allows you to confirm the activity with the contacts involved and then send the meeting as an attachment in an ACT! and/or Outlook format.

7. **Click OK.**

You now have a real, live scheduled activity!

After you create activities, ACT! is a worse nag than your mother! You can see your activities — and ACT! reminds you to complete them — in a number of ways:

✔ If you set a Reminder when scheduling an activity, the ACT! Alarms window (Figure 8-2) appears each time that you open ACT!.

✔ The Activities tab for a selected contact enables you to see what specific activities you've scheduled with that particular contact.

✔ The Task List shows a listing of everything you've scheduled for all your contacts during a specified time period.

✔ All ACT! calendars include a listing of the current day's events.

Figure 8-2:
The Alarms
window
reminds
you of
scheduled
activities.

Alarms window screenshot showing:

Alarms

Ringing alarms: 6

8/2/2002 - 8:00 AM Greg Hart
[1] 310-555-2626
Send proposal

8/6/2002 NONE Chris Huffman
[1] 212-555-6756
Read ACT! Quickstudy Guide

8/9/2002 - 1:00 PM Greg Hart
[1] 310-555-2626
Discuss proposal

8/13/2002 - 2:30 PM Steve Reese
[1] 480-555-1987
Negotiate price

9/25/2002 NONE Mike Underwood

Select All
Snooze..
Clear Alarm
Clear Activity...
Reschedule...
Go to
Hide Details

Activity information
Activity Type: To-do   Date: 8/2/2002   Time: 8:00 AM
With: Greg Hart
Company: The Mad House
Phone: [1] 310-555-2626
Regarding: Send proposal
Details: Suggest:

- modified samplers
- special packaging

Later in this chapter, in the section "Exploring Activities," I show you how to view, edit, clear, and share your scheduled activities.

Regardless of your method of viewing your activities, remember this tip from my friend Liz Hendon (which I mention also in Chapter 7): "When frustrated, check your filters." If you're just not seeing everything that you know is supposed to be showing in your calendar, do as Liz suggests — check your filters! Not seeing anything scheduled for the future? Maybe your date range is set to show the activities for today only. Seeing too much? Perhaps your filters are set to show *everyone's* task list or calendar. Not seeing *any* of your activities at all? Perhaps your filters are set to include everything *except* your own activities!

Working with the ACT! Calendar

The various ACT! calendars are great for viewing scheduled tasks. Here are a couple of ways to get to your calendars:

- ✔ Click View and specify the type of calendar that you'd like to view.
- ✔ Click a calendar icon on the View bar.

You can view your calendar in any one of three different ways, depending on which way you feel the most comfortable:

- ✔ **Daily Calendar:** Shows you the time-specific activities of the selected day as well as a listing of the day's tasks (see Figure 8-3). The day is divided into half-hour intervals.

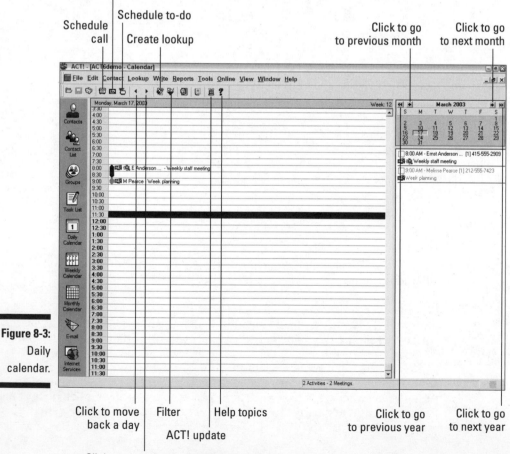

Figure 8-3: Daily calendar.

Schedule meeting

Schedule call

Schedule to-do

Create lookup

Click to go to previous month

Click to go to next month

Click to move back a day

Filter

Help topics

Click to go to previous year

Click to go to next year

ACT! update

Click to move forward a day

✔ **Weekly Calendar:** Shows you the time-specific activities of the selected week as well as a listing of the day's tasks (see Figure 8-4). Each day is divided into one-hour intervals.

✔ **Monthly Calendar:** Shows you the time-specific activities of the selected month as well as a listing of the day's tasks (see Figure 8-5).

✔ **Mini-calendar:** Displays three months at one time (see Figure 8-6). The Mini-calendar works a little differently from the Daily, Weekly, and Monthly calendars. Press the F4 key to access the Mini-calendar directly from the Contacts view. Right-click the day that you want to check, and a small window appears, displaying all activities scheduled for that day.

After you access any of the ACT! calendars, you can navigate to a different date in one of the following ways (refer to Figure 8-3):

✔ Go to Today's Date by right-clicking the name of the currently selected month and choosing Today from the pop-up menu.

✔ Go to a different year by clicking the double arrows.

✔ Go to a different month by clicking the single arrows.

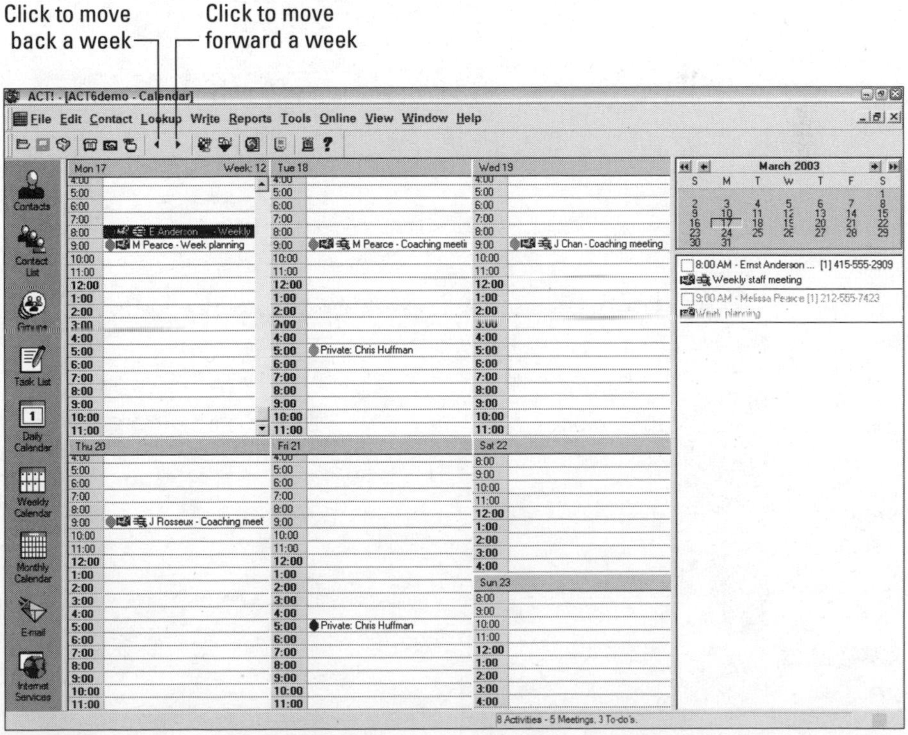

Click to move
back a week

Click to move
forward a week

Figure 8-4:
Weekly
calendar.

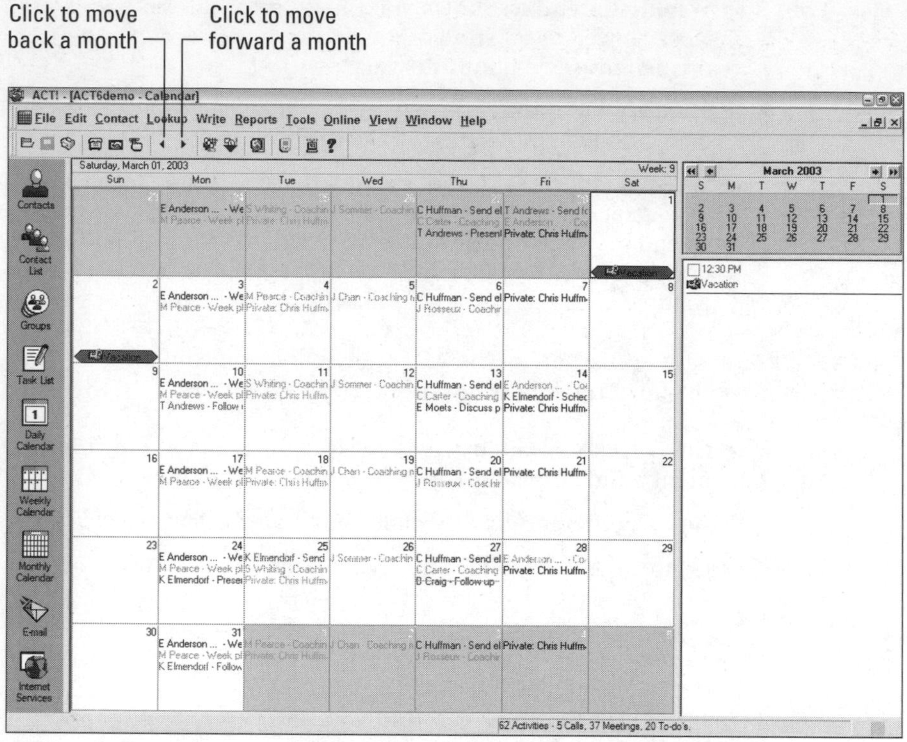

Click to move
back a month ⌐⌐ Click to move
forward a month

Figure 8-5:
Monthly
calendar.

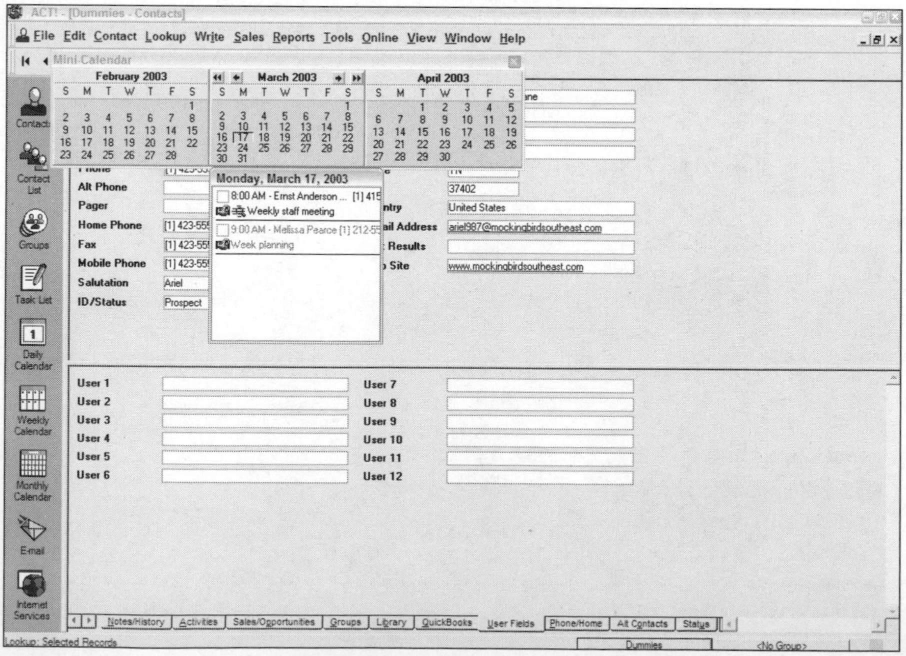

Figure 8-6:
Mini-
calendar.

Using the Task List

Like the *Honey Do list* hanging from my husband's work bench, the ACT! Task List gives you a listing of *all* the activities for *all* of your contacts.

The Task List is readily accessible by clicking the Task List icon on ACT!'s View bar. A sample Task List is shown in Figure 8-7.

You're able to filter the Task List by using different criteria (see Figure 8-7):

✔ The type of activity

✔ The priority of the activity

✔ The date range of the activities

✔ The cleared status of the activities

✔ The users whose activities you want to view

Filter the Task List using these criteria.

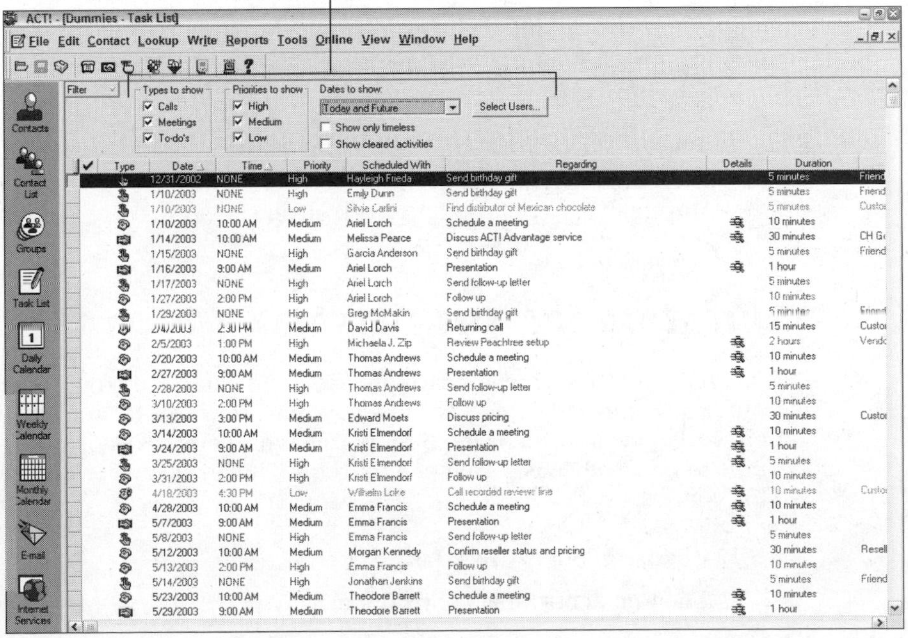

Figure 8-7: The ACT! Task List.

Creating a lookup from the Task List

Here's the scenario. You wake up bright-eyed and bushy-tailed, ready to face another new day. You get to the office, view your Task List, and stop dead in your tracks: The length of your Task List is so long that you don't even know where to begin. Consider creating a lookup directly from the Task List. By spending the first hour of your day sending out all those faxes and brochures that you promised — and then the next hour returning your phone calls — you get everything done.

When you break down your tasks into manageable pieces — instead of having a breakdown yourself — the Task List becomes less intimidating.

Having said all that, I feel compelled to add that Rome wasn't built in a day, and you might not be able to complete *all* your tasks in a single day, either. ACT! has a preference that enables you to *roll over* your tasks to the next day if necessary. Check out Chapter 3 for a quick refresher on changing ACT! preferences.

1. **To open your Task List, click the Task List icon on ACT!'s View bar.**

2. **Select the activity types in the Types to Show area to indicate the activities that you want to work with.**

3. **Select the date range of the activities for which you want to create a lookup.**

4. **Right-click the Task List and select Create Lookup.**

   ACT! creates a lookup of the selected activities. You can now scroll through your contacts and work on all similar tasks at the same time.

Printing the Task List

As great as ACT! is, it can be totally useless if you don't have access to a computer or hand-held device. Or maybe you work with a technically challenged co-worker (your boss?) who prefers to have a copy of his or her Task List *printed* on a daily basis. No need to fret; ACT! can easily perform this task for you:

1. **Choose Reports⇨Task List.**

   The Run Report dialog box opens.

2. **From the Include Data for Contacts Managed By drop-down list, choose the user whose Task List you want to view and print.**

3. **On the Activities/Notes/Histories tab, specify the types of activities that you'd like to include in the Task List and also the date range for the Task List.**

4. **Click OK to print the Task List.**

Exploring Activities

In the first section of this chapter, "Scheduling Your Activities," I show you how to do exactly that. After scheduling an activity, you'll probably want to take a look at it. Or edit it. Or clear it. Or maybe even share it with others. So in this section, I show you how to do all these things.

Viewing the Activities tab

If you click the Activities tab at the bottom of the Contacts view, ACT! displays all the activities scheduled with the current contact. This is a great way to have a list of all the activities that you've scheduled with a contact.

You can *filter* your activities so that only certain activities show on the Activities tab. Your choices include (notice the similarity between these filters and the ones shown for the Task List in Figure 8-7)

✔ Types to show

✔ Priorities to show

✔ Dates to show

✔ Select users

✔ Timeless activities

✔ Cleared activities

After you set your filters, you can also determine the columns that you want to appear on the Activities tab. These are the possibilities:

✔ The type, date, time, and duration of the activity

✔ The priority that you set for the activity

✔ The regarding information and any details that you entered for the activity

✔ The company associated with the current contact

   ✔ The name of the group that the activity might be associated with

   ✔ The contact's phone number

   ✔ Who scheduled the activity

   ✔ What ACT! user the activity was scheduled for

   ✔ What contact the activity was scheduled with

After you determine the columns that you want to view onscreen, you can easily print a down-and-dirty report. In Chapter 5, I give you all the juicy details for rearranging the columns on the Activities tab — or on any other ACT! list for that matter — and turning it into an instant report.

Editing your activities

Like all the best-laid plans of mice and men, your activities will change, and you will need a way to make note of these changes in ACT!. Changing an activity is all in the click — or in this case, the *double-click* — of the mouse. If you can *see* an activity, you can *edit* it. The only activities that you can't change are those that you've already *cleared*.

ACT! also has a way of *rescheduling* several activities at a time. Say, for example, that your flight was delayed by bad weather and that you need to move all of Monday's activities to Tuesday. You accomplish this by following these steps:

1. **Click the Task List icon on the View bar.**

2. **Click the Activity Selection button at the left side of the activity that you want to change.**

3. **Hold down the Ctrl key while selecting additional activities.**

4. **Press F4 to bring up the Mini-calendar.**

5. **Drag the highlighted activities to the new date on the Mini-calendar.**

   ACT! changes the date for all activities that you selected.

Clearing activities

After you've completed a task, *clearing* the task is very important. When you clear a task, ACT! does several things:

  ✓ Stops reminding you about the activity

  ✓ Allows you to add some additional details about the activity

  ✓ Lets you schedule a follow-up activity if necessary

  ✓ Automatically updates the Last Reach, Last Meeting, or Last Attempt fields with the current date

  ✓ Creates an entry on the Notes/History tab of the contact with whom you had scheduled the activity

WARNING!

If you don't clear your activities, you're treated to a long list of alarms each and every time that you open ACT!. Not only is this annoying, it can also be dangerous because you might also ignore *current* alarms!

To clear an activity, follow these steps:

1. **Select the activity that you want to clear by doing one of the following:**

   • In any Calendar view, select the check box next to the activity in the Daily Checklist.

   • In the Task List or the Activities tab, click the check mark column.

   • Right-click the activity and then choose Clear Activity.

   Using any method, the Clear Activity dialog box appears (see Figure 8-8). The current date and time appear automatically. The regarding information that you had originally entered for the activity appears as well. This information later appears in the regarding column of a note that is automatically created when you clear an activity.

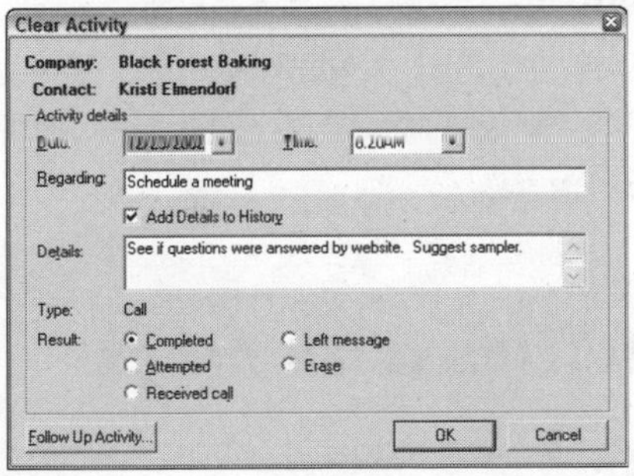

Figure 8-8:
Clearing an
activity.

The Clear Activity dialog box enables you to clear just one activity at a time. You can clear multiple activities from the Activities tab or the Task List:

    a. Click the Selection button to the left edge of the window to select an activity.

    b. Hold down the Ctrl key while selecting additional activities to clear.

    c. Right-click the selected activities and then choose Clear Multiple Activities from the shortcut menu.

2. **Select the Add Details to History check box if you want to edit or add activity details.**

   Changes that you make to the Add Details area appear in the Regarding field in the Notes/History tab for the contact.

3. **Select a Result option.**

   The result determines the type of note that's added to the Notes/History tab as well as the system field that is affected. For example, if you indicate that a call was completed, two things happen:

   - A note is added to the Notes/History tab with Call Completed showing in the Type column.

   - The Last Reach field is changed to include today's date.

4. **Click the Follow Up Activity button to schedule a follow-up activity (if you want).**

   This is a very cool concept. When you *clear* an activity, ACT! gives you the option of scheduling a *follow-up* activity. Schedule a follow-up exactly as you would an original activity.

5. **Schedule the follow-up activity in the Schedule Activity dialog box and then click OK to return to the Clear Activity dialog box.**

6. **Click OK again, and you're done.**

Sharing your activities with others

If you're looking for a way to print your calendars, I show you how in Chapter 9. However, you might also want to electronically share your calendars with remote users. You can send remote users a copy of your tasks by creating an ACT! report and then sending the file as an attachment. Here's what you need to do:

1. **Choose Report⇨Activities/Time Spent from the ACT! Contacts view.**

   The Run Report dialog box opens.

2. **From the Send Output To drop-down list, choose File-Editable Text.**

   The resulting file has the .rtf (rich text format) extension rather than appearing onscreen or in the printer.

3. **On the Activities/Notes/Histories tab, set the filter to show activities for a specific week or month.**

4. **Return to the General tab and click OK to run the report.**

5. **Attach the file to an e-mail message and send it to your remote user.**

   The remote user can open the file with any word processor.

Part III
Sharing Your Information with Others

The 5th Wave   By Rich Tennant

"IT'S ANOTHER DEEP SPACE PROBE FROM EARTH, SEEKING CONTACT FROM EXTRATERRESTRIALS. I WISH THEY'D JUST INCLUDE AN E-MAIL ADDRESS."

In this part . . .

Entering contacts into ACT! is only half the fun. The other half consists of communicating with the outside world. So here you'll find out how to run and create reports for your internal purposes and also how to reach an audience of one or thousands through the use of snail mail or e-mail. You'll even find a large collection of commercial forms for printing (buried deep inside of ACT!).

Chapter 9

Printing Non-Reports

· ·

· ·

*W*ith the advent of a plethora of handheld devices, techies often assume that the paper address book, calendar, or Rolodex has become extinct and that all should be placed in the Smithsonian somewhere between the dinosaurs and World War I fighter planes. Well, guess what folks? Printouts of the various aspects of your daily life are alive and well and probably hanging slightly above your PDA cradle.

No man is an island; everyone needs to communicate with the outside world at some point. Conversely, sometimes you need to carry information about the outside world with you or refer to it when you're not chained to your computer. ACT! provides you with more things to print than you can shake a stick — or tree — at! So in this chapter, I show you how to print various commercial forms, including address books, calendars, and labels. Or, if you prefer, you can print that same information on a plain, ordinary sheet of paper. I also show you how to create un-reports from various ACT! lists.

You might have wondered about the title of this chapter: "Printing Non-Reports." I've chosen that title because ACT! makes a clear distinction between *reports* and *other printable material*. (Chapter 10 deals with the exciting world of ACT! reports, and Chapter 11 even shows you how to modify existing reports — or create new ones of your own.) In this chapter, I focus on printing things other than reports. You'll find this information in the File menu — not in the Report menu.

Printing Address Books

Printing an address book is probably one of the more common tasks used by ACT! users, and ACT! makes the chore an extremely simple one to perform.

Creating a hard copy of your ACT! address book is basically a three-step process:

1. Add all your contact information into your ACT! database, making sure that your information is as complete as possible.

2. Create a lookup of the contacts that you want to include in your address book.

   Of course, you may want to include *all* your contacts in the print copy of your address book. You might even want to print separate address books for each of the different types of contacts in your database.

3. Choose the format for your address book.

Those are the basic steps. Following is a step list that includes all the down-and-dirty details for creating your own printed address book:

1. **Create a lookup if you intend on printing only a portion of your address book.**

   Refer to Chapter 6 if you need a refresher course in creating an ACT! lookup.

2. **In the Contacts view, choose File➪Print.**

   Okay, I know you're probably scratching your head wondering why I'm asking you to print when you haven't created anything yet. That's the concept with these non-reports: They aren't actually reports by definition, so ACT! just threw them into the Print menu. Go figure!

   You can see a sample of the File menu in Figure 9-1.

Figure 9-1:
ACT!'s File menu.

ACT! - [Karen - Contacts]

File Edit Contact Lookup Write Sales Repor

🗋 New...		Ctrl+N
🖻 Open...		Ctrl+O
■ Close		Ctrl+W
🖫 Save		Ctrl+S
Save Copy As...		F12
Data Exchange	▶	
🗐 Synchronize...		
🗐 Synchronize Setup...		
Backup...		
Restore...		
Administration	▶	
Set Reminders...		
🗢 Print...		Ctrl+P
Print Notes/Histories		
1 C:\ACT Databases\Karen.dbf		
2 C:\ACT Databases\...\HSRC.dbf		
3 C:\ACT Databases\ACT6demo.dbf		
4 C:\ACT Databases\Dummies.dbf		
🗈 Exit		Alt+F4

3. **Choose Address Book from the Printout Type drop-down list (Figure 9-2).**

   ACT! enables you to print contact addresses and phone numbers in a variety of commonly used paper formats, including

   - Avery
   - Day Runner
   - Day Timer
   - Deluxe
   - Franklin
   - Time System

   If you are currently using an address system from one of these manufacturers, choose it from the Printout Type drop-down list. You're able to print all your ACT! information onto preformatted addressing systems. ACT! provides you with the most popular, commercially available, addressing systems. The preprinted forms are available at any of the large office supply warehouse stores.

   Figure 9-2 shows you some of your choices. You might notice that the Edit Template button is grayed out. That's because you can't make changes to the Address Book *templates*.

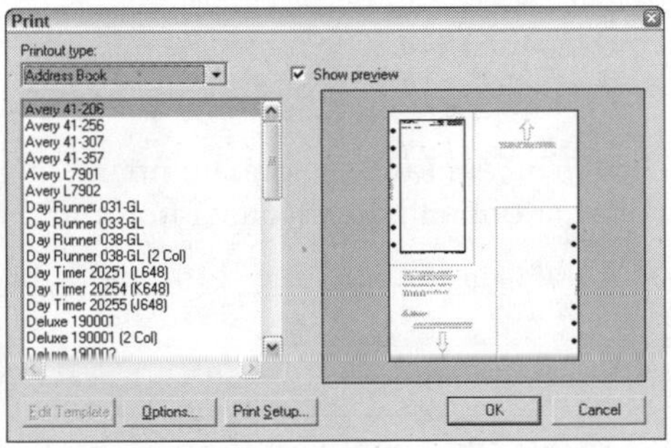

Figure 9-2:
Using
commer-
cially
available
formats.

   Of course, if you don't want to spend the money on preprinted forms, or you'd just like a printout of your address book on a plain sheet of paper, you can always use my particular favorite form for printing an address book: Plain paper.

4. **Select the format for printing the address book from the list of printout types on the left of the dialog box.**

   A preview of the selected printout appears in the preview pane on the right.

5. Click the Options button to specify the information to include in the address book.

The Address Books Options dialog box opens, as shown in Figure 9-3.

Address Book Options

Print

☑ Primary address   Additional fields:
☑ Secondary address   [None]
☑ Phone numbers   [None]
☑ Alternate contacts   [None]
☐ E-mail addresses

Print settings
☐ Double sided printing
☐ Break page on new letter
☑ Letter at top of page
☑ Lines between contacts
☐ European postal format

Sort order
● Company name
○ Last name

Create printout for
○ Current contact
● Current lookup
○ All contacts

OK   Cancel   Font...

6. In the Print area of the Address Books Options dialog box, select the fields that you'd like to include in your address book:

- *Primary Address:* Prints the contact's main address.

- *Secondary Address:* Prints the contact's home address.

- *Phone Numbers:* Prints all contact's phone numbers, including Work, Alt, Phone, Fax, Mobile Phone, Home Phone, and Pager.

- *Alternate Contacts:* Prints the second and third contacts' names and phone numbers.

- *E-mail Addresses:* Prints the contact's e-mail addresses.

7. In the Additional fields drop-down boxes, add up to three additional fields.

The choices in Step 6 are based on the default fields that come with ACT!. If you've added several new phone number fields, they won't appear in the printout of your address book, but ACT! allows you to add up to three additional fields.

If you're truly unhappy with the format of the address books, or you have the need to add more fields, you can design a custom report to accommodate your exact needs. Find out how to create brand-new reports in Chapter 11.

8. **In the Print Settings area of the Address Books Options dialog box, select your printing option.**

   Here's where you get to determine how your address book is going to print:

   - *Double Sided Printing:* Prints the address book on both sides of the page.

   - *Break Page on New Letter:* Starts a new page for each letter of the alphabet.

   - *Letter at Top of Page:* Prints the current alphabetic letter at the top of each page.

   - *Lines between Contacts:* Prints a line between contact entries.

   - *European Postal Format:* Prints the postal code before the city.

9. **In the Sort Order area, select the order in which you want entries to appear in your address book — alphabetically either by company name or contact last name.**

10. **In the Create Printout For area, specify whether to include the Current Contact, the Current Lookup, or All Contacts in the Create Printout For box.**

11. **Click the Font button to specify the typeface.**

12. **Click OK.**

    The Print dialog box appears.

13. **Click OK in the Print dialog box.**

14. **Click OK in the Windows Print dialog box.**

15. **Run to your printer and admire your newly printed Address Book.**

Creating Mailing Labels and Envelopes

All right. You've created a brochure that's guaranteed to knock the socks right off of your customers — and potential customers. Now all you've got to do is send those puppies out in the mail. There is no easier method to do this than by creating mailing labels or envelopes using ACT!.

Some of you might be snickering about now because you're much too sophisticated to be using snail mail. You've probably already raced over to Chapter 12 and learned how to create HyperText Markup Language (HTML) templates. You might still use the ACT! labels to create everything from file tabs to name badges.

You print out labels and envelopes in ACT! in exactly the same way. At first glance, printing envelopes in ACT! to match a customized letter template seems like a great idea. After all, they look a lot more personalized than an ordinary mailing label. However, if your mailing entails sending personalized letters to a large number of people, you may want to rethink your decision. Unless you have a specially designed envelope tray, you're probably going to have to print your envelopes in batches. But remember that 30 envelopes are much bulkier and harder to store than a page of 30 labels. While you print each batch of envelopes, you'll have to make sure that they remain in the exact same order as your letters or matching them to the corresponding letter could become a nightmare.

If you're printing envelopes, I suggest limiting the number of envelopes that you print at any one time. If you're just printing an envelope for one person to go with a letter that you just created using a document template, using your word processor to create the envelope is probably easier than using ACT!. ACT! automatically asks if you'd like to print an envelope after you create a document using a document template (see Chapter 12 for the details).

To create labels or envelopes using ACT!, just follow these steps:

1. **Create a lookup of the contacts for whom you want to create labels or envelopes.**

   If you're creating a personalized mailing, I'd guess that you've already created a lookup of the contacts that will get the mailing. By creating the corresponding labels using the existing lookup, you're guaranteed to have the same number of contacts and to have your labels print in the same sort order.

2. **From the Contacts view, choose File➪Print.**

3. **Choose Labels or Envelopes from the Printout Type drop-down list.**

   From this point forward, I focus on creating labels, but these directions work for envelopes. Just substitute the word *envelope* for the word *label* in any of the directions.

   If you're wondering where the label menu is in ACT!, wonder no more — it's there, but it's hiding. ACT! automatically defaults to address book whenever you access the Print menu.

4. **Select a template from the list.**

   The available label templates are listed on the left of the dialog box.

Notice that the majority of the labels listed correspond to Avery labels. Chances are that even if you're using a generic label, you'll find the magic words *Same as Avery Label #XX* printed on the side of the box.

5. **Click Edit Labels to make modifications to an existing label template (if you want to make modifications).**

   The Label Designer dialog box opens. The Label Designer tool palette also opens; you'll recognize this tool palette if you've designed layouts or reports in ACT!. Go to the Cheat Sheet (at the beginning of this book) to see the tool palette's many tools identified.

6. **Before making adjustments to the existing label formats, save the template using another name by choosing File⇨Save As, typing the name of the template in the File Name field, and then clicking OK.**

7. **Modify the label formats to your heart's content:**

   • *To delete a field:* Click the Selection tool in the tool palette, click a field, and then press Delete.

   • *To move a field:* Click the Selection tool in the tool palette and drag a field to a new position.

   • *To change the font for a field:* Double-click a field and then choose the Font tab to specify a different font, size, or attribute.

   • *To add a field:* Click the Field tool and draw a rectangle where you want to place the field.

   • *To close the template:* Choose File⇨Close and then click Yes to save.

   The next time that you run a set of labels, the template that you created will appear as one of the label template choices.

If the label that you ordinarily use isn't listed, changing your labels to correspond to one of the labels listed in ACT! is probably your easiest choice. But if you rely on a special label, you could create a document template that corresponds with the dimensions of your labels. Check out Chapter 12 to find out how to create custom templates.

8. **Click OK.**

   The Run Label dialog box appears, as shown in Figure 9-4.

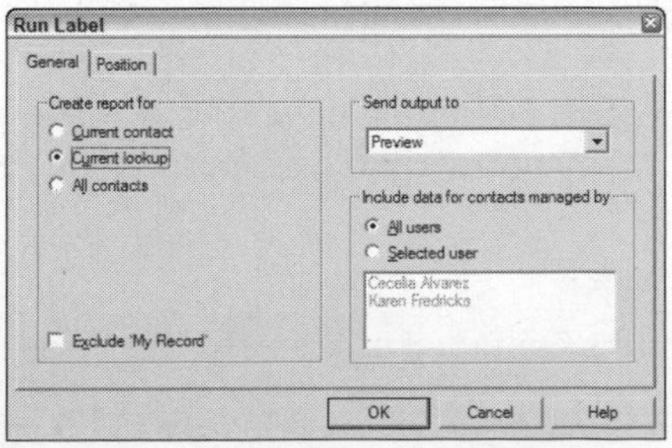

Figure 9-4:
The Run Label dialog box.

9. **In the Create Report For area, specify whether you want to create labels for the Current Contact, the Current Lookup, or All Contacts.**

10. **In the Send Output To drop-down box, select to immediately print or to first preview the labels.**

    If you're using a partially used page of labels, go to Step 11; otherwise, go to Step 12.

11. **If you're using a partially used page of labels, specify on which label to start printing on the Position tab.**

    For example, if you used five labels on a sheet of Avery 5160 labels, you may want to start printing on the third label in the second row of labels. In this case, enter **2** in the Row field and **3** in the Column field. Figure 9-5 shows you how to specify the label that you want to start printing on.

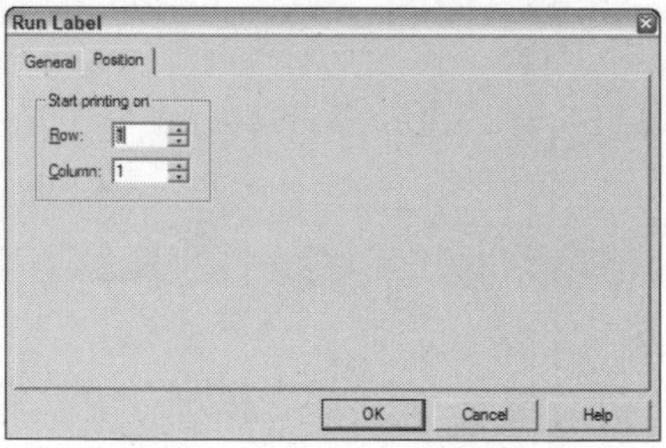

Figure 9-5:
Specifying
the starting
label
position.

12. **Click OK.**

    You're now the proud owner of a beautiful set of labels.

Creating a List View Report

I like to think of the ability to print the various ACT! lists as somewhat of a secret weapon. By being able to print these lists, you can report quickly on just about anything that you can view throughout your database. This ability enables you to quickly create a report based on the specifications and criteria that you need immediately.

You're able to create list view reports for the following ACT! lists:

- ✔ The Contact List
- ✔ The Task List
- ✔ The Activities tab in both the Contacts view and in the Group view
- ✔ The Notes/History tab in both the Contacts view and in the Group view

✔ The Sales/Opportunities tab in both the Contacts view and in the Group view

✔ The Groups tab in the Contacts view

✔ The Contacts tab in the Group view

Basically, if you're in a *list* view, such as the Contacts view or the Task List, ACT! can print the list. If you're viewing a *tab* that contains a list of items, such as the Notes/History or the Sales/Opportunities tab, ACT! can print those items.

To create a list view report:

1. **Display the list view or tab that you want to print.**

    • To display a tab, click the tab.

    • To display a view, such as the Task List or Contact List, click the appropriate icon on the View bar.

2. **Arrange the columns exactly as you want them to appear on your hardcopy printout.**

    If you need help adding or removing columns, or changing the order or size of existing columns, check out Chapter 5.

    All lists that you see in ACT! work in exactly the same way.

3. **Change the font of the currently displayed list by choosing Edit⇨Preferences and then following these steps:**

    a. **On the Colors and Fonts tab (Figure 9-6), make sure that the correct list view is selected and then click the Font button.**

    b. **Change the size to the desired size.**

    c. **Select the Show Grid Lines check box if you want grid lines to appear in the View List report.**

    d. **Click OK.**

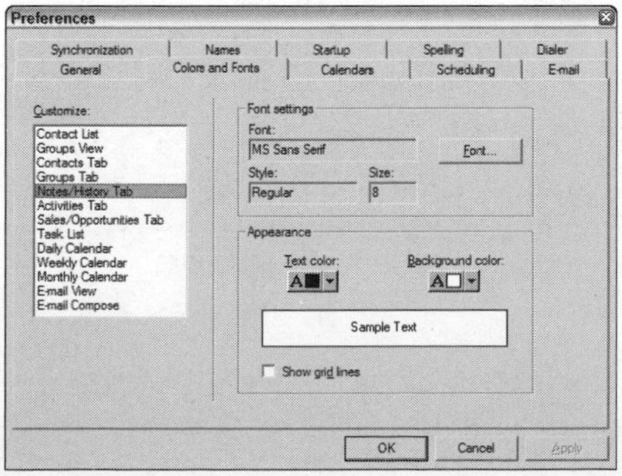

Figure 9-6:
Changing
font size.

4. **Choose File⇨Print *Window/Tab Name*.**

   You aren't actually going to see the words *Window/Tab Name* when you look at the File menu. The Print command automatically shows the name of the window or tab that you're currently looking at. So if you're in the Contact List, the menu item reads Print Contact List. If you're viewing the Notes/History tab in the Contacts view, the menu item reads Print Notes/History.

5. **Click OK.**

   At this point, one of two things happens: either a lovely report floats out of your printer, or ACT! asks you for a little more information. Printing your report is only one of your concerns; the other is being able to read it. If all columns of your report fit neatly across your monitor, chances are that what you see is what you'll get on your report.

6. **If the columns can't fit across the page, a Print dialog box appears in which you must select one of these options and then click OK:**

   • *Print Only Those Columns That Fit on One Page:* Prints the columns that fit on the page but not the remaining columns.

   • *Shrink to Fit:* Reduces the text size so that all the columns fit on the page.

   • *Print All Columns:* Prints the columns that fit on the first page and then prints the remaining columns on additional pages.

Chapter 10

Using the Basic ACT! Reports

After you build your database, the fun part is sitting back and using it. If paper is your game, then ACT! is surely the name — at least of the software that you should be using for any type of reporting. In Chapter 8, I talk about printing calendars, in Chapter 9, I show you how to print address books and labels, and in Chapter 11, I demonstrate how to design your own reports. Here in this chapter, I discuss the various ACT! reports that are available.

I show you everything you always wanted to know about ACT! reports but were afraid to ask. After reading this chapter, you'll be familiar with the various reports and how to run them. I also show you techniques for sharing those reports with colleagues.

Knowing the Basic ACT! Reports

ACT! comes with a menu of 34 basic reports right out of the box. In Chapter 11, I show you how to customize existing reports or create new ones. Here I list the basic reports, briefly describing each. Chances are good that at least one of the basic ACT! reports will give you exactly the information that you're looking for.

The first three reports in the ACT! reports menu are probably among the most useful because they supply you with information for each of your contacts. You can determine which one best suits your needs by deciding whether you'd like to view a page, a paragraph, or simply one line of information about your contact.

- **Contact Report:** A one-page report showing all the contact information for each contact, including the notes, history, and activities.
- **Contact Directory:** Prints the primary address and home address for each contact in paragraph form.
- **Phone List:** Prints the company name, company phone number, phone extension, and mobile phone number for each contact; the report displays one line of content for each contact.

The next several reports display information that's pertinent to you and your notes and activities:

- **Task List:** Shows you the scheduled and completed calls, meetings, and to-do's scheduled with each contact during a specified date range. The Task List is sorted by contact so that you can see a listing of all the time that you've spent — or are scheduled to spend — with any given contact.

  Figure 10-1 shows a sample of the top part of an ACT! Task List.

  REMEMBER

  If you want to see a more traditional task list sorted by date, create one on the fly by clicking the Activities tab in the Contacts view and then running a List View report. (I show you how in Chapter 9.)
- **Notes/History:** Displays the notes and history items for each contact during a specified date range. It looks just like the Task List except that it gives you details about the notes and histories that you've created in ACT!.
- **History Summary:** Produces a list of every attempted call, completed call, meeting held, letter sent, and field changed for each contact during a specified date range sorted by contact. Figure 10-2 shows you the top part of an unfiltered History Summary report.

Task List

Karen Fredricks Tech Benders
Boca Raton FL

Date Range: All Dates

Contact: Colleen McCarthy Ace Pet Service [1] 541-555-3648

Type	Cleared Status	Date	Time	Regarding	Scheduled For
Call	Open	8/9/2002	10:00 AM	Schedule a meeting	Chris Huffman
				See if questions were answered by website.	
				Suggest sampler.	
Meeting	Open	8/19/2002	9:00 AM	Presentation	Chris Huffman
				Show gourmet chocolate and gift baskets.	
To-do	Open	8/20/2002	NONE	Send follow-up letter	Chris Huffman
				Liked the coffee.	
Call	Open	8/26/2002	2:00 PM	Follow up	Chris Huffman
Call	Cleared	9/17/2002	NONE	Follow up	Chris Huffman
Call	Open	9/19/2002	NONE	Follow up	Chris Huffman
Call	Open	9/24/2002	10:48 AM	Follow up	Chris Huffman

Contact: Jackie Jorgensen Arcadia Ave. Florist [1] 602-555-8169

Type	Cleared Status	Date	Time	Regarding	Scheduled For
To-do	Open	8/15/2002	8:30 AM	Send "thank you for your patronage" letter	Chris Huffman

Contact: Dylan Nguyen Bechtel Corp. [1] 602-444-5410

Type	Cleared Status	Date	Time	Regarding	Scheduled For
Call	Open	10/23/2002	1:45 PM	Follow up on order	Chris Huffman

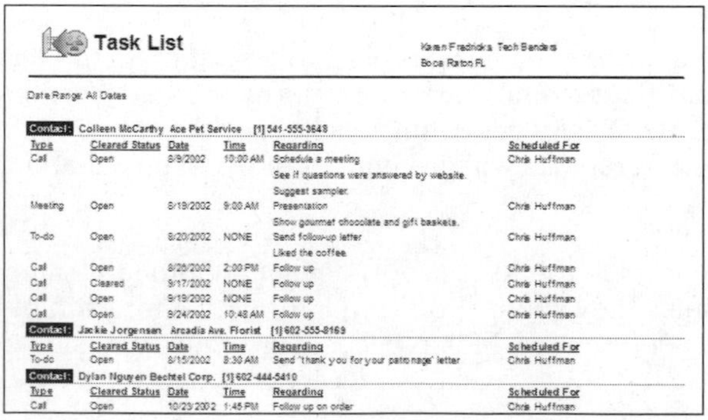

Figure 10-1: A sample ACT! Task List report.

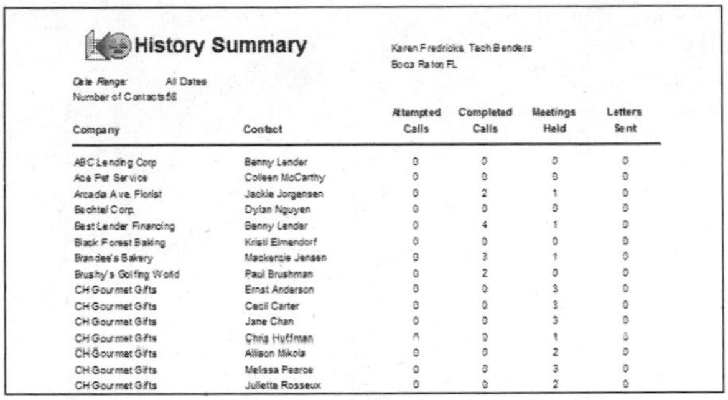

History Summary

Karen Fredricks, Tech Benders
Boca Raton FL

Date Range: All Dates
Number of Contacts 58

Company	Contact	Attempted Calls	Completed Calls	Meetings Held	Letters Sent
ABC Lending Corp	Benny Lender	0	0	0	0
Ace Pet Service	Colleen McCarthy	0	0	0	0
Arcadia Ave. Florist	Jackie Jorgensen	0	2	1	0
Bechtel Corp.	Dylan Nguyen	0	0	0	0
Best Lender Financing	Benny Lender	0	4	1	0
Black Forest Baking	Kristi Elmendorf	0	0	0	0
Brandee's Bakery	Mackenzie Jensen	0	3	1	0
Brushy's Golfing World	Paul Brushman	0	2	0	0
CH Gourmet Gifts	Ernst Anderson	0	0	3	0
CH Gourmet Gifts	Cecil Carter	0	0	3	0
CH Gourmet Gifts	Jane Chan	0	0	3	0
CH Gourmet Gifts	Chris Huffman	0	0	1	0
CH Gourmet Gifts	Allison Mikola	0	0	2	0
CH Gourmet Gifts	Melissa Pearce	0	0	3	0
CH Gourmet Gifts	Julietta Rosseux	0	0	2	0

Figure 10-2: An ACT! History Summary report.

- **History Summary Classic:** Shows the numerical total of attempted calls, completed calls, meetings held, and letters sent for each contact during a specified date range sorted by contact.

  TIP

  The History Summary report displays only those contacts that you've contacted during a specific date range. The History Summary Classic report, however, displays a list of all your contacts, including contacts that you *have contacted* as well as those that you *have not contacted.* If you end up producing a 50-page report, I suggest creating a Contact Activity lookup before running the report. If you need help with creating a lookup, turn to Chapter 6.

- **Activities/Time Spent:** Shows the date, time, duration, and information regarding activities scheduled with each contact during a specified date range. You'll get a subtotal of the time that you've spent with each contact as well as of the time that you're still scheduled to spend with them — if you assign a time duration to your meetings, calls and to-do's.

The next two reports are based on information in two of the key ACT! fields:

- **Contact Status:** Shows you the ID/Status, last reach, last meeting, and last results for each contact during a specified date range. You'll likely want to create a Contact Activity lookup before running this report to avoid having a lot of empty contact information in your final report.
- **Source of Referrals:** I mention in Chapter 14 that changing certain default fields isn't a good idea. Here's one reason why: The Source of Referrals report relies on the information in the Referred By field. Figure 10-3 shows you an example of the Source of Referrals report and plainly shows what happens if you don't enter data consistently. *Dave* Davis and *David* Davis are probably the same person, yet they show up in two different spots in the report.

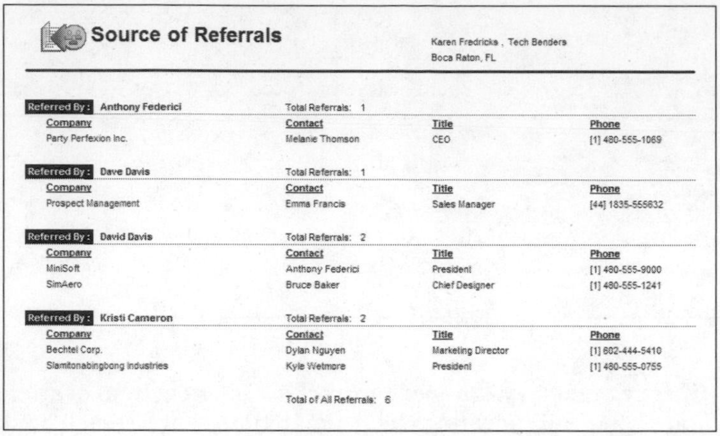

Source of Referrals

Karen Fredricks , Tech Benders
Boca Raton, FL

Referred By : Anthony Federici	Total Referrals: 1		
Company	Contact	Title	Phone
Party Perfexion Inc.	Melanie Thomson	CEO	[1] 480-555-1069
Referred By : Dave Davis	Total Referrals: 1		
Company	Contact	Title	Phone
Prospect Management	Emma Francis	Sales Manager	[44] 1835-556632
Referred By : David Davis	Total Referrals: 2		
Company	Contact	Title	Phone
MiniSoft	Anthony Federici	President	[1] 480-555-9000
SimAero	Bruce Baker	Chief Designer	[1] 480-555-1241
Referred By : Kristi Cameron	Total Referrals: 2		
Company	Contact	Title	Phone
Bechtel Corp.	Dylan Nguyen	Marketing Director	[1] 602-444-5410
Slamtonabingbong Industries	Kyle Wetmore	President	[1] 480-555-0755
	Total of All Referrals: 6		

Figure 10-3: ACT!'s Source of Referrals report.

You can find the Group reports together in a subsection of the main Reports menu or in the Reports section if you're in the Group view. These reports give you different ways to view the information in your groups. If you aren't using groups (which I explain fully in Chapter 20), these reports don't hold any benefit for you.

- **Group Membership:** Lists all groups and their members.
- **Group Summary:** Lists the notes, histories, and activities for all groups or for specific groups.
- **Group/Subgroup Summary:** Lists notes, histories, and activities for all groups and subgroups.
- **Group/Subgroup Membership:** Lists all groups and subgroups and their members.
- **Group Comprehensive:** Lists all information (including notes, histories, and activities) for each group, subgroup, and their respective members.
- **Group List:** Lists all groups and their description from the Group Description field.
- **Group/Subgroup List:** Lists all groups, subgroups, and their respective descriptions from the Group Description field.

ACT! provides you with a variety of sales reports, funnels, and graphs. The Sales Reports use information inputted into the Sales/Opportunities tab. If you aren't using the Sales/Opportunities feature (head to Chapter 19 for the lowdown), you aren't able to use these reports. The eight Sales Reports are all housed in a separate Sales section in the Reports menu.

✔ **Sales Totals by Status:** Garners totals of all sales opportunities and sorts them by Closed/Won Sales, and Lost Sales.

✔ **Sales Adjusted for Probability:** Lists all sales opportunities by contact, with totals.

✔ **Sales List:** Lists information for sales opportunities, Closed/Won Sales, and Lost Sales.

✔ **Sales Pipeline Report:** Gives information about sales opportunities at each stage in the sales process.

✔ **Sales by Record Manager:** Lists sales opportunities, Closed/Won Sales, and Lost Sales sorted by Record Manager.

✔ **Sales by Contact:** Provides complete sales information for each contact with a sales opportunity or a closed sale.

✔ **Sales Graph:** Gives forecasted or closed sales, in a bar or line graph.

✔ **Sales Pipeline:** Gives the number of sales opportunities at each stage of the sales process, in a graphical form.

For more information on the Sales Reports, check out Chapter 19.

ACT! 6 adds four brand-new reports to ACT! but unfortunately didn't add them to the Reports menu. In Chapter 22, I tell you how to find these reports and describe them in more detail. The new ACT! reports are

✔ **Count of Group Membership:** Displays group information. This particular report shows you the number of primary and subgroups, the name of each primary and subgroup, and the number of contacts in each primary and subgroup.

✔ **E-mail List:** Prints out the company name, contact name, and e-mail address of the contacts in either your current lookup or in your entire database.

✔ **Fax List:** Prints out the company name, contact name, and fax number of the contacts in either your current lookup or in your entire database.

✔ **Call and Meeting Summary Report:** Counts your attempted calls, completed calls, meetings held, and messages left. Filter the report by date and/or record manager; run the report for either your entire database or for the current lookup.

Running an ACT! Report

The following directions apply to all ACT! reports. The dialog box is the same for all reports. Depending on the report that you're running, however, some of the options may be unavailable and thus appear grayed out.

To run an ACT! report, just follow these steps:

1. **Perform a lookup or display the contact record or records that you want to include in the report.**

   All roads in ACT! lead — or at least pass by — the lookup. Before running a report, decide which contact's or group's data you want to include in your report. For example, you may run a History Summary Report for a single contact or a Contact Report for all contacts in a state or region. You can include data from the current contact or group record, the current contact or group lookup, or from all contacts or groups.

2. **Sort the contacts before running the report if you want the contacts in the report to appear in a particular order.**

   Do you want the contacts to appear alphabetically by company name or by last name? If you have numerous contacts with the last name Smith, do you then want to sort them by company or state? You must make these decisions *before* running an ACT! report.

   Sort your contacts in one of two ways: Sort by up to three criteria by choosing Edit➪Sort, or sort your contact by a single criterion by clicking the appropriate contact heading in the Contact List.

3. **Click Reports and then click the name of the report that you want to run. To run a report that doesn't appear in the menu, choose Reports➪Other Report and select the appropriate report.**

   The Run Report dialog box opens, as shown in Figure 10-4. The General tab is identical for any and all ACT! reports that you create.

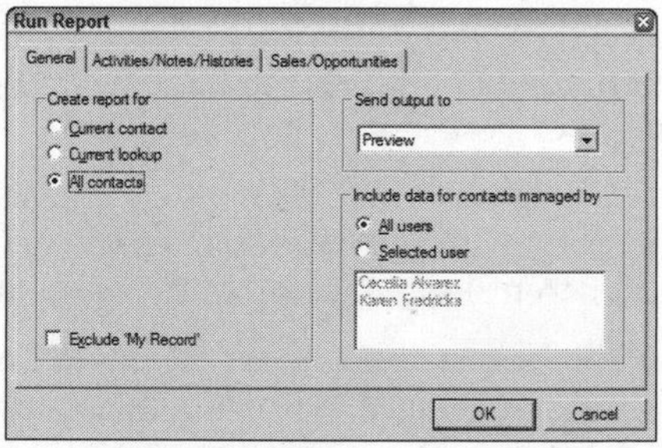

Figure 10-4:
The Run
Report
dialog box.

4. **In the Create Report For area, specify the contacts to include in the report.**

   The choices are self explanatory.

If you sorted the contacts, select the Current Lookup radio button, even if you want to include all contacts in the database. If you don't select this option, the contacts in the report don't appear in the sort order that you specified.

5. **Select the Exclude 'My Record' check box to exclude information from your My Record in the report.**

   This option is not available for all reports.

6. **In the Send Output To drop-down list, select an output for the report.**

   • **Printer:** If you're fully confident that your report will print correctly the first time, go for it! This option sends the report directly to your default printer.

   • **Preview:** Choose the Preview option if you're at all hesitant about your reporting capabilities. A preview of the report appears onscreen. After previewing the report, print it or run it again if it isn't looking exactly the way that you intended it to look.

   • **Fax:** Sends the report as a fax using your selected fax software.

   In order to send a fax from ACT!, you need to have two things present in your computer: access to a fax/modem either on your local or network computer; and a piece of faxing software, such as WinFax Pro.

   • **E-mail:** Sends the saved report as an attachment to an e-mail message. The attachment has an .rpt extension and can only be read by recipients who have ACT! installed on their computers.

   • **File: ACT! Report:** Allows you to save the report as a file with the .rpt extension that you can later open, view, and print. However, you can't edit the contents of an .rpt file.

   • **File-Editable Text:** Lets you save the report in .rtf or .txt format. After you save the report, you can edit it saved as an .rtf or .txt file in the ACT! word processor or Microsoft Word. This is a great option if you need to embellish an ACT! report with information obtained from another source.

7. **In the Include Data For Contacts Managed By area, select the Record Manager of the contacts that you're including in your report.**

   • **All Users:** Includes contact records managed by all users of the database.

   • **Selected Users:** Includes contact records managed by selected users of the database. If you're the only user of the database, only your name appears in the list.

   The Record Manager options are not available for Group and Sales reports.

8. **On the Activities/Notes/Histories tab (Figure 10-5), make the appropriate selections.**

   If the report you have chosen includes sections for activities and notes/history, those options are available. If not, the options will be grayed out.

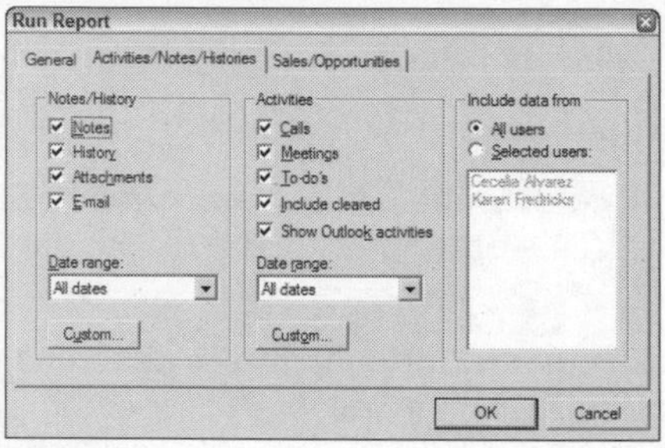

Figure 10-5:
The
Activities/
Notes/
Histories
tab.

- In the Notes/History area, select the type of notes and the corresponding date range of the notes that you're including in your report.

- In the Activities area, select the type of activities and the corresponding date range of the activities to include in your report.

- In the Include Data From area, select the users whose information you want to include in the report.

Don't be surprised if the options in the Activities/Notes/Histories tab appear grayed out for most reports that you attempt to run. One of ACT!'s limitations is that these options are available only in their entirety for the following reports:

- Contact Report

- Group Summary Report

- Group Comprehensive Report

The Notes/Histories area is where you designate whether you want to include notes, histories, attachments, and e-mail information in your reports based on the date range during which you created these notes and entries. The following reports allow you to view the Notes/Histories but *not* the Activity portion of the Activities/Notes/Histories tab:

- Notes/History Reports

- History Summary Report

- History Summary Classic Report

- Call Meeting Summary Report

The Activities portion enables you to include calls, meetings, and to-do's in your report as well as include activities that are either cleared or that were created in Outlook. As with Notes/Histories, the Activities portion of the Activities/Notes/Histories tab is available only in certain reports:

- Task List
- Activities/Time Spent Report
- Contact Status Report

The Crystal Clear Reports (CCR) program helps you overcome some of the ACT! report limitations by providing you with additional ACT! reports. Read more about CCR in Chapter 24.

9. **Click the Sales/Opportunities tab — if you're running a Sales report.**

Figure 10-6 shows the Sales/Opportunities tab that appears in the various sales report. This tab is grayed out if you aren't running a sales report.

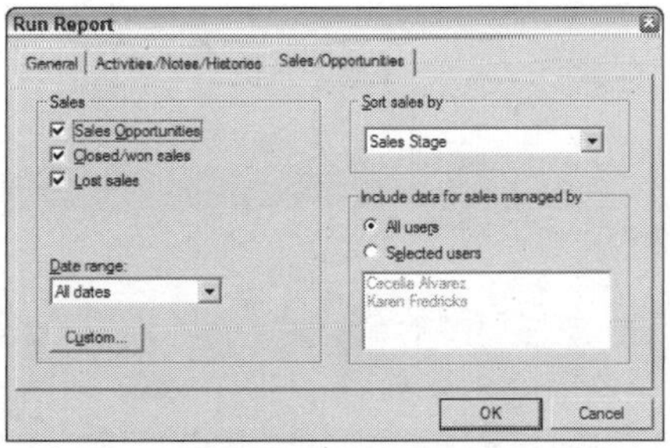

Figure 10-6:
The Sales/
Opportu-
nities tab.

- In the Sales area, select whether you want to include Sales Opportunities, Closed/Won Sales, and/or Lost Sales in your report.

- In the Date Range area, specify the date range of the Sales Opportunities to include in the report.

- In the Sort Sales By area, select a sort order for the report. A sales report can be sorted by numerous criteria, including sales stage, amount, and probability.

- In the Include Data for Sales Managed By area, choose to include information from All Users or Selected Users of your database.

10. **Click OK.**

ACT! runs the report. If you aren't happy with the results, run the same report a second time using different criteria, or try running a different report. Better yet, read Chapter 11 to discover how to create your very own ACT! reports.

Chapter 11

Designing Your Own Reports

ACT! comes with more than 20 reports right out of the box. Surely one of these reports will give you exactly the information that you need. Chapter 10 shows you how to run any of the existing ACT! reports. In this chapter, I show you how to create brand new reports or modify an existing one. If, after designing a report, you'd like to add it to the Report menu, head to Chapter 3 where I show you how.

Before you jump into modifying reports, check out the "Five Reports You Must Save in a Different Way" section in this chapter, where I list the five reports that behave differently from the other ACT! reports. This section contains information that can save you grief and time.

If you want to more than double the amount of reports that are contained in ACT! — without having to create them yourself — flip to Chapter 24 where I show you how to add over 30 additional reports by using a handy little product called Crystal Clear Reports.

Creating an ACT! Report

Designing a database report can be a bit intimidating if you've never done it before. Being familiar with the structure of your existing database will prove helpful when you attempt to create a report. So you'll need to know the *names* of the fields that you'll be working with as well as their location in ACT!. For example, if you want to include the name of a company, you must know that the field is called Company and that you find the field on the Contacts view. If you want to include notes that you've added, you must know to include the Details field from the Notes/Histories tab.

Create a lookup of the contacts that you're including in your report. This is an optional step but can be timesaving. As you design your report, you'll notice that sometimes certain fields won't be large enough to contain their data or that columns won't line up correctly. By creating a lookup, you're able to check the progress of your report-designing efforts each time that you add a new element to your report.

1. **From within the Contacts view, choose File⇨New⇨Report Template.**

    The ACT! Report Designer opens.

    Yikes! The problem with designing an ACT! report from scratch is that you have to create the report from scratch. As shown in Figure 11-1, a blank template with Header, Contact, and Footer section titles appears on the left.

Report Designer's tool palette

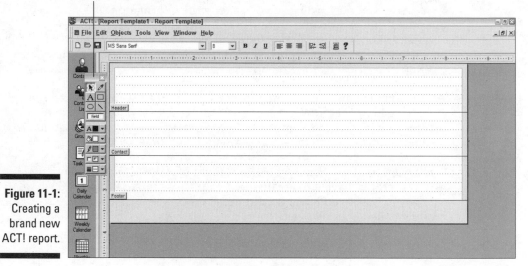

Figure 11-1:
Creating a
brand new
ACT! report.

2. **Choose File⇨Save As.**

    Later in this chapter, I show you how to modify existing reports. When you're creating a new report, it needs a new unique name.

3. **Fill in a name for your new report and then click Save.**

4. **Choose Edit⇨Define Sections to add a new section.**

    The Define Sections dialog box opens. You can see it in all its glory in Figure 11-2. Report templates contain sections of information. You can add, change, or delete sections. The sections will contain the various fields that you include in your report.

A new report template starts with three main sections:

- **Header:** Information that appears at the top of every page, such as the report's title and creator.

- **Contact (or Group):** The area that contains one or more of your contact or group fields. Every report contains a single Contact section or Group section, but not both. This is the meat and potatoes of the report where you'd find pertinent information such as the contact's name, address, and phone number.

- **Footer:** Information that appears at the bottom of every page, such as a page number or the date that you run the report.

Each section has a section title that appears in the report template but doesn't appear in the report itself.

5. **Click the Add button.**

Figure 11-2:
The Define
Sections
dialog box.

6. **Select a section and then click OK.**

   At this point, the only new sections that you can add are the Title Header and the Title Footer. Both appear only on the first page of the report.

7. **Choose Edit➪Define Sections.**

   The Define Sections dialog box opens again.

8. **Select the section for which you'd like to create a subsection.**

   In most cases, you'll create subsections for the Contact section. Subsections can be created under primary sections or under other subsections. For example, the Contact section might have a Notes/ History subsection showing all notes and histories that you created for each contact. The Note/History subsection can contain a Summary sub-subsection that gives you a count of all those notes.

9. **Click the Add button.**

   The Add Sections dialog box opens.

Mostly, the basic subsections are self explanatory, but some are not:

- **Notes/History:** Includes information from the fields in the Notes/History tab. That's straightforward enough.

- **Sales:** Includes information from the fields in the Sales/Opportunities tab. No surprises here.

- **Group or Contact:** A Group section can contain a Contact subsection, and vice versa. A-ha! — this is important to know.

- **Activities:** Includes information from the fields found in the Activities tab. Almost redundant, isn't it?

- **Summary Sorted By:** Defines the order in which you want your report sorted. You can sort your report based on any of the contact fields. For example, you can sort your report alphabetically by company or by contact last name. A very handy tool, indeed.

- **Summary:** Includes counts, totals, averages, and minimum and maximum values. Summary sections can display statistics for primary sections or subordinate sections.

10. **Select a section from the Sections area of the Add Sections dialog box.**

    If a section name is grayed out, ACT! is telling you that you can't add that particular subsection to a section.

    Depending on the subsection that you want to add, you might have to select a corresponding field. For example, if you select Summary Sorted By, you must also select a field from the list on the right to choose the field that determines the sort order.

11. **Specify other subsection options.**

    Depending on the type of subsection that you're adding to your report, you can now specify any of the following options:

    - **Page Break Before Each Section:** Starts a new page at the beginning of the section.

    - **Allow Section to Break Across Multiple Pages:** Displays and prints all information in a section, even if it doesn't fit on a single page. If you turn off this option, a page break is inserted before the section if the section doesn't fit on the page.

    - **Collapse Blank Lines:** Eliminates lines in a section that contain only fields with no data or that are duplicated. Graphic objects whose upper-left corners fall within the line are also eliminated.

    - **Collapse Blank Section:** Eliminates sections in the report that contain no data. Graphic objects whose upper-left corners fall within the section are also eliminated.

12. **Click OK to close the Add Section dialog box.**

13. **Click OK to close the Define Sections dialog box.**

14. Familiarize yourself with the Report Designer's tool palette.

If you've worked with the Layout Designer, you're probably scratching your head and muttering to yourself that you know you've seen those tools somewhere else. You have. The tool palettes for the ACT! Report and Layout Designers are identical. Refer to the Cheat Sheet (located at the beginning of this book) for a listing of its tools. The tool palette consists of a dozen icons; simply click an icon to work with a different element in your report.

If you initially thought that the tool palette was in your way and closed it, make it reappear by choosing View➪Show Tool Palette.

15. Click a section or subsection title and drag it up or down to allow you more room to work with.

For now, visualizing what your report will look like is difficult. After you add a few fields to your report, however, you can determine whether you have left enough — or too much — room in a section and then resize the section as necessary.

16. Click the Field tool on the tool palette.

The cursor is transformed into a big plus sign.

17. Place your cursor on the template where you want to insert a field and drag down and to the right to define the field's length and position.

When you release the mouse button, the Field List dialog box appears. You can now place any of your existing ACT! fields into the report templates.

18. Click a tab and select the field that you want to add.

You must place the appropriate fields in the appropriate section of the report. For example, place Activities fields in the Activities section, the Group fields in the Group section, and so on.

Clicking the System tab allows you to add page numbers, dates, and date ranges to your reports.

19. Select options for each field that you're adding.

- **Add Field Label:** If you don't want to include a field label for a field in the template, deselect the Add Field Label option.

- **Use My Record:** On the Contact tab, select Use My Record to include data from your My Record in the report. For example, to include your name in the Header section, select the Contact field and the Use My Record option. If you don't select this option, data for the report comes from the information in the contact or group records.

- **Detail Field:** This creates a field that will contain data.

- **Summary Field:** This summarizes the results of all the records.

    If you indicate that a field will be a summary field, you must also determine the type of summary field it will be.

- **Count:** This counts the number of records for the selected field.

- **Total:** This calculates the total of all values in the selected field.

- **Average:** This calculates the average of all values in the selected field.

- **Minimum:** This finds the lowest number or earliest date in the selected field.

- **Maximum:** This finds the highest number or latest date in the selected field.

20. **Click the Add button.**

21. **Click the Close button.**

    The Report Designer now contains the fields and field labels that you added. Figure 11-3 shows you an example of a report template that contains several sections, subsections, and fields.

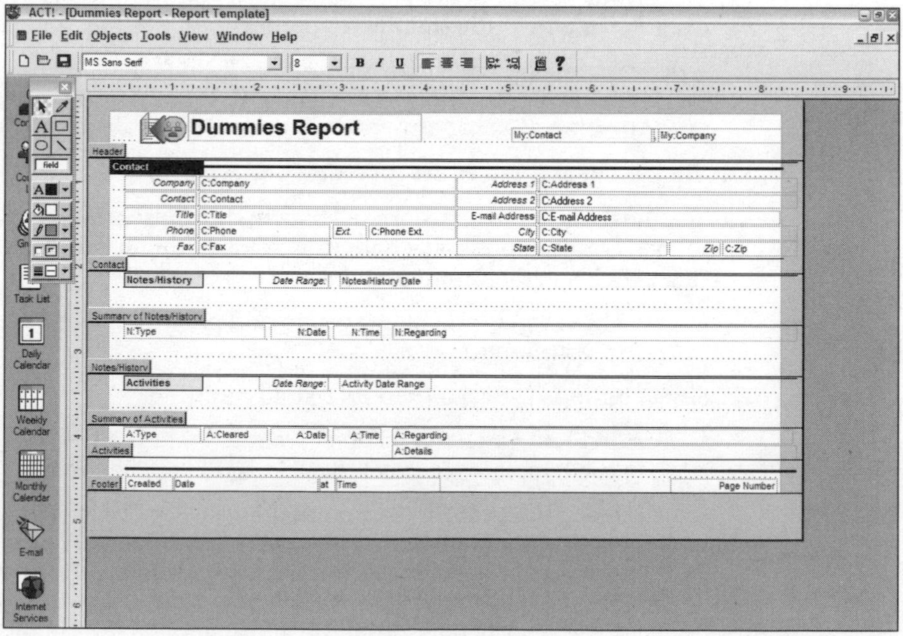

Figure 11-3:
A sample report template as shown in the Report Designer.

Notice that there appears to be duplicate fields. The first field that you see is the field label. You can edit any of these labels by clicking the Text icon on the tool palette, clicking the label, and then typing in any desired changes.

You can distinguish the field itself by the colon that appears in each field. This is where the actual data from your ACT! database appears when you run the report. The letter in front of the colon indicates the field type. For example, if you add your name in the Header section, the field appears as My:Contact. If you added a contact's company, it appears on the report template as C:Company.

22. **Choose File⇨Preview to test the report each time that you add a few new elements to the report template.**

    By previewing your report, you can view the outcome of your report while you design it.

23. **If at first you don't succeed, click Close to return to your template and make the appropriate changes.**

24. **When you're satisfied with your report, choose File⇨Save to save it.**

Modifying an Existing Report

Until you really get the hang of creating customized reports, I recommend that you modify an existing report that gives you most of the information that you need. Modifying an existing report is much easier than creating a new one from scratch. Just make sure that you use the Save As command to give your modified report a new, unique name. That way, if your changes don't have the desired effect, you can still revert back to the original report!

Follow these steps to renovate existing ACT! reports:

1. **Do a little research to determine which ACT! report comes closest to filling your needs.**

   I admit it — I'm a schoolteacher by nature and believe in doing a bit of research before attempting to write a report (pun intended). You might also consider these basic rules:

   - The *Contact Report* produces an entire page for each contact.

   - The *Contact Directory* produces a paragraph for each contact.

   - The *Phone List* produces one line for each contact.

2. **Choose Reports⇨Edit Report Templates.**

3. Double-click the name of the report that you want to modify.

Probably one of the hardest things about customizing existing reports is figuring out the names of the corresponding files. All the ACT! reports end with the `.rep` extension. Many of the report names are rather obvious; for example, the filename of the Contact Report is `Contact6.rep`. However, some of the report names may throw you for a loop. For example, the name of the Group/Subgroup List Report is `ACCLIST6.rep`. Go figure!

Table 11-1 lists the ACT! reports and their corresponding filenames. Chapter 10 contains descriptions of these reports' content.

Table 11-1	ACT! Report Filenames
Report	*Filename*
Contact Report	`CONTACT6.rep`
Phone List	`PHONELS6.rep`
Task List	`TASKLIS6.rep`
Notes/History	`NOTEHIS6.rep`
History Summary	`HISTORY6.rep`
History Summary Classic	`HISTCLA6.rep`
Activities/Time Spent	`ACTIVIT6.rep`
Contact Status	`STATUS6.rep`
Source of Referrals	`REFERRA6.rep`
Group Membership	`GRPMEMB6.rep`
Group Summary	`GROUP6.rep`
Group/Subgroup Summary	`ACCSUMM6.rep`
Group/Subgroup Membership	`ACCMEMB6.rep`
Group Comprehensive	`CCCOMP6.rep`
Group List	`GRPLST6.rep`
Group/Subgroup List	`ACCLIST6.rep`
Sales Totals by Status	`SLSTOTA6.rep`
Sales Adjusted for Probability	`SLSFRCS6.rep`
Sales List	`SLSDTAI6.rep`
Sales Funnel Report	`SLSFUNL6rep`

Report	Filename
Sales by Record Manager	SLSBYMG6.rep
Sales by Contact	SLSCNTC6.rep
Count Group Membership	COUNTGROUPMEM.rep
E-mail List	E-MAILLIST.rep
Fax List	FAXLIST.rep
Calls and Meeting Summary	CALLMTGSUM.rep

4. **Choose File⇨Save As and give your new report a new name.**

   I hope that I sound like a broken record because you must realize the importance of renaming reports *before* you start to modify them. Just in case!

5. **After you save your report *using a different name*, add or delete fields and sections to your heart's content.**

   Follow the same procedures that I detail in the previous section to modify this report. Then preview your report, save it, and relax — after you do the initial work, your new report will continue to work for *you*!

Five Reports You Must Save in a Different Way

Although it's generally a good idea to rename an existing ACT! report and modify it rather than create a brand-new report from scratch, a few of the ACT! reports are written in such a way that you may encounter difficulties if you try to modify and save them with a new filename. These reports are

- Notes/History
- Contact Report
- Task List
- Sales by Record Manager
- History Summary Classic

Typically, these reports work correctly until you make even the slightest modification, at which time the report ceases to function properly. This happens because the filtering for certain reports is hard coded into the program. Using the original filename for the modified report and moving it to another folder solves the problem. Here's how you do it:

1. **Use Windows Explorer to create a new subfolder within the ACT! report folder.**

2. **Choose Reports⇨Edit Report Templates.**

3. **Open the file that you want to modify and then choose File⇨Save As.**

   The next step is where you do things a little differently. Proceed carefully.

4. **Save the file as the original report name but save it to the new reports folder that you created in Step 1.**

5. **Modify the report in its new location.**

   Refer to the steps where I detail modifying reports in the section "Creating an ACT! Report."

6. **To run the report, choose Reports⇨Other Report and navigate to the folder that now holds the new report.**

7. **Select your modified report and click OK.**

Chapter 12

Merging Your Information into a Document

A particularly useful ACT! feature enables you to create customized document templates. These templates are forms in which ACT! fills in your selected data fields. You can send these forms to a thousand people as easily as you can send them to just one person. You can send out routine documents one at a time on a continual basis, or you can send out the document one time to all or part of your database. After you create a form, you can send it out via snail mail, e-mail, fax, or Pony Express.

Mail Merge Isn't Just about Mailing

Poor mail merge! Folks often have two common misconceptions about mail merge. Some people think that the term *mail merge* is synonymous with *junk mail*. Also, the word *mail* makes some folks think that one requirement for a mail merge is a postage stamp. However, neither of these common misconceptions is true. A mail merge simply takes the content of one or more fields and puts that content into a template or form.

A good way to understand the concept of mail merge is to visualize this simple equation:

template + data field(s) = personalized document

Note the (s) at the end of data field, suggesting that you can use either one name or many names. Some of you may think that you will never perform a mail merge because you have no desire to send out a mass mailing. Others of you may have already perfected the art of mass mailing but never realized that a mail merge can be directed to one person or to thousands of people. I hate to be the one to break your bubble, but if you have any kind of routine documents that you're generating repetitively, you should be using ACT!'s mail merge to do it.

The three things necessary to create a mail merge are

- ✔ **A name or a list of names:** By now you're the happy owner of a database and know how to create a lookup. (Don't know how to create a lookup? Better check out Chapter 6.) You can merge a document with your current contact, your current lookup, or the entire database.

- ✔ **A document template:** A *document template* is a letter or form that substitutes *field names* in place of names and addresses or whatever other information that will come directly from your database. ACT! comes with a number of document templates that you can either use as is or modify. You can also create your own document templates by using a word processor.

- ✔ **A program that will combine the names into the template:** After you have a list of names and a document template, you need something to combine them. You could try to use your food processor, but I prefer to use the mail merge feature in ACT!.

Picking Your Word Processor

ACT! can use either its own word processor or Microsoft Word to create document templates. By default, ACT! is set to use its own word processor. Most ACT! users prefer using Word as their word processor, and I assume that you're no different. Although the ACT! word processor will get the job done, chances are you're already using Word and using an application that you're already familiar with is preferable.

If your word processing preferences inside ACT! aren't set to use Microsoft Word as your default word processor, you can't use existing Word templates or any templates that you created by using Word. To change your word processor settings, follow these handy-dandy directions:

1. **Choose Edit⇨Preferences from the Contacts view.**

2. **On the General tab, select a word processor from the Word Processor list.**

   In this case, you're choosing Microsoft Word.

3. **Click OK.**

Each time that you begin to use Word through ACT!, you might notice a slight delay. Leaving Word open *without having any documents open* can alleviate this delay.

Occasionally, users running ACT! on a network encounter one of the following error messages when trying to access Word:

```
Word processor not found on system

The word processor driver is not running

ACT! failed to add ACT.DOT to Word
```

If you encounter any of these messages, your network administrator will need to change the macro security level in Word before you can run the program with ACT!.

Creating a Document Template

Before you can win friends and influence prospects with your dazzling display of personalized documents, you need two basic elements: the data and the document template.

Remember — you're creating a template, not a document, to perform your mail merge. A *document* is a plain old file that you create and use in Word. You use it once, save it, and store it away for posterity, or delete it as soon as you're done with it. A *template* is a form that will be merged with your contact information. The convenience of templates is that you use them over and over again.

Because you've already got your data tucked away nicely in your database, all you have left to do is to create the document template, which involves creating a form document. Your document template will contain blank areas that are then filled in with information from your database after you perform a merge. Create a document template by following these steps:

1. **Choose File⇨New.**

   The New dialog box opens. You're given a list of choices, as shown in Figure 12-1.

2. **Select Microsoft Word 2000 or 2002 (XP) Template.**

   Try not to look too surprised when Word opens. You've already demanded that ACT! use Word as your default word processor. Like an obedient contact manager, your wish is ACT!'s command.

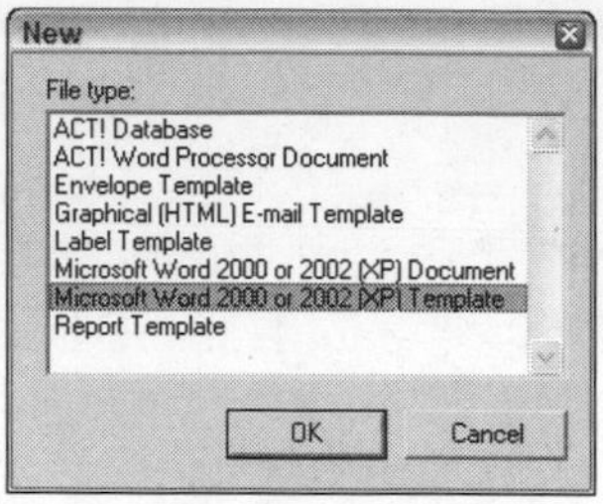

Figure 12-1:
Creating
a new
document
template.

3. **Resist the urge to close the Mail Merge Fields window that's obscuring a portion of Word.**

The Mail Merge Fields dialog box, shown in Figure 12-2, is the main event of this little procedure. If you scroll through the Mail Merge Fields, the various field names should ring a bell. After all — they're all your database fields.

You can drag those pesky fields out of your way by placing your mouse pointer on the Merge Fields title bar and dragging it out of the way.

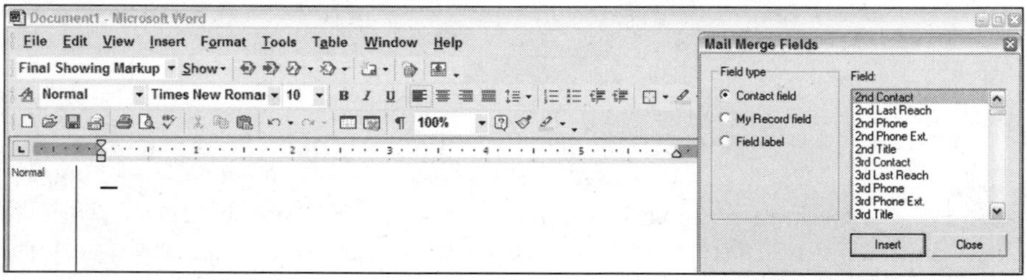

Figure 12-2:
The Mail
Merge
Fields dialog
box.

4. **Change all your page settings.**

Go ahead and change your font, margins, and other formatting items exactly as if you were working in a regular ol' Word document.

5. **Create the body of your letter or form.**

Nothing new under the sun here. You can backspace, delete, and type just like you would in a non-template document.

6. **Determine what type of field you'd like to insert into your template.**

The Mail Merge Fields dialog box allows you to insert three different types of field information:

- **Contact Field:** If you want your contacts' information to appear when you perform a mail merge, then you need to insert a contact field into your template. In a letter, the name at the top that you're sending the letter to would be the *Contact* field.

Whatever information you've entered into a field appears in the merged document. If any of the fields in the contact record are empty, ACT! skips that field; you won't see a blank line. In Figure 12-3, I've inserted the company field; if your contact isn't associated with a company, that line is skipped.

- **My Record field:** If you'd like your own contact information to appear, select the My Record Field radio button. If you're creating a letter document template, the name on the bottom is your name and is represented by the *My Record* field option.

Your My Record information resides on the first contact record that appears when you log on as yourself in the ACT! database.

- **Field Label:** Selecting the Field Label radio button inserts the name of the field, not the information contained in that field. You might wonder why you would want to go through the effort of scrolling through the list of field names to insert a label when you could just as easily type in the field label. I am wondering the same thing!

7. **Insert fields where you would like contact information to appear.**

Here's where the fun begins. Every time you get to a part that could be populated with ACT! information, you must scroll down that long list of fields, select the one that you'd like to insert into your template, and click the Insert button.

The field name will appear in your document set off by a set of lovely brackets. Treat these field names exactly as you would any other words in your template. For example, if you'd like to see them set in bold, bold the field name. If the contact information appears at the end of a sentence, follow it by a period.

8. **Choose File⇨Save As.**

Okay, I know that you probably already know how to save a document in Word, but I'd like to draw your attention to a couple of interesting phenomena that occur when saving an ACT! document template in Word. If you look at Figure 12-4, you'll see that the filename appears inside quote marks and has .adt already filled in as the extension — even though the Save As Type indicates that you're creating a file with the .doc extension. My advice is to ignore the extensions and just type in the filename of your choice. Your document is automatically saved with the .adt extension. And, unless you specify otherwise, your template is saved to your default template folder. In Chapter 3, I show you how to determine the location where you'd like to use to save your templates, and also how to add a document template to the Write menu.

Document templates created with the ACT! word processor will end in the extension .tpl.

Figure 12-3:
Sample
document
template.

Figure 12-4:
Saving the
document
template.

9. Check your document for accuracy and edit as necessary.

After a template is created, you can change your templates whenever the
need arises. There are a variety of reasons why you may need to go back
and edit an ACT! template. After using it, you may discover a spelling
mistake. The contact fields that you're using may not be working correctly
or may lack the proper punctuation. You might even want to make changes
to the wording in the template. The procedure for editing your document
template varies only slightly from that of creating the document:

a. **Choose Write⇨Edit Document Template.**

b. **When the Open dialog box appears, select the document template that you want to open and then click Open.**

The template opens in Word, and the Mail Merge Fields dialog box automatically appears.

When you're editing an existing template, you'll see your field names rather than your data. If you see actual data, you aren't editing the template, and the changes that you make affect only the current document that you're in; your document template remains unchanged.

c. **Make the appropriate changes to the template.**

d. **Click Save when you're finished editing.**

In general, using an existing template is easier than creating a new template from scratch. Basically, to create a new template, you simply open a similar template and follow the same procedure as if you were editing an existing template — but save the file to a *different name*. Or, if the document already exists in Word, you might want to first open the existing document in Word, highlight the information that you'd like to appear in your template, copy it to the Clipboard, and then paste it into the new template.

Initially, ACT! comes with a default letter, memo, and fax template. You can access them by clicking Write from any ACT! screen and choosing letter, memo, or fax. You can easily modify these templates in the same way you'd modify any other template: Choose Write⇨Edit Document Templates and choose `letter.adt`, `memo.adt` or `faxcover.adt`, respectively. Your personalized templates then appear as Letter, Memorandum, or Fax Cover Page in the ACT! Write menu.

Creating HTML (Graphical) E-mail Templates

HyperText Markup Language (HTML), or graphical e-mail templates as ACT! calls them, differ slightly from regular document templates in several ways. For starters, you typically create graphical e-mail templates by using the ACT! word processor. Graphical e-mail templates are essential if you want to

✔ Send personalized documents via e-mail (rather than through snail mail)

✔ Include hyperlinks to Web sites or e-mail addresses

✔ Include graphics that are stored on your Web site

Creating a true HTML template can be confusing for many of you and beyond the scope of this book. If you'd like to include graphics in your template that aren't currently stored on your Web site, your Web designer can create a special page for you to store your graphics. You can also create graphical e-mail templates by using other products, such as Microsoft FrontPage or Macromedia Dreamweaver, although you'd need some knowledge of HTML to do so (also beyond the scope of this book).

To create a graphical e-mail template, follow these steps:

1. **From the Contacts view, choose File⇨New.**

   The New dialog box opens.

2. **Select Graphical (HTML) E-mail Template and then click OK.**

   You are now in the ACT! word processor, as shown in Figure 12-5. This is where things start to vary slightly from creating traditional templates.

3. **Type in the body of your document template as you would in any other word processor.**

   Although it might at first look a little foreign to you, the ACT! word processor works pretty much just like Word does — it just lacks some of Word's functionality. Here are a couple of suggestions to get you started:

   • To change the margins, page orientation, or paper size, choose File⇨Page Setup.

   • To center, insert bullets, or use other styles, choose Format⇨Paragraph and then select an option (Figure 12-6).

   • Although you can change the basic fonts, sizes, and attributes from the toolbar, you have to hunt a little deeper to change the color of the font. (Choose Format⇨Font to access the Font dialog box that's shown in Figure 12-7.)

I recommend sticking with the fonts that come with Windows. Even if the font displays properly on your computer, the same font must also be installed on the recipient's computer. If the recipient doesn't have that font installed, another font will be substituted, and who knows how that final outcome will look.

4. **Insert a hyperlink to a Web site if desired.**

   You might want to send out an e-mail to all your clients directing them to a special promotion or an article of interest on your Web site. When you insert a hyperlink, you need to include the complete address — including the `http://` — or your readers won't end up at the correct site.

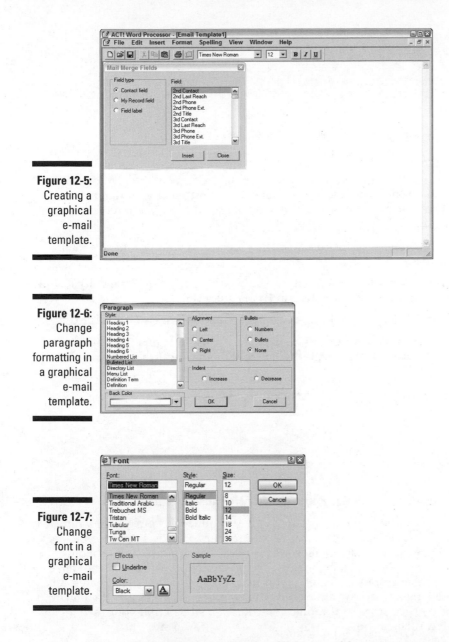

Figure 12-5:
Creating a graphical e-mail template.

Figure 12-6:
Change paragraph formatting in a graphical e-mail template.

Figure 12-7:
Change font in a graphical e-mail template.

To insert a hyperlink to a Web site address into your graphical e-mail template:

a. Place your cursor where you would like to insert your hyperlink and then choose Insert⇨Hyperlink.

The dialog box shown in Figure 12-8 appears.

Figure 12-8:
Insert a
hyperlink.

> **Hyperlink** [?][X]
>
> Hyperlink Information
>
> Type: http: [▼]   [OK]
>   [Cancel]
> URL: http://www.techbenders.com

       b. Fill in the URL (Web site address) of the site.

5. **Insert a hyperlink to an e-mail address if desired.**

   You might want your readers to respond to items of interest, or you
   might want to include a disclosure at the bottom of your document
   giving them the choice of opting out if they don't wish to receive future
   mailings.

   To insert a hyperlink to an e-mail address into your graphical e-mail
   template:

       **a. Place your cursor where you would like to insert your hyperlink
   and then choose Insert⇨Hyperlink.**

       b. Click the Type drop-down list box and then choose Mailto.

       **c. Type in your e-mail address, as shown in Figure 12-9, making
   sure to keep the mailto: in front of your address.**

Figure 12-9:
Inserting an
e-mail link.

> **Hyperlink** [?][X]
>
> Hyperlink Information
>
> Type: mailto: [▼]   [OK]
>   [Cancel]
> URL: mailto:karen@techbenders.com

6. **If desired, insert a graphic by choosing Insert⇨Image.**

   And now the fun really begins. Adding graphics to your e-mail templates
   makes them more attractive to your readers. However, before you
   plunge in, take note of a few words of caution: You would probably be
   pretty safe in assuming that the recipient of your e-mail does not have
   the same graphics located on his machine as you do. This creates a
   dilemma — you can either send the graphics to him as an attachment,
   or you can store the graphics on your Web site so that your reader can
   view them in the same way he would view a Web site.

   If you send an e-mail with an attachment, many virus protectors will at
   the very least warn your reader that your e-mail might contain a virus
   (because of the attachment it carries). Other virus protection software
   will block your e-mail entirely. This obviously is not a good thing!

   Figure 12-10 shows you the "more better" way to insert a graphic.
   I insert the graphic by indicating the path to my Web site. The recipient
   will receive the template without an attachment.

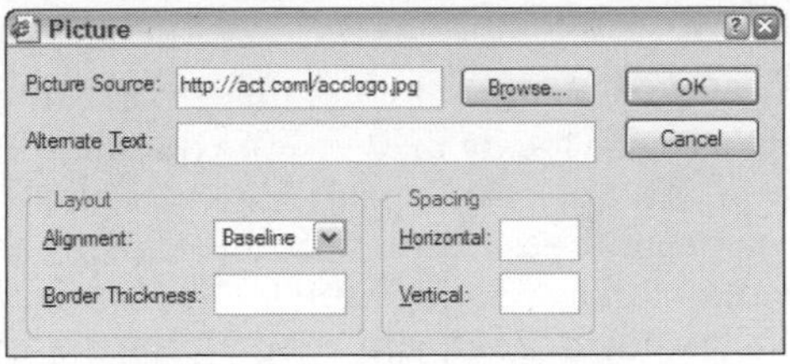

Figure 12-10:
Inserting a
graphic as a
link to your
Web site.

To find the path to a graphic that can be found on your Web site, right-click the graphic and choose Properties. The Properties dialog box will display the correct address for your graphic.

7. Choose File➪Save As and give your graphical e-mail template a name.

ACT! automatically assigns the `.gmt` extension to the filename.

Reaching an Audience of One

Many of you might think creating a mail merge implies sending out a single message to thousands of people at one time. However, a mail merge can also be used to automate the most mundane and routine of tasks. You can use ACT!'s document templates to write a thank-you letter every time that you land a new client or to write an inquiry letter each time that you receive a new lead. After you discover this timesaver, I guarantee that you'll never go back to your old way of creating documents again!

To send a document to a single member of your database, follow these steps:

1. Create a lookup to find the contact to whom you want to send a letter.

Feel free to turn to Chapter 6 if you need help creating a lookup

The current contact record that you have displayed will be the one whose information will fill into your template.

2. Click Write and then choose Letter, Memorandum, Fax Cover Page, or Other Document.

This procedure doesn't work when you're sending a graphical e-mail template. To do that, you'd have to perform a mail merge — even with only one recipient.

You can modify any of the ACT! menus. You might want to modify the Write menu to include some of your own templates. Flip over to Chapter 3 if you need a little refresher course in adding new items to an ACT! menu.

3. Complete the body of the document.

Depending on the type of document that you chose to create and the modifications that you had previously made to the document template, you will be looking at the start of a document. For example, by choosing to create a letter, the name, address, salutation, and closing are already provided. You just need to add the body of the letter to complete it. If you chose to create a fax coversheet, you need merely to add the number of pages in the transmittal and an optional comment to proceed.

If you choose Other Document, you're able to choose one of your own templates. These, of course, already include the body as well.

4. (Optional) Save your document.

After you complete your document, you can save it to the location of your choice. If you don't think that it's necessary to save the document that you create from your own templates (because you can so easily re-create them), you aren't required to.

5. Print, fax, or e-mail your document.

If you are using Word as the default word processor to create your ACT! documents, you can now print, fax, and e-mail exactly like you're already used to doing in Word.

If you chose to print, the Create History dialog box appears after printing is complete. Now this is cool. I like to refer to this as the "Would you like fries with that?" step. After you create a document using a document template, ACT!, at your discretion, can create a record of the document in the Notes/History Tab. You now have a history of the date on which you sent a document. Better yet, other people in your organization are also aware of your interactions with the contact. A dialog box like the one you see in Figure 12-11 appears, ready to take your order:

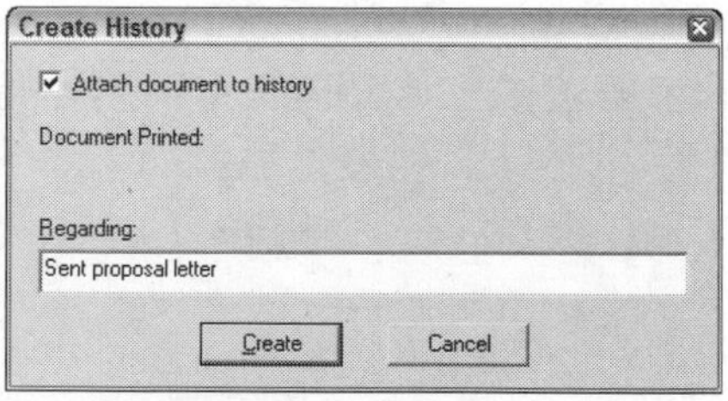

Figure 12-11:
Adding a
document
to Notes/
History.

> **Create History**   ⊠
>
> ☑ Attach document to history
>
> Document Printed:
>
> Regarding:
> Sent proposal letter
>
> [Create]   [Cancel]

- If you do not want to create a history for the document, click the Cancel button.

- If you want to attach the document to a note on the Notes/History tab, select the Attach Document to History check box option (if it isn't already). When this option is enabled, a shortcut to the document is automatically added to the Notes/History tab; you can access the document by double-clicking the attachment.

- If you want to have additional information appear in the note that will be added to the Notes/History tab, enter a description of the document in the Regarding field and then click the Create button. This description will appear on the Notes/History tab regardless of whether you saved the document.

6. **Print an envelope for this selected contact.**

   You have to hand it to ACT!: The program really tries to be as accommodating as possible. After you have worked your fingers to the bone creating your latest tome, ACT! gently asks you whether you'd like to print an envelope (Figure 12-12).

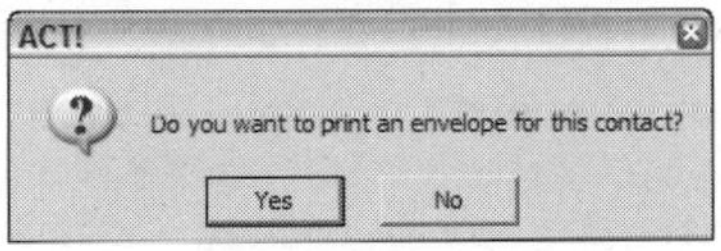

Figure 12-12:
Printing an
envelope.

Do you want to print an envelope for this contact?

Yes   No

Specify whether to print an envelope for the contact. If you click No, you're done with the letter-writing process. Close Word and return to ACT!. If you click Yes to print the envelope, the Print dialog box appears; you can select the type of envelope that you want to use.

If you do not want this dialog box to appear each time that you print a letter, turn off the When Printing Letters, Prompt to Print an Envelope option in the General tab of the Preferences dialog box.

We're Off to See the Mail Merge Wizard

When you create a mail merge to multiple contacts, follow these four basic steps:

1. Select the contacts to whom you're sending the letter.

2. Select the template that includes both the contact fields that you want to merge into the letter and the body of the letter itself.

3. Send the output to your word processor, printer, fax machine, or e-mail program.

4. Perform the mail merge.

Luckily, ACT! has taken the laborious task of mail merging and simplified it. Throughout the process, you'll encounter just four easy-to-navigate windows. Trust me — there's no chance of losing your way; ACT! holds your hand during the entire journey.

To perform a mail merge, follow these steps:

1. **Select the contacts that you would like to be the recipients of your mail merge.**

   To do so, either use a lookup to select certain contacts (such as all contacts in a specific state, city, or company) or select contacts from the Contact List.

   If you're creating one of those charming Christmas newsletters telling all about your two kids who just graduated from Harvard Medical School and your recent month-long excursion to purchase two Mercedes — leave me off the list!

2. **From the Contacts view, choose Write⇨Mail Merge.**

   The Mail Merge Wizard opens and demands to know, in a loud booming voice, what contacts. All right, you caught me in one of my Judy Garland flashbacks. You can't actually hear the question, but it comes across loud and clear in the Mail Merge Wizard - What Contacts? screen that's shown in Figure 12-13.

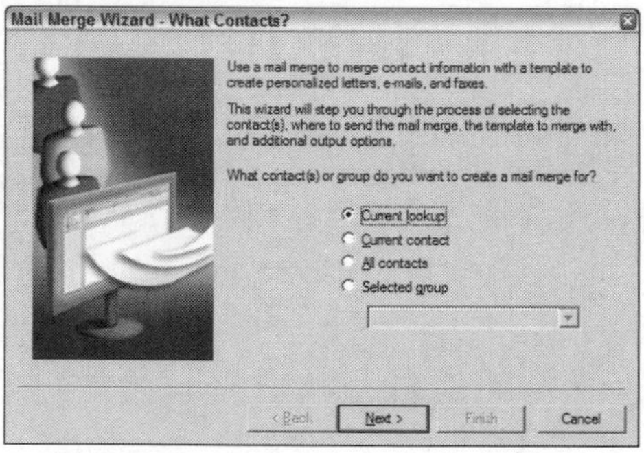

Figure 12-13: Choosing the contacts to include in a mail merge.

3. **Choose to whom you want to send the mail merge to (see following list) and then click Next.**

   - *Current Lookup* merges your document with the contact records that you chose in Step 1.
   - *Current Contact* sends the merge only to the contact currently showing in the Contacts window.
   - *All Contacts* goes to everyone in your database.
   - *Selected Group* enables you to merge your document with a specific contact group.

4. **Decide how you want to send the merge.**

   Decisions, decisions! The four choices on today's menu are

   - *Word Processor* saves all the merged documents into a single word processing document. This is a good choice if you want to review your merged documents before printing them out.

   - *E-mail* sends all the merged documents as e-mail messages.

     If you choose to send out a mail merge via e-mail, each recipient will receive an e-mail that is specifically addressed to that person. No one will see a list of the other recipients.

   - *Printer* is a good choice if you're sure that your contact information and your template is perfect, as in *error-free*. This is also a popular choice if you like to chop down trees in the Amazon. This option sends all the merged documents directly to the printer.

   - *Fax* sends all the merged documents as fax transmissions. If this option is grayed out, you don't have fax software installed on your computer.

   You cannot fax directly from your computer if you don't have access to a fax/modem.

5. **Pick your template.**

   As shown in Figure 12-14, you can now indicate the template you'd like to use in your mail merge by clicking the Browse button, selecting the name of the document template that you want to use, and then clicking Open.

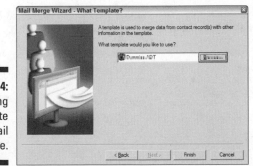

Figure 12-14: Choosing the template in a mail merge.

If, in Step 4, you indicated anything but e-mail, you're finished:

- If you chose the printer option, you should now be hearing the happy sound of your printer spitting out 1,001 personalized letters to your dearest friends and relatives.

- If you chose the word processor option, you can now spend the next two hours reviewing 1,001 personalized letters to your dearest friends and relatives, ensuring that all the information therein is accurate.

- If you chose the fax option, your faxing software opened, and you're ready to fax.

6. **You have a little more work ahead of you if you chose the e-mail send option.**

   Try not to be discouraged. Your e-mails are going to arrive at their intended destination long before those people choosing one of the other options has even finished stuffing envelopes or deciphered the new area code rules for a fax transmittal. Besides, you're treated to the options that you see in Figure 12-15.

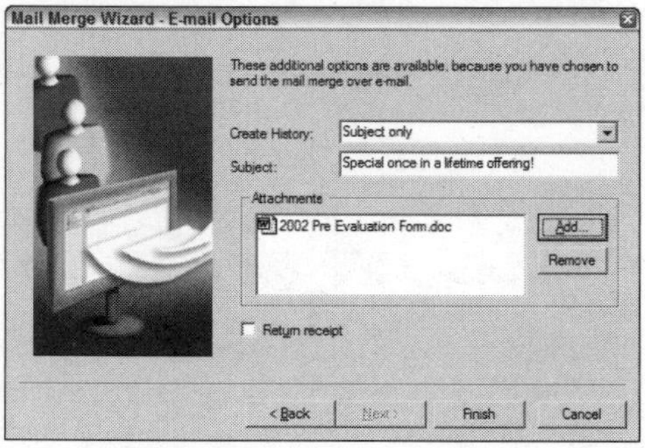

Figure 12-15: E-mail merge options.

- You can create a history of your e-mail by including the subject or the subject and message of your e-mail in the Notes/History tab. You also have the option of attaching the entire e-mail message to a note.

- Type in the subject line of your e-mail.

- If you'd like, you can send an attachment along with your e-mail blast.

- Specify that each recipient of your e-mail send you back a Return Receipt.

Chapter 13

ACT! E-Mail

*I*n this chapter, I show you how to integrate ACT! with your existing e-mail client. ACT! enables you to send e-mail through it to contacts who are in your database, people who are not in your database, and to a selected group of contacts in your database. Finally, you'll discover the various preference settings that are crucial in order to e-mail successfully.

Getting Started with ACT! E-Mail

ACT!'s e-mail capabilities are probably the most misaligned of all the ACT! features. The e-mail portion was totally revamped in ACT! 6 and works much better than it did in previous versions. However, understanding a few of its quirks makes transmitting e-mail through ACT! a much less aggravating experience.

To fully understand the e-mail portion of ACT!, you must understand the concept of the e-mail client. An *e-mail client* is an application that runs on a personal computer or workstation and enables you to send, receive, and organize e-mail. A senior executive at Best, CRM once told me, "ACT! is not in the business of designing e-mail clients." What that means is that ACT! isn't built to replace your existing e-mail client; rather, ACT! works on top of it.

As of this writing, ACT! 6 supports the following e-mail clients:

✔ Outlook

✔ Outlook Express

✔ Lotus Notes

✔ Internet Mail (an internal e-mail client that supports the use of your SMTP and POP3 settings)

TIP

I didn't include America Online (AOL) in this list because ACT! doesn't support it. AOL utilizes its own proprietary e-mail client that does not use the SMTP and POP3 setting that are common to most other e-mail clients. For that reason, and for many other limitations of the AOL e-mail client, your needs are better served by using an alternative method of e-mail for your business purposes.

The two most commonly used e-mail clients are Outlook and Outlook Express in the Windows environment. For business purposes, Outlook is probably the e-mail client of choice. It has more features than Outlook Express and is more attuned to the business environment. Outlook comes bundled with most versions of Microsoft Office and is a common fixture on most office computers. Outlook Express comes as part of the Windows operating system. Because it is a much more basic program, Outlook Express isn't as often used for business e-mailing.

Setting your e-mail preferences

If you initially set up your database using the QuickStart Wizard (see Chapter 3, where I show you how to work your way through the wizard), you already specified your e-mail client. If you're working on an existing database, here's what you must do to configure ACT! for e-mail:

1. **Test to make sure that your e-mail is functioning correctly outside of ACT!.**

    Before you configure your e-mail preferences in ACT!, I recommend testing your e-mail to make sure that it's working correctly. Send a test e-mail to your significant other using Outlook or Outlook Express. Doing so helps eliminate possibilities if, for some reason, you have trouble e-mailing in ACT!.

2. **Choose Edit⇨Preferences.**

    The E-mail Preferences dialog box appears, as shown in Figure 13-1.

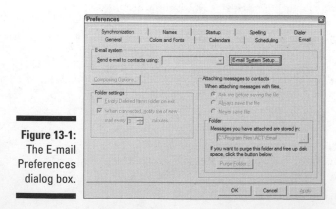

Figure 13-1:
The E-mail
Preferences
dialog box.

3. On the E-mail tab, click the Composing Options button (grayed out in Figure 13-1)

The Composing Options dialog box opens, shown in Figure 13-2, where you set preferences for your ACT! e-mail.

Figuro 13 2: E-mail composing options.

[Composing Options dialog box showing:]

Composing Options

New message settings

Signature text:

Send messages in: HTML

Default priority: Normal

History options: Subject only

☐ Return receipt

☑ Use type ahead for entering recipients

Reply & Forward settings

☑ Close original message on reply or forward

☑ Include message body on reply or forward

☐ Include attachments on reply

☑ Include attachments on forward

OK   Cancel   Apply

- **Signature Text:** Here you type your signature and any other information that you want to appear on all new e-mail messages. If you want to include a hyperlink to your Web site, include the entire URL starting with http://www. For your e-mail address, you must insert **mailto:** before the e-mail address, like this:

mailto:karen@techbenders.com

The signature options appear every time that you compose a brand-new e-mail in ACT! to a new contact or send an *e-mail blast* (a mass e-mailing that's sent to several recipients at once) without using a template. When you send an e-mail to an existing contact, ACT! relies on the email-body.gmt template. Check out Chapter 12 to read about editing .gmt templates.

- **Send Messages In:** Lets you select HyperText Markup Language (HTML) or plain text for the default format type of new messages.

- **Default Priority:** Allows you to select either a low, normal, or high priority as the default preference for all your new e-mail.

- **History Options:** Allows you to select the history type that will be recorded after you send an e-mail. You can choose to have nothing, only the subject, the subject and full body, or an attached copy of your message recorded on the Notes/History tab.

- **Return Receipt:** Prompts the recipient of your message to automatically send a notification when he or she receives your e-mail.

- **Use Type Ahead for Entering Recipients:** If you select this option, ACT! supplies the rest of a recipient's name after you type the first several letters of it.

- **Close Original Message on Reply or Forward:** Closes the original message window when replying to or forwarding e-mail.

- **Include Message Body on Reply or Forward:** Select this option so that ACT! includes the original message text when you reply to or forward a message.

- **Include Attachments on Reply:** Select this option so that an attachment is included when you reply to a message that includes an attachment.

- **Include Attachments on Forward:** Same as preceding bullet, except that this option applies to messages with attachments that you forward.

4. **After you've set all your preferences, click OK.**

   The E-mail Preferences dialog box reappears.

5. **Click the E-mail System Setup button.**

   The E-mail Setup Wizard opens, as shown in Figure 13-3.

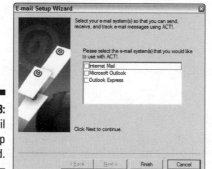

Figure 13-3:
The E-mail
Setup
Wizard.

6. **Select your preferred e-mail client and then click Next.**

   - If you select Outlook, you're asked whether you want to use your default Outlook settings; on the next screen that appears, click Always Use Default Outlook Profile to indicate yes.

   - If you select Outlook Express, you receive the warning shown in Figure 13-4 telling you that you won't have full e-mail functionality in ACT! if you use Outlook Express.

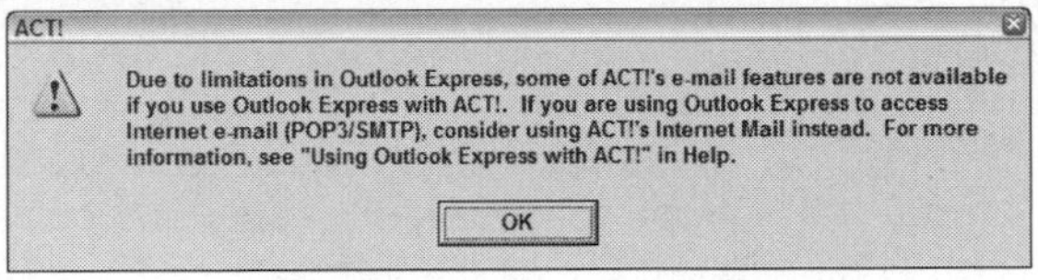

Figure 13-4:
Outlook
Express
warning.

> **ACT!**
>
> ⚠ Due to limitations in Outlook Express, some of ACT!'s e-mail features are not available if you use Outlook Express with ACT!. If you are using Outlook Express to access Internet e-mail (POP3/SMTP), consider using ACT!'s Internet Mail instead. For more information, see "Using Outlook Express with ACT!" in Help.
>
> [OK]

• If you select Internet mail, you're prompted to enter the username, e-mail address, and SMTP and POP3 that were assigned to you by your e-mail service provider.

7. **On the final screen of the E-mail Setup Wizard, click the Finish button.**

Editing e-mail addresses

After you set your e-mail preferences in ACT!, you need e-mail addresses so that you can actually send some e-mails. No doubt you've already added many e-mail addresses to your ACT! database, but I'm guessing that you haven't yet discovered a good way to correct or change existing e-mail addresses.

ACT! is designed to launch the e-mail window when you click the e-mail field in the contact window. This feature makes it very easy to send e-mail in ACT!, but makes it very hard to edit existing addresses.

To edit the e-mail field, try one of these methods:

✔ Use the Tab key to move the cursor to the e-mail field. After the cursor is in an e-mail field, you're able to edit it by clicking the e-mail field's drop-down arrow.

✔ Move the mouse pointer over the e-mail field and right-click. You can now edit the e-mail field.

E-Mailing Your Contacts

A benefit of sending e-mail from within ACT! is that a history of the event is added to your contact's Notes/History tab each and every time that you send an e-mail. E-mail is an increasingly popular form of communication, so having a history of all the e-mail that you sent to each of your contacts will help you keep track of it all. You can send e-mail messages to one or more contacts and attach contact records, group records, or files to your messages. Using an HTML or a graphical template, you can also use a mail merge to send a pre-set message to one or several contacts at a time.

Depending on how you'd like to reach your contacts, there are a variety of ways that you can send e-mail to them using ACT!. You might be writing a one-time e-mail to an individual contact, or you might be sending a form e-mail to either an individual or a whole group of your contacts. You might also want to send a spur-of-the-moment message to one contact — or even thousands of your contacts. Explore the possibilities.

E-mailing an individual contact

To send an e-mail to the current contact, follow these steps:

1. **Create a new e-mail message with one of these methods:**

   • Click the contact's e-mail address.

   • Choose Write⇨E-mail Message.

   • Click the E-mail icon on the View bar and click New.

   All methods result in a new message (Figure 13-5) with the contact's name appearing in the To field.

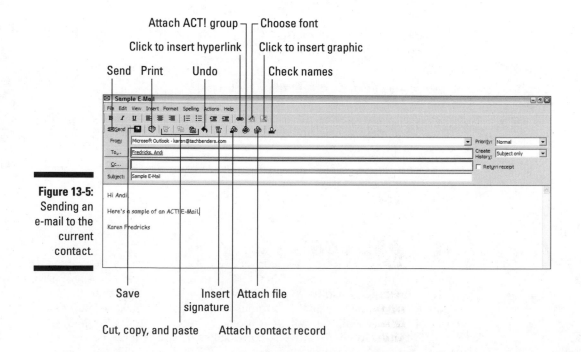

Figure 13-5:
Sending an e-mail to the current contact.

If you choose one of the first two options to create a new e-mail message, ACT! automatically uses the `emailbody.gmt` template. If you modify the template to include your own contact information and a link to your Web site, those changes appear each time that you write a new e-mail.

If you choose the third method, the signature that you set up in the e-mail preferences appears. You can change the data that appears for any of the options.

2. **In the Subject field, type a subject.**

3. **Type your message in the text box.**

4. **Feel free to pick an option or two from the New Message toolbars, depending on how fancy you want to get with your e-mail.**

   When you create an e-mail in ACT!, two toolbars appear in the New Message window. If you hover your mouse over the various tools, a tool tip appears, explaining the function of each button.

   The top toolbar enables you to make changes to the text formatting exactly as you would in any word processor. Notice also two buttons (refer to Figure 13-5) that allow you to insert either a graphic or a hyperlink into your e-mail message.

   The bottom toolbar enables you to send attachments along with your e-mail. You're probably already familiar with the concept of file attachments. ACT! also allows you to send either a single contact record or a group of contact records to recipients (if they're using ACT!).

5. **If you'd like, change the default options for Priority, History, and Return Receipt.**

   See Step 3 in the section "Setting your e-mail preferences," where I explain these options.

6. **Click Send.**

Sending mass e-mails

ACT! makes a distinction between sending e-mail and sending *merged* e-mail. Merged e-mails all share the following characteristics:

✔ When you send a merged e-mail, ACT! relies on the `.gmt` mail template.

✔ When you send a merged e-mail, you must include at least one contact field in your template.

✔ E-mail merging in ACT! allows you to send e-mail in true HTML format.

Important things to consider when sending a mass e-mail

Before jumping head first into the world of mass e-mailing, consider the following important points:

- **Test your e-mail preferences:** You should test your e-mail preferences before sending your missive out to thousands of people. If you don't, you might find yourself with a thousand e-mails in your outbox that can't be sent. Try sending a sample e-mail to a friend or colleague.

- **Test your e-mail template:** Again, testing your message before sending it across the universe is always a good idea. Try sending the message to a co-worker or colleague first.

- **Check with your ISP:** Many Internet Service Providers (ISPs) have implemented safeguards against *spam*. Before you send an e-mail to all of the contacts in your database, call your ISP to find out how many e-mails you can send at a time. If your ISP limits the number of e-mails you can send at one time, you'll need to send your mailings in smaller groups or purchase an add-on product that sends your e-mail in batches.

Sending non-merged mass e-mails

If you're not entirely comfortable with the concept of HTML, you might want to start out by sending an e-mail to your contacts rather than attempting an actual e-mail merge. This is a great way for less computer-oriented ACT! users to reach a large number of contacts.

To send an e-mail to any number of your contacts, here's all you have to do:

1. **Create a lookup (Chapter 6 shows you how) to find the contacts to whom you want to send the e-mail.**

   For example, if you want to send an e-mail to all customers in the Southeastern Region, create the lookup and then narrow it to include only those contacts that have an e-mail address.

   Narrow your lookup by choosing Lookup⇨E-mail Address; next click Narrow Lookup and finally click Non-empty Fields. Voilà! Your lookup is narrowed.

2. **Click the E-mail icon on ACT!'s View bar.**

   The ACT! E-mail dialog box opens.

   If you've set your e-mail preferences to either Outlook or Outlook Express, you should now see a mirror image of either your Outlook or Outlook Express Inbox.

3. **Click the New icon on the e-mail window's toolbar.**

   The New icon is easy to spot — it's the icon that says *New* on it!

4. **Click the To, Cc, or Bcc button.**

   The Select Recipients dialog box opens, as shown in Figure 13-6. Here's where you choose multiple contacts who will all receive your e-mail blast.

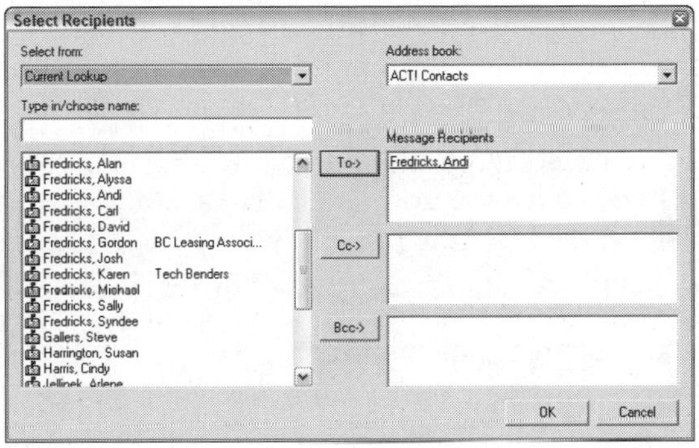

Figure 13-6: Selecting recipients for an e-mail blast.

5. **In the Address Book list, select the address book that you'd like to use.**

   This is where you can select to use either the currently opened ACT! database or your Outlook e-mail addresses.

6. **In the Select From drop-down list, choose All Contacts, Current Lookup, or Groups.**

   • **Current Lookup:** Limits the list of recipients to contacts in your current lookup.

   • **Groups:** Displays a list of the groups in your current ACT! database.

7. **Select one or more names from the list on the left.**

   • To select a *single* name, click it.

   • To select a *continuous list* of names, click the first name in the list, hold down the Shift key, and then click the last name in the list that you want to select.

   • To select *multiple (non-continuous)* names in the list, click the first name that you want to select, and then hold down the Ctrl key while clicking any and all names that you want to select.

8. **Click the To button.**

   The names that you select appear in the Message Recipients box.

9. **Click OK.**

   You're returned to the New Message window.

10. If you'd like, change any of the e-mail options.

Go for it! Insert a link to your Web site or attach a file.

11. Click Send.

You might want to pat yourself on the back, content with the knowledge that you have mastered the art of sending an e-mail blast.

Sending a merged mass e-mail

Using ACT! to create an e-mail merge enables you to send an *HTML e-mail*. This means that your e-mail will have the look and feel of a Web page instead of just displaying boring black-and-white text. In ACT!, you create these HTML e-mails by using a graphical mail template with the .gmt extension. In Chapter 12, I discuss in detail how to create a graphical mail template that you can send to any number of your contacts using a mail merge.

Using the mail merge allows you to send e-mail that has been personalized for the recipient(s). For example, if you want to send a birthday e-mail to one of your contacts, this is your e-mail of choice. Figure 13-7 shows how the message was personalized to include both the contact's name and the birth date.

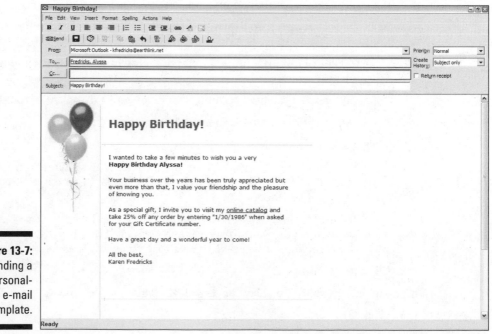

Figure 13-7: Sending a personalized e-mail template.

Ready

Mail merge must include at least one mail merge field. If you aren't personalizing your e-mails, you need to choose a different method of e-mailing. Also keep in mind that you'll probably want to create a lookup of the contacts you want to e-mail *before* starting the e-mail merge!

Working with Incoming E-Mail

Now that you're proficient in sending e-mail, you need to know how to read an e-mail message. Although you can continue to view your mail using your existing mail client, you'll find a couple of advantages in using ACT!:

- **Open messages.** Double-clicking the message does the trick.

- **Read messages in another folder.** Simply click the folder in the Folder List.

- **Sort your e-mail messages.** Click the E-mail icon on ACT!'s View bar and messages display in the message list, for your default e-mail system, in order from newest to oldest. You can change the order by clicking a column header.

- **Create a new contact record from an incoming e-mail (if the contact isn't already in your database).** This is a particularly timesaving feature of ACT! and ensures that potential contacts don't get lost in the shuffle.

    1. **Choose Actions⇨Create Contact from Sender.**

       The Add Contact dialog box appears, as shown in Figure 13-8. ACT! automatically inserts the sender's name and e-mail address.

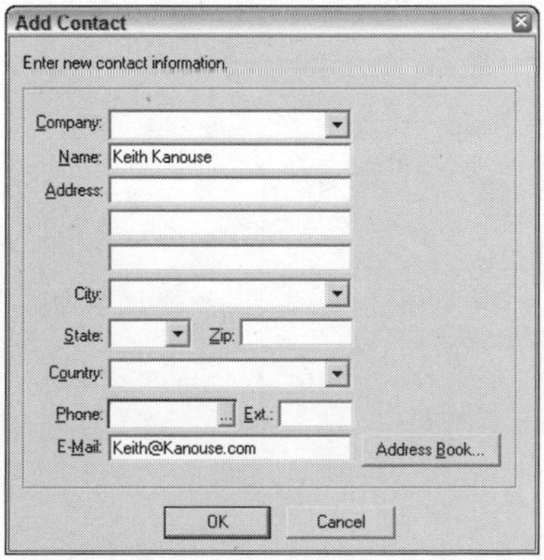

Figure 13-8:
Adding a
contact
record from
an e-mail
message.

2. Enter the rest of the contact's information.

The fields are self explanatory.

3. Click OK.

If you receive lots of e-mail that you'd like to convert into contact records, I recommend that you consider one of the E-Grabber programs. E-Grabber captures addresses and phone numbers from the body of an e-mail. For more information about the E-Grabber line of products, see Chapter 24.

✔ **Attach the e-mail to a contact's Notes/History tab.** Just like you can create an automatic history record each time that you *send* an e-mail to a contact, you can also create a history each time that you *receive* an e-mail from a contact:

1. Choose Actions⇨Attach to Contact.

2. On the Attach E-mail to Contact dialog box that appears, click the name of the contact(s) that you'd like to associate with the e-mail message.

3. Click the To button and then click OK.

ACT! places a note on the contact's Notes/History tab indicating that you received an e-mail from the contact.

Part IV
Advanced ACT!ing

The 5th Wave   By Rich Tennant

"Your database is beyond repair, but before I tell you our backup recommendation, let me ask you a question. How many index cards do you think will fit on the walls of your computer room?"

In this part . . .

On the surface, ACT! is a deceptively easy program to master. However, those of you who are so inclined — or didn't run fast enough — might want to add ACT! Database Administrator to your current job description. The database administrator is the one in charge of adding new fields to the database and making sure that the database remains in perfect working condition. Best of all, when things go wrong, guess who everyone will turn to? Not to worry, though — just turn to this section for help.

Chapter 14

Creating Contact Fields

• •

• •

1 am a firm believer that a little knowledge is a dangerous thing. Although adding a field to your ACT! database is not a hard thing to do, it is something that should be well thought out and planned in advance. This is particularly true if you plan on sharing your database with other users. Planning is important because you usually have a goal in mind for your database. If your goal is to create a report with three columns — one for the contact name, one for the birthday, and one for the Social Security number — you need to make sure that all those fields exist in your database. Planning also prevents you from adding thousands of contacts to your database, only to find that you have to modify each record to include information that was omitted the first time around!

To add a field to your database, you must have administrative rights to the database; the makers of ACT! made this a requirement so that you'd understand the importance of this responsibility. So unless you have administrative rights to the database, you don't even have to read this chapter! I suppose you still could, just for curiosity's sake, but it isn't necessary.

In this chapter, I show you (all of you who have administrative rights to your databases anyway) not only how to add new fields to an ACT! database, but also how to set the various field parameters to help users use the database more effectively and efficiently.

Before getting started, I want to briefly outline the three steps involved with adding fields to a database:

1. Understand why you want to add fields and what purpose these fields will serve.

2. Determine what fields you're going to add and what drop-down lists will be available in each.

I can't stress enough the importance of this step. Plan ahead! Or you might end up with a big mess. . . .

3. Add the fields.

And, voilà! You're done. (Okay, this one has a whole bunch of steps, but you get what I mean.)

Understanding the Concept of Fields

For most of you, adding a field to your database will be easy. After all, you're good at following directions. However, for some of you, knowing *why* to enter a field will prove to be more challenging.

To explore the question of why, I first want to reiterate the basic concept of fields. What the heck is a field? As I mention in Chapter 1, a *field* is a single piece of information. In general, a field contains just one piece of information. For example, you have only one business Zip code; therefore, you have one business Zip code field. Alternatively, you probably have at least eight phone numbers: home, business, toll-free, cellular, fax, beeper, and the list goes on. Each of these phone numbers requires a separate field.

A good field holds one fairly specific piece of information. A bad field contains too much information. For example, having a separate field for your street address, city, state, and Zip code is a good thing. These separate fields allow you to perform a lookup based on any of the criteria: You could find clients by Zip code, by city, or by state. An example of a bad field would be lumping all the address information into a single field; you then lose your ability to perform a lookup by Zip code, city, or state. (Need a refresher on performing lookups? Head to Chapter 6.)

You might want to consider the following basic rules when determining the criteria for adding a field to your database:

✔ A field contains an important tidbit of information.

✔ A field can be used to perform a query or sort. For example, you may want to send a mailing to all your customers in New York and sort your mailing by Zip code. To do this, you need separate fields for contact type, state, *and* Zip code.

✔ A field can be used to insert information into a report or template. If you want to create letters thanking one person for buying a purple polka-dotted vase and another for buying a leopard-print vase, you need a vase type field.

Do Your Homework!

Okay, I admit it — I'm a former secondary school teacher, and I guess that background just naturally spills over into my ACT! consulting. Well class, pretend you're back in school because you're now going to be assigned some homework. To be politically correct, I could have said you're now entering the *pre-planning stage of your ACT! implementation.* But I still consider it as important homework that you must complete *prior* to jumping in and adding new fields to your database, so your assignment is as follows:

1. **Jot down all the fields that you want to see in your database.**

2. **Scurry around the office and collect any documents that you want ACT! to create for you. This includes both forms and form letters.**

   You're going to have to get a little high tech here, but I think you can handle it. Get out your trusty highlighter pen and highlight any of the information in each document that is contact specific. For example, each contact has its own unique address. Maybe you're thanking particular contacts for meeting to discuss purchasing widgets (as opposed to gadgets, which you also sell). This means that you need a Product field.

3. **Think of how you'd populate the fields with drop-down lists, and then on the list that you started in Step 1, jot them down to the side of each of the fields.**

   For example, if you run a modeling agency, you might need a field for hair color. The drop-down choices could contain red, blonde, black, and punk pink.

4. **Sketch out any reports that you'd like to create from ACT!, and add the column headings to the now rather long list that you created in Step 1.**

   The idea here is to get your thoughts down on paper so that you can visualize what you want your ACT! report to look like. If you already have a sample of your report in Excel, you can use that. If not, get out your trusty pencil and outline what you'd like your report to actually look like on a piece of paper.

5. **Get out a red pen, and at the top of your paper, write 100%, Well Done, and draw a smiley face. Hang your list on your refrigerator.**

   Okay, that last step wasn't really necessary, but you're now well on your way to having the database of your dreams!

Add a New Field to Your Database

Believe it or not, after completing your homework (see the preceding section), you're done with the hard part of the task. The actual addition of fields is relatively easy; just follow the steps.

Only an ACT! user with administrative privileges is able to add new fields to an ACT! database. If the Define Fields option is grayed out in Step 1, you aren't logged in as an administrator.

1. **In the Contacts view, choose Edit⇨Define Fields.**

   The Contacts view is generally a good place to start for most of your customization projects. The Define Fields dialog box appears, as shown in Figure 14-1. The Record Type box will indicate that you're adding new *Contact* fields to the database. You can also add new group fields to your database by switching the Record Type to *Group*.

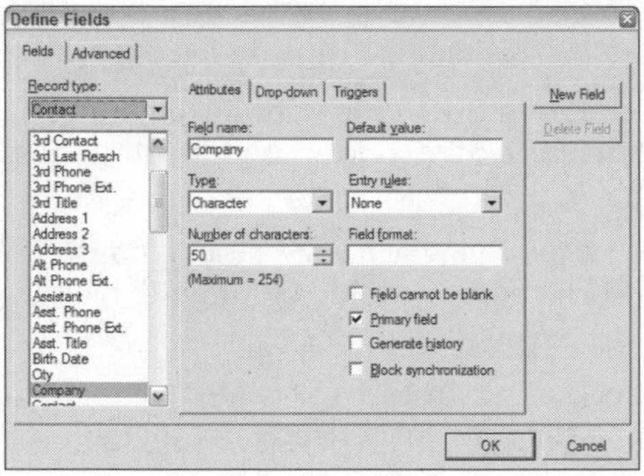

Figure 14-1:
The Define Fields dialog box.

ACT! will not allow you to add new fields or edit existing fields while other users are logged into the database. If you see the warning shown in Figure 14-2, you know that other users are indeed currently logged into the database. What to do? Storm over to their workstations in a huff and demand that they exit out of ACT! immediately. If that doesn't work, consider bribery.

2. **Start by renaming the 15 User fields (listed along the left side of the attributes area on the Fields tab).**

   This is where you need to drag your homework off the refrigerator and type in one of the fields that you had planned to create in the Field Name box. ACT! supplies you with 15 user fields that you can customize to better serve the needs of your business. After all, Social Security number is a lot more meaningful than User 12.

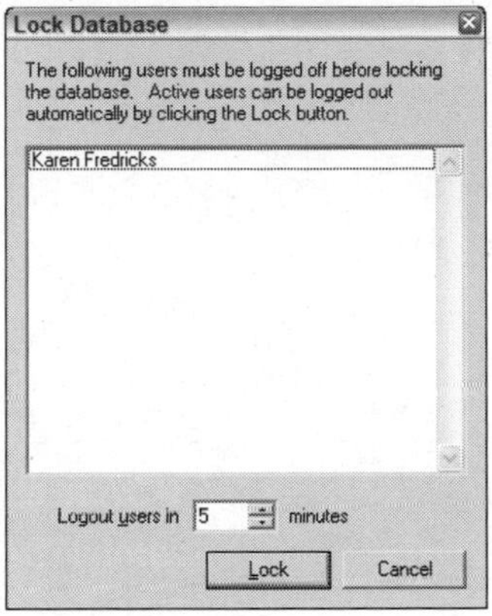

Lock Database

The following users must be logged off before locking
the database. Active users can be logged out
automatically by clicking the Lock button.

Karen Fredricks

Logout users in 5 ⬍ minutes

[Lock] [Cancel]

Figure 14-2:
Another
user is
using the
database.

3. **When you run out of User Fields to rename, click the New Field button.**

   ACT! rewards you with a blank, new field in the Field Name box and
   assigns it the name *New Field* until you can think of something better to
   call it.

   Try not to get too fancy or long-winded when naming your fields. Using
   special characters such as <, >, $, or : can cause problems when creating
   queries and mail merges, so I recommend that you not use them. You can
   use spaces in the field name, but don't end a field name with a space. Long
   field names can be hard to place into mail merge templates and layouts,
   so you're better off keeping field names as short as possible.

4. **From the Type drop-down menu (refer to Figure 14-1), choose a field
   type for the field that you're adding.**

   You can create a variety of different types of fields. Among the choices are

   - **Character:** This is probably the most common of the field type
     choices; a character field can contain both numbers and characters.
     It's kind of a one-size-fits-all kind of field.

   - **Currency:** As its name implies, this is for fields relating to cold,
     hard cash. The field comes equipped with a dollar sign, appropri-
     ate commas, optional decimal places, and a sunroof (optional).
     Check out the neat options in Figure 14-3.

   - **Date:** A really cool thing happens when you make a field a date field.
     When the time comes for you to enter information into a data field,
     you'll see a tiny little calendar that enables you to select a date. The
     calendar is cute, but, more importantly, it supplies a useful purpose.
     If you create a field for a birthday and make it a Character field, the
     other local yokels using the database might get creative and input
     anything from Jan 1 and January 1st to 01/01 and 1/1. Finding all
     birth dates in the month of January would become an exercise in
     futility.

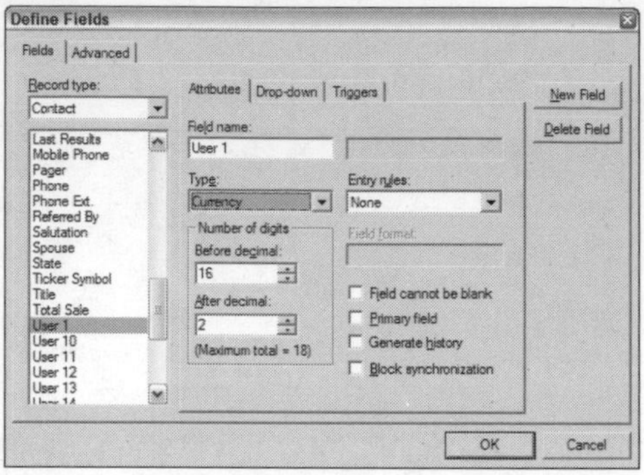

Figure 14-3:
Currency
field
options.

You can also designate a date field as an *Annual Event* field; brush up on the various benefits of annual events in Chapter 6.

- **Initial Capitals:** At first glance, this seems like a nifty option. The idea behind the Initial Capitals option is that you can turn *KAREN FREDRICKS* into *Karen Fredricks*. Seems like a great idea on paper. In reality, however, you'll end up with *Ibm Corporation* and *Marcus Welby Md.*

- **Lower Case:** i suppose you might want to type in all lowercase. i just can't imagine why.

- **Numeric:** This option enables you to enter only numbers into a field. Let's say you want to find all your customers that have more than 30 employees. You can easily search for a number greater than *30,* but you can't possibly search for a number greater than *thirty.*

- **Phone:** In Chapter 4, I show you all those nifty things that ACT! does to speed up the data input process. If you designate a field to be a *phone* field, you'll automatically get a year's supply of dashes.

- **Time:** If time is of the essence, this is where you can input a time.

- **Upper Case:** I NEVER TYPE IN ALL UPPERCASE BECAUSE I FEEL LIKE I'M SCREAMING. BESIDES, I'M AFRAID I MIGHT DEVELOP POLYPS ON MY FINGER TIPS.

- **URL Address:** Use this field type if you need to add Web address or e-mail fields into ACT!.

ACT! already comes equipped with e-mail and Web site fields for your viewing pleasure. And, you can add several additional e-mail addresses to the existing ACT!'s e-mail field. Add a new URL field with caution!

5. **Select the field's length (Number of Characters box in Figure 14-1).**

   Your fields can contain as many as 254 characters. That's roughly 50 words. That should be more than long enough. If you need more than 254 characters to accommodate all that you need to input into any given field, you probably need more than one field!

6. **Assign a Default Value if you feel so inclined.**

   For instance, if 80 percent of your database consists of customers, you might assign *customers* as the default value of the ID/Status field.

7. **Assign an entry rule.**

   This is a great way to really lock down your database by limiting the choices that users have in inputting data. Your three choices are

   - **Protected:** Although the database users will be able to *see* the contents in this cell, they will not be able to add or edit information in this field. If you do want to add or edit information in this field, the administrator will be required to change the entry rule to None before anyone can make a change to the field.

   - **Only from Drop-Down:** Users are required to enter data based on the choices in the drop-down menu. This is a good choice if you want to ensure that your database users don't become too creative when entering data.

   - **None:** This is the default value of any ACT! field.

8. **Assign one of the four optional attributes:**

   - **Field Cannot Be Blank:** Use this option if you want to require that information be entered into a certain field.

   - **Primary Field:** When you duplicate a contact record, the primary fields are the fields that are duplicated.

   - **Generate history:** This is a neat little feature that generates a history in the Notes/History tab when you change the contents of the field.

   - **Block Synchronization:** This will cause the field not to be synchronized, meaning that if you're synchronizing with a remote user, that user won't receive any updated information in that particular field.

9. **If the field is a drop-down, click the Drop-down tab in the Define Fields dialog box.**

   Figure 14-4 shows you the Drop-down tab. From here, you can build a drop-down list by clicking New and entering the choice for each drop-down item. You can also type in an optional description. For example, if you're using initials to indicate a Sales Rep, you might want to include the rep's full name in the description area.

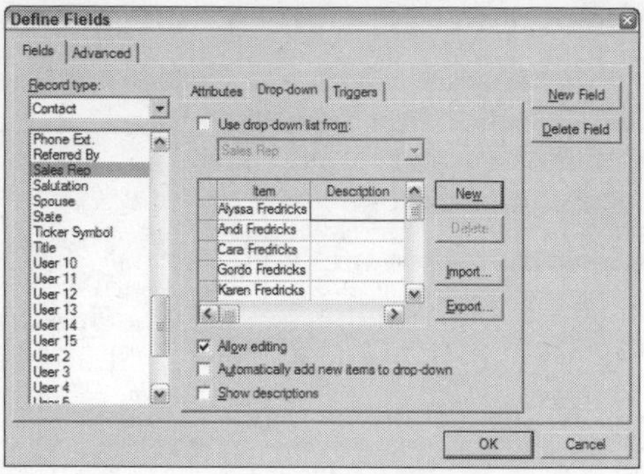

Figure 14-4:
Defining
drop-down
lists.

The Drop-down tab also allows you to define two other attributes for your drop-down fields:

- **Allow Editing** enables any of your users to add new items to a field's drop-down list as she is entering contact information.

- **Automatically Add New Items to the Drop-down** is a good way to let your users help to define the items that will be used in a drop-down list.

  If you decide to allow users to automatically add new items to a drop-down list, you might want to do so only temporarily. The mess that will be created is directly proportional to the number of users you have.

10. Click OK.

Congratulations! You are now the proud owner of a brand-new field. Depending on the number of contacts in your database, you might have to wait a minute or two as ACT! applies all your changes to the database.

You might feel cheated that I didn't touch on the Advanced tab. Don't worry, in Chapter 16, I explain how the Advanced tab helps you to clear out all those pesky duplicates from your database. And, although the triggers area is a little beyond the scope of this book, I talk about some add-on products in Chapter 24 that will help you use the ACT! triggers.

Chapter 15

Customizing Layouts

Many ACT! users are confused about the concept of the layout. In fact, some of you might have ended up renaming a layout label when you wanted to rename fields. As I tell you in Chapter 14, a *field* is a place to store information. A *layout* refers to how you actually see those fields. Your layout determines both the order of the fields and the format of each field. A layout is the name for a file that determines which fields you see and in what order those fields appear. After you add new fields to your ACT! database, the next step is to stick them into an existing layout (or design a new one).

The layout confusion is further compounded by users who are sharing their database across a network. Problems occur if the layouts are not stored on the network, and the users are accessing different layouts. Depending on the layout that they are using, some users may not be able to see all the fields of the database. Chapter 3 tells you how to set your preferences to access a shared layout on your network

In this chapter, I show you how to use the Layout Designer to modify an existing layout. Here you'll master adding or replacing tabs on your layout, reordering all the fields when you're finished, and finally, sharing your masterpiece with others.

Modifying an Existing ACT! Layout

Before you begin modifying an existing layout, think about how you want your fields arranged on your layout. Why not try out all the layouts that come with ACT!? This way, you'll get a feeling for the one that's most comfortable to you. Don't worry about colors or the names on the tabs — all that can be changed.

Designing a new layout completely from scratch is possible although more trouble than modifying an existing one. If you feel the urge to design a new layout from scratch, you need to know that you'll start with an entirely blank canvas. If you'd like to have a go at it, choose File⇨New from the Layout Designer, and a brand-new — absolutely blank — layout appears. You have a lot of work ahead of you. And I'm guessing a lot of headaches, too. So why bother with creating a new layout from scratch? I can't think of a good reason. I recommend just making changes to an existing layout — you'll save yourself a lot of time and grief and probably be very happy with the results.

Here's what you do to modify an existing layout:

1. **Choose the layout that's closest to the one that you'd like to have.**

   If you need help with switching layouts, take a peek at Chapter 2.

2. **Choose Tools⇨Design Layout.**

   The Layout Designer opens. Each field consists of four elements (see Figure 15-1):

   • The *field label* is an optional element but usually appears immediately to the left of a field.

   • The *field* itself is identified by the two little gray boxes that appear at the field's right edge.

   • A *group stop* is the gray box directly to the right of the field. If a field is set as a group stop, a red dot appears in the gray box. Group stops allow you to use the Enter key to move quickly from one area of your layout to another by skipping some of the fields. For example, you might use your Enter key to advance from the phone field to the address field without having to stop at the fax and mobile phone fields. You can also set group stops to allow you to flip between your various tabs with a press of the Enter key.

   • A *tab stop* determines the field that you move to when using the Tab key while entering data; it is identified with a number in the Layout Designer window.

   Another important element of the Layout Designer is its tool palette. You can move the tool palette by dragging it with the mouse, but stifle your desire to close it — it's essential to the layout design process. (Take a look at the Cheat Sheet at the very beginning of this book to find out the names of its tools.)

3. **Choose File⇨Save As and give your layout a new name.**

   ACT! layouts are given the extension .cly. I recommend renaming your layout so that you can later go back to your original layout (if you totally annihilate this one) and easily identify your layout (if you choose a recognizable name).

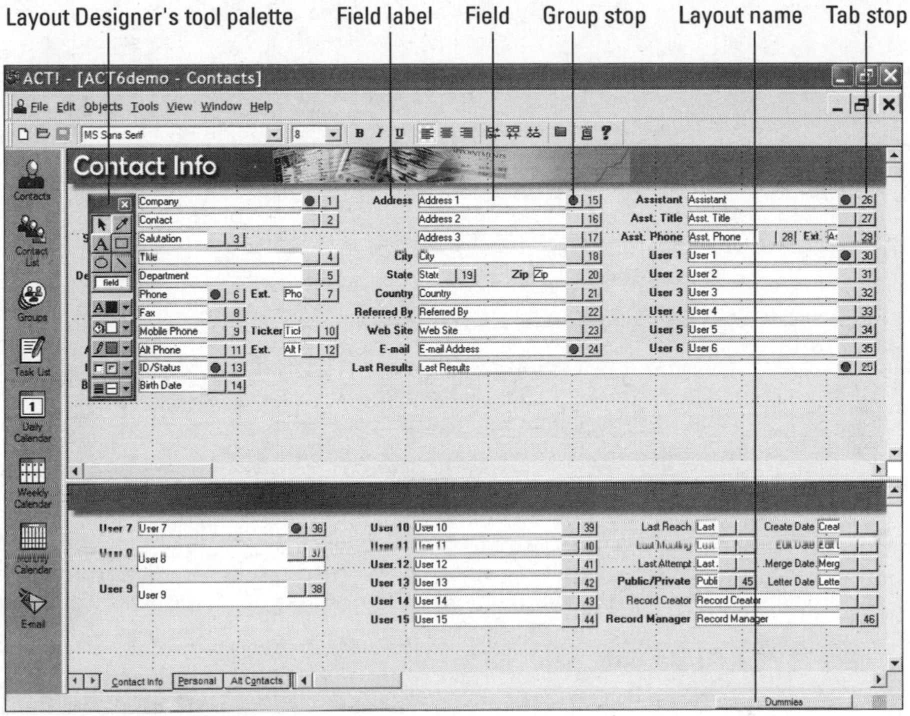

Layout Designer's tool palette   Field label   Field   Group stop   Layout name   Tab stop

Figure 15-1:
The ACT!
Layout
Designer.

The name of your layout appears in the bottom-right corner of the screen (refer to Figure 15-1).

As you make changes to your layout, the Save icon on the Layout Designer toolbar comes to life. Click it to save your work. Relying on the old undo standby (Edit⇨Undo) is an option, but it will only undo the very last change you made and sometimes isn't capable of undoing anything at all. So save your layout early and often!

4. Click the Selection tool on the tool palette.

The Selection tool, the tool that you'll probably use most often, enables you to select fields so that you can move, change, or remove them.

5. With the Selection tool, select fields and field labels that you want to remove from the layout.

Removing unused fields can simplify a layout and make room for other fields that you want to add. I recommend removing what's unwanted before moving on to other aspects of the layout design process.

Make your selections by any of these methods:

- Click any field or field label to select it.

- Click any field and then hold down the Shift key while clicking additional fields to select multiple fields and labels.

- Create a box around the desired labels and fields by holding down the left mouse button and then dragging to create a selection box.

When you select a field, a border of small boxes appears around the field indicating that it is selected.

6. **Press the Delete key.**

   The unwanted fields go away.

   Removing a field from the layout does not remove the actual field from the database. The field remains in your database but isn't visible in the layout from which selected fields have been removed.

7. **To move fields around, select them with the Selection tool and then drag them to a new location on your layout.**

   If only it were this easy to rearrange the living room! The idea is to *drag* the selected fields and their corresponding labels to the place on your layout that seems the most logical to you. When you hold your mouse over selected fields, your cursor transform into a plus sign, indicating that you're ready to move the field.

8. **To change the look and feel of any field, right-click the field and then choose Properties from the pop-up menu that appears.**

   The Object Properties dialog box opens, as shown in Figure 15-2.

Using layouts to restrict access to key fields

If you have certain fields in your database that you don't want other database users to have access to — for example, a record of your customers' credit card information — you can't restrict your users from viewing selected fields because ACT! doesn't have field-level security. You can create specific layouts, however, that don't include the fields that you are concerned about.

What you do is create a custom layout based on your current one, *remove* the fields that you don't want other users accessing, and then distribute the new layout to your staff. As long as your users don't have access to *other* layouts that include these fields, these fields remain invisible to them.

Although this method of securing your database isn't foolproof, creative use of your layouts can help you add more security to your database.

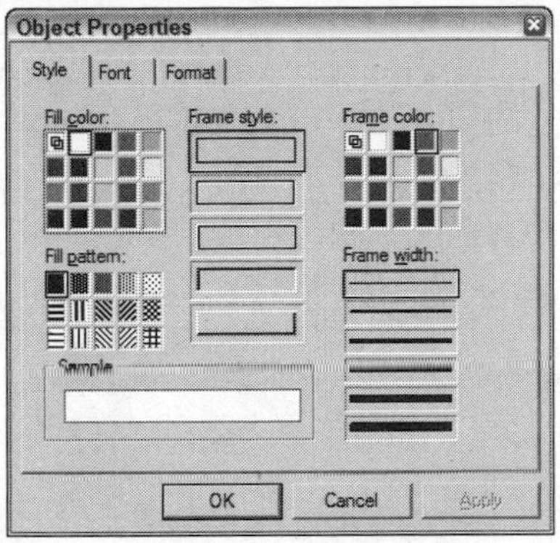

Figure 15-2:
The Layout
Designer
Object
Properties
dialog box.

9. **On the Style tab, change fill color, pattern, and other style items; on the Font tab, select a new font, font style, and size. Click OK to apply your changes.**

10. **To add a new field to your layout, click the Field icon (it's named Field) in the tool palette.**

    Your cursor takes the form of a plus sign.

11. **Hold down the left mouse button and drag the cursor to the right to define the field's size.**

    Figure 15-3 shows the Fields dialog box that opens, presenting a list of all fields that do not appear on the current layout.

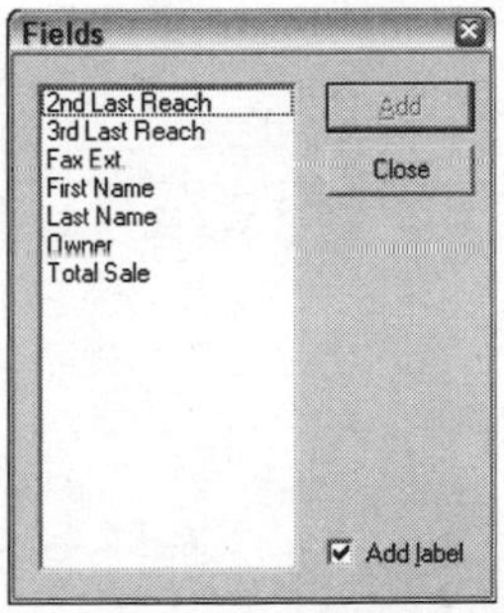

Figure 15-3:
Adding a
new field to
an ACT!
layout.

12. **Select the field that you want to add to the layout, deselect the Add Label check box (if you don't want the field to have a label), and then click the Add button**

    The field is added to your layout. You can add as many fields to your layout as you'd like, but you're allowed to use each field only once.

13. **When you're done adding fields, click the Close button in the Fields dialog box.**

14. **To add or rearrange layout tabs, choose Edit⇨Tabs.**

    The Define Tab Layouts dialog box appears (Figure 15-4), where ACT! gives you several tab customization options:

    - Click the Add button to add an additional tab to your layout. Enter a name for the new tab in the Add Tab Layout dialog box and then click OK.

    - Click the Rename button to give the tab a new name.

    Several of the layout tabs are an intrinsic part of ACT! and cannot be moved, renamed, or modified, including the Notes/History, Activities, Sales/Opportunities, Groups, and Library tabs. Customize the rest of the tabs to your heart's desire, and feel free to add additional tabs should you require more space to hold your newly added fields.

    - Click the Delete button to remove a tab from your layout.

    When you remove a tab from a layout, all the fields that are located on that tab are removed as well. Consider moving — or removing — all the fields from a tab *before* you delete the tab itself!

    - Click the Move Up button to move a tab so that it appears *before* another tab.

    - Click the Move Down button so that a particular tab appears *after* another.

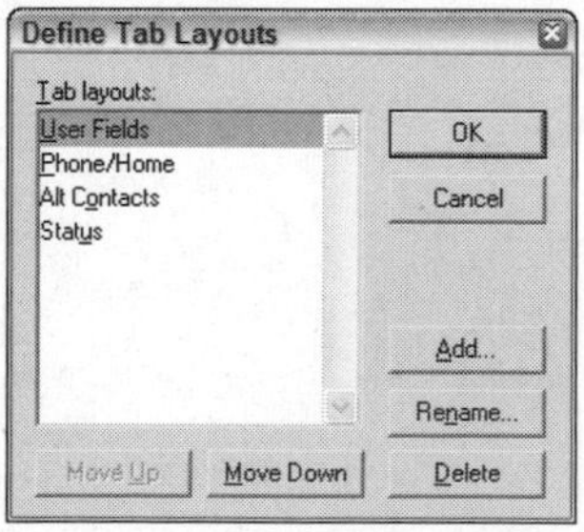

Figure 15-4:
Editing tabs
in an ACT!
layout.

15. **After you make all desired changes to your layout, click through the fields' tab stops in the order that you want to set as the field entry order.**

If you click the tab stop number (refer to Figure 15-1, where the fields are numbered sequentially) on the fields whose field entry order you want to change, the number disappears. If you click the tab stop again, the next available number is assigned to the field.

Note: You can't renumber fields until after you've removed the number that you want to use from another field. In other words, you're allowed to use each number only once.

Modifying layouts generally renders the field entry order non-sequential (see Figure 15-5). Although having out-of-sequence field ordering doesn't damage your database, it does make inputting data difficult. Each time that you press the Tab key, your cursor skips to the next *numbered* field instead of to the next field that you see on your layout.

If the tab and group stops are not appearing on your layout, choose Edit⇨Field Entry Order⇨Show (from the Layout Designer menu) to display them.

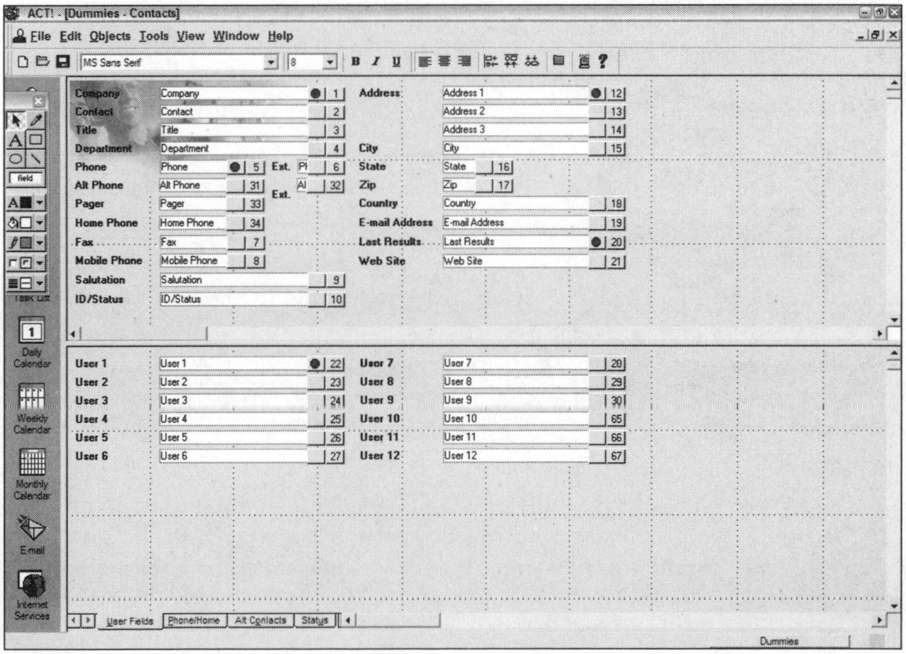

Figure 15-5:
A layout without sequential field order numbering.

Look but don't touch: The wonders of Plexiglas!

If you have occasion when you want all your employees to have full access to all the contacts in the ACT! database, but you don't want them to be able to change certain key pieces of existing information, ACT! layouts are here to help.

For example, if Social Security numbers are vitally important to you, you wouldn't want to risk having this information changed. Unless you use ACTforWeb, which I discuss in Chapter 18, you have no way to limit a user's ability to edit or view specific fields. However, there's a fairly easy workaround that accomplishes your goal through the use of layouts.

Tip: You'll be using tools from the Layout Designer's tool palette in this step list, so have the Cheat Sheet handy to help you identify the necessary tools.

1. **Choose Tools➪Design Layouts to open the Layout Designer.**

2. **Click the field's tab stop number to remove the number.**

   The object is to deny access to this field. Leaving in the tab stop number would allow users to access the field by tabbing into it.

3. **Click the Rectangle tool (on the tool palette) and then draw a square around the field or fields that you don't want your users to be able to edit.**

   Before beginning this step, consider how much caffeine is coursing through your blood stream. The object here is to draw the rectangle so that the edges are in the exact same position as the edges of the field you're trying to protect. A steady hand is essential!

4. **With the Selection tool, right-click the rectangle that you just drew and choose Properties.**

5. **Change the fill color to No Color by clicking the double-box icon to the left of white, and then click OK.**

6. **Right-click your rectangle and choose Move to Front.**

7. **Save the layout and distribute it to your employees.**

   Make sure that this now becomes the *only* layout that your users have access to. If they do have access to other layouts, make sure that the protected fields have either been removed from that layout or are protected.

If your layout is in need of a massive renumbering of tab stops, removing all the existing tab stop numbers is a good idea. Simply choose Edit➪Field Entry Order➪Clear from the Layout Designer menu to renumber. You'll now need to click each field *in sequential order* to assign new field order numbers.

16. **Add a group stop by clicking a Group Stop button that doesn't contain a red dot.**

    A red dot then appears.

    Remember that a group stop is designated by a red dot in the gray box to the immediate right of a field (refer to Figure 15-1 and Step 2).

17. **Remove a group stop by clicking a Group Stop button that contains a red dot.**

    The red dot disappears.

18. **When you're happy with your layout, close the Layout Designer by clicking the bottom of the two X's in the upper-right corner of the Layout Designer window.**

    If you haven't already saved your layout, you're prompted to do so.

19. **Click Yes to save your layout and exit the Layout Designer.**

    For more tips on beautifying your layout, sneak a peek at Chapter 23.

Sharing Layouts with Other Users

If you're working with ACT! in a multi-user environment, you need to distribute your layout to other users of your ACT! database. In Chapter 3, I show you how to change your layout preferences to make sure that ACT! is looking for the layout in the correct location. You, however, have to make sure that the layout gets to that designated locale.

If you sync with remote users, take note: Fields that you add to your database are sent to remote users as part of the synchronization process, but layouts are not. The folks with whom you synchronize data must either add any newly created fields to their existing layout or be sent a copy of the newly designed layout.

Here's a couple of different ways to get your layout to your various users:

- ✔ **Copy the file to a shared network folder that's accessible to all users.** Make sure that you change the default location for layout files to the shared folder.

- ✔ **Copy the layout file to a floppy disk or a network folder.** Then have the other users copy the file to their default layout folders.

- ✔ **Attach the layout file to an e-mail message and send it to your remote users.** The users can then save the file to their default layout folders.

Chapter 16

Zen and the Art of Database Maintenance

. . . .

In This Chapter

▶ Performing routine maintenance

▶ Avoiding database corruption

▶ Backing up the database

▶ Restoring the database

▶ Editing and replacing field data

. . . .

*I*n this chapter, I show you how to take care of your motorcycle . . . er, I mean your database. Would you believe that your ACT! database is very similar to a motorcycle? Both are made up of many moving parts that require maintenance. Failure to provide routine maintenance can result in big problems — for a motorcycle as well as for your database. If something does go wrong, having a backup is nice and, in most cases, necessary to keeping your job. Sometimes your motorcycle gets dirty; likewise, your database is prone to clutter. You'll sometimes have to bite the bullet, roll up your sleeves, and do a little cleaning — and clear out old or duplicate contact records from ACT!.

Regular maintenance keeps your database running efficiently. When you don't provide routine maintenance for a motorcycle, things get corroded; when you don't provide maintenance for your database, your records become corrupted. Quite simply, a *corrupted database* is one in which weird things start happening. No, you won't see a ghost, but you might not see a note that you know you created the day before. Or that note just might pop up again later — in the wrong place!

Understanding the Need to Compress and Reindex

In ACT!, basic maintenance is referred to as *compressing and reindexing*. This procedure is very similar to the ScanDisk and Disk Defragmenter procedures that you might already perform on your PCs. The *compress* part means that you are squeezing out all the little empty spaces that were left in your database when you deleted contact records. Compressing your database helps it to run more efficiently.

An *index file* refers to any one of several files that work in the background to enable you to perform lookups in a jiffy. (I discuss lookups in Chapter 6.) Without indexed data files, a simple search for a contact might take an inordinate amount of time. As ACT! performs various lookups, these index files get pulled in all directions, and ultimately your lookups take longer and longer to complete. *Reindexing* whips the index files back into shape.

I love to change the messages on my voice mail, and one of my favorite choices is, "Have you compressed and reindexed today?" Users often offer up a variety of excuses for why they didn't compress and reindex. These excuses range anywhere from "I didn't have time" to "I didn't know I was supposed to." Of course, many of you give these excuses *after* your database has already been damaged. By then, of course, it may be too late for compressing and reindexing — if that's the case, peruse Chapter 17, where I give you pointers on repairing your database.

Database maintenance should be done at the very least on a weekly basis. Multi-user databases and large databases should be re-indexed more often. There is no such thing as doing too much maintenance — only too little!

If you're the administrator of your ACT! database, you will probably be treated to a reminder to perform database maintenance on a regular basis. If not, Chapter 3 tells you how to set those reminders. The default reminder setting in ACT! is set to remind you to compress and reindex every 30 days. If you are a little old lady who uses her database only once in a blue moon, this setting is probably sufficient. However, if the data in ACT! is extremely important to you, head to Chapter 3 so that you can find out how to change that setting (if you haven't done so already) so that ACT! reminds you to compress and reindex your database at least every *seven* days.

Reminders are not-too-subtle hints that you are supposed to *do* something! When you start ACT!, you should be reminded to compress and reindex your database at regular intervals. Do not ignore these reminders!

Are you shaking in your boots right now, wondering whether other situations require compression and reindexing? My answer is that you should compress and reindex whenever you think about it and if you recently

- ✔ Experienced a power outage
- ✔ Had network problems
- ✔ Added new fields to your database
- ✔ Made changes to the drop-down lists in your database
- ✔ Added or deleted contact records to your database
- ✔ Imported another database into your existing ACT! database
- ✔ Added — or deleted — users to your database
- ✔ Were in a network environment and/or had several simultaneous users accessing the database

If your database is located on a network, I recommend compressing and reindexing on a daily basis.

- ✔ Suspect that your database is corrupted

What are the warning signs of a corrupted database? I give you a very long list of warning signs in the next section (appropriately named "A little shopping list of database horrors").

A little shopping list of database horrors

Database corruption comes in many shapes and sizes. The following is a rather long list — but please read it all! — of some of the more common indications of a corrupted ACT! database:

- ✔ While trying to open a database, you receive an error message or ACT! stops responding. Smoke might be seen rising from the back of your CPU.

Sometimes it's difficult to determine whether the corruption is in the *database* or in the ACT! *program* itself. To determine this, try opening the `act6demo` database that was installed on your computer when you installed ACT!. If the `act6demo` opens and runs correctly, the problem lies with your database. If you encounter the same problems in the `act6demo` database that you were having in your own database, you might need to reinstall ACT!.

- ✔ You can't log into the database as a particular user.

✔ ACT! crashes every darned time that you click on a particular field. Or you might receive a *fatal error*.

This corruption commonly occurs when your drop-down list has become corrupted. To remove the contents of the drop-down list, do the following:

1. **Choose Edit⇨Define Fields from the Contacts view.**

2. **Highlight the appropriate field.**

3. **Click the drop-down list.**

4. **Delete all the entries from the drop-down list.**

Deleting the contents of a drop-down list does *not* delete that information from your contact records. In other words, doing this does *not* result in data loss. Whew! Deleting the entries in the drop-down list just means you're going to have to add new items back into the drop-down list later.

✔ Notes and histories appear to be missing, or mysteriously appear attached to the incorrect contact record.

✔ Sales opportunities disappear.

✔ Activity details do not print when printing your Task List.

✔ You notice a significant drop in the number of contact records in your database.

✔ Your database is acting funny or running slower than usual.

✔ The name of your database has become *truncated*. For example, the name of your database was originally My Important Stuff; it's now magically renamed to Myimpo~1.

Creating a shortcut by dragging a copy of the .dbf file onto the desktop is a great way to impress your friends while corrupting your database and increasing your circle of enemies. In many versions of ACT!, it also results in the truncation of the original filename.

✔ You open your database and receive a reminder to do something fun, such as back up, perform database maintenance, run group membership rules, synchronize, or update your ACT! calendar. You click OK like a good ACT! user and do as you're told. Because your reminders are set for seven-day intervals, you heave a sigh of relief knowing that you now have one less thing to worry about. Then, the next day when you open the database, the reminder(s) appear again — telling you that you haven't performed your civic duty in 1,079 days.

If you notice one — or heaven forbid, more than one — of the preceding warning signs, I'm sorry to say that the time has come to either perform CPR on your faint-hearted co-workers or perform some simple database maintenance. In the next section, I give you the details on performing the simple database maintenance (that is, compression and reindexing). You're on your own with the CPR.

Performing a compress and reindex

So here you go — performing the ever-important compress and reindex. I have a few things for you to keep in mind as you go through this process. These are important reminders, so read the next couple of paragraphs before jumping into the steps.

Various ACT! add-on products, including WinFax, ACT! Link for QuickBooks Pro, Wired Contact, and PhotoACT, actually log on to the database and fool ACT! into thinking that they are users of the database. ACT! senses these pseudo-users lurking in the background and prevents you from performing routine maintenance.

If the Administration command is grayed out from ACT!'s File menu, it means that you don't have sufficient administrative rights to perform that option. You might want to peek at Chapter 3 to see about changing your permissions — or jog your database administrator's memory a bit to remind him that his salary is directly proportional to the efficient performance of your database!

In Chapter 17, I include a tip on how to *undelete* contacts you might have deleted in error. After you compress your database, you're no longer able to undelete any contact records.

To compress and reindex your ACT! database, you must be *logged in* as the administrator and all other users must be *logged out*. Follow these steps to perform a compress and reindex:

1. **Choose File➪Administration➪Database Maintenance.**

   If the users of the database are taking their sweet time getting out of the database when you demanded that they exit immediately, you'll see a list of names, as shown in Figure 16-1. A-ha! — the culprit caught red-handed. Unfortunately, you aren't able to continue until all users am-scray from the database.

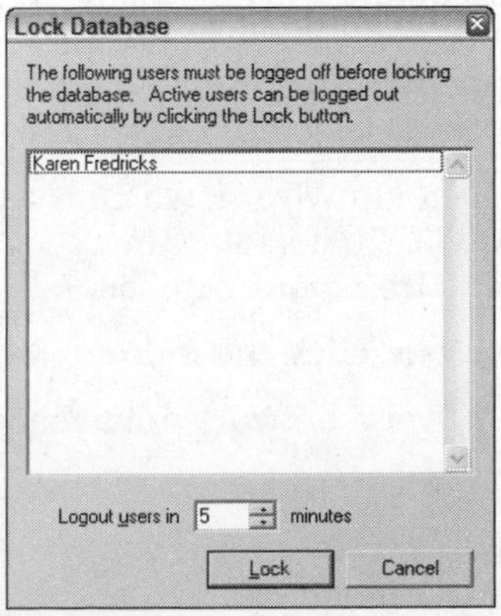

Figure 16-1:
Uh-oh —
another
user is
in the
database.

> **Lock Database**
>
> The following users must be logged off before locking the database. Active users can be logged out automatically by clicking the Lock button.
>
> Karen Fredricks
>
> Logout users in [5] minutes
>
> [Lock] [Cancel]

Even though Figure 16-1 suggests that you can log other users out of ACT! (notice the Logout Users in xx Minutes check box at the bottom of the dialog box), chances are that it won't happen if the other users remain logged onto the database. It's a buggy feature. Be prepared to get up and wrestle control of their computers away from them!

If all systems are go, you're ready to compress and reindex your database, and you should be looking at the screen that's shown in Figure 16-2.

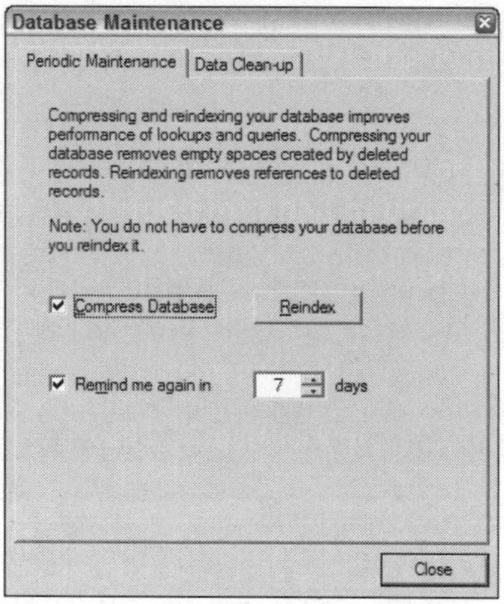

Figure 16-2:
Compres-
sing and
reindexing
the ACT!
database.

2. **In the Database Maintenance dialog box, click the Periodic Maintenance tab and then make sure that the Compress Database check box is selected.**

3. **Click the Data Clean-up tab.**

   The Database Clean-up tab enables you to set preferences to clean out some of your old data, including notes and histories, lost or old sales opportunities, and transaction logs. As shown in Figure 16-3, you can specify various *Older Than* dates to determine how many of the notes and histories and things you want to keep. If you're not sure what you'd like to clean out of the database, you're probably safer to just leave all the options on the Data Clean-up tab deselected (unchecked).

   In Chapter 24, I mention the Data Cleanup Wizard, which is a neat utility that enables you even greater flexibility in deciding the types of notes and histories that you want to delete from your database.

4. **Back on the Periodic Maintenance tab, click the Reindex button.**

   If the database is large or accessed over a network, reindexing may take more than 15 minutes. Be patient!

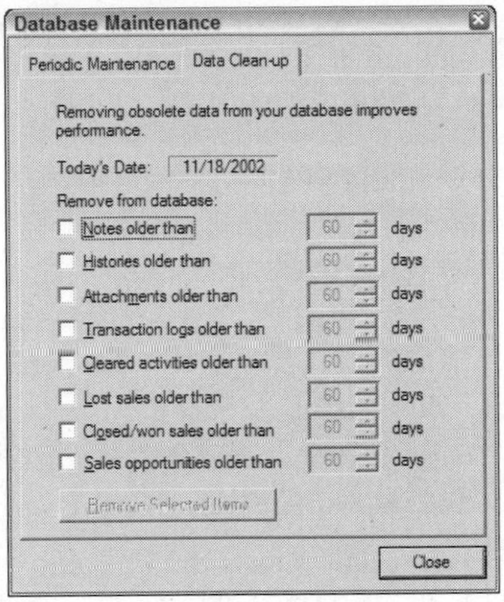

Figure 16-3:
The Data
Clean-up
tab.

WARNING! Do not mosey over to the Windows Task Manager by pressing Ctrl+Alt+Delete while ACT! is whirring and hissing and doing its compress and reindex thing. Task Manager will only inform you that your database is not responding, and you may be tempted to click the End Task button. Suppress the urge to do this at all costs! Forcing ACT! to shut down while compressing and reindexing can cause serious harm to your database.

TIP If, after you compress and reindex, you are still having trouble with your database, the corruption may be tied to a single user's login. You can generally determine this if you can log in as other users without difficulty but have trouble logging in as a specific user. To resolve this problem, create a new user to replace the corrupt user and then delete the corrupt user, being sure to reassign the records to the new user. Chapter 3 tells you how to add new users — and delete existing ones.

Backing Up the ACT! Database

You probably already know the three rules of real estate: location, location, location. Similarly, the three basic rules of computing are backup, backup, backup! With the proliferation of viruses, as well as the poor construction of many computers, it is imperative that you back up on a daily basis. Failure to do so can result in loss of data — as well as time and money!

REMEMBER *Only administrators* of the ACT! database get to back up a database. Because every database requires an administrator, you automatically landed the job if you are the only user of the database. If you need to back up the database and find that the backup option is grayed out on the File menu, you must find a database administrator and wheedle him or her into changing your permissions. In Chapter 3, I explain the various ACT! user permissions.

If you're going to be making major changes to your database, such as importing new records, deleting old contact records, or modifying existing fields, I recommend creating a backup before you start — just in case!

Very often, the ACT! database resides on a network drive and is backed up to a tape drive on a daily basis. In this case, it is not necessary to back up your database using ACT!. However, you might be feeling a false sense of security knowing that this backup is taking place. Don't find out too late that your tape backup was backing up the ACT! program and not the ACT! data files themselves. Chapter 3 explains how to create a folder for your database on a shared network; make sure that the folder is being included as part of your backup. Feeling scared? Remind your IT person that your data files are the important files that should be included as part of the backup.

When you back up your database, ACT! compresses the data into a `.zip` file. You can choose the type of data you want to back up, such as templates, layouts, documents, or reports. You can also set a reminder for backing up your database, which I discuss in Chapter 3.

In this section, I first show the basics of performing a backup in ACT!. I then — ever so briefly — touch on two backup options (floppy drives versus Zip drive). What good is a backup if you don't know how to restore it? Don't worry — I show you how to do that, too.

If you use backup software or store your data on an Internet site, remember that an ACT! database consists of more than a single file. You must back up all files whose filenames begin with the name of the database, as well as any related files, such as documents and report templates.

Performing the basic ACT! backup

Remember, you must have an administrator security-level password to back up your ACT! database. Open the ACT! database that you want to create a backup copy of and follow these steps:

1. **Choose File⇨Backup.**

   The Backup dialog box appears displaying the name of the open database and assigns a name and location for the backup database, as shown in Figure 16-4.

2. **To back up the database to a different location from what's showing, click the Browse button.**

3. **Select a new location for your backup file and then click Save.**

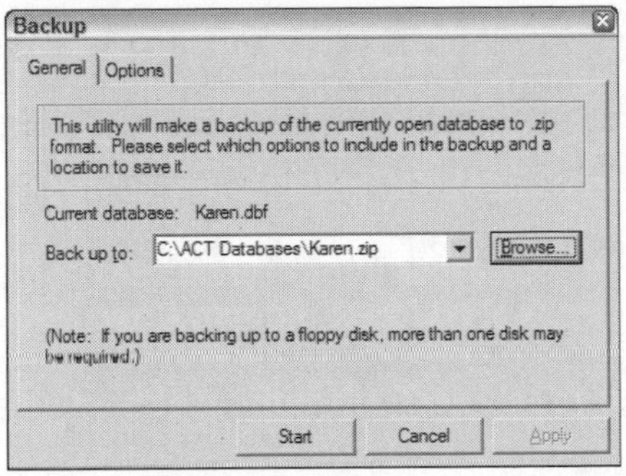

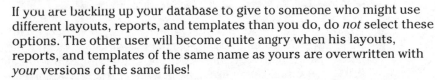

Figure 16-4:
The Backup
dialog box.

4. **On the Options tab, select the items that you want to include in your back up.**

The Options tab of the Backup dialog box (shown in Figure 16-5) offers various choices, such as Attached Mail and Envelopes. I think you'll agree that these are self explanatory.

When you use ACT!'s backup option, you're able to include the various other files that you have created with ACT!. For example, you might want to include any reports, layouts, and templates that you've customized in ACT!.

If you are backing up your database to give to someone who might use different layouts, reports, and templates than you do, do *not* select these options. The other user will become quite angry when his layouts, reports, and templates of the same name as yours are overwritten with *your* versions of the same files!

You are also given the option to set up a reminder to back up your database on a regular interval.

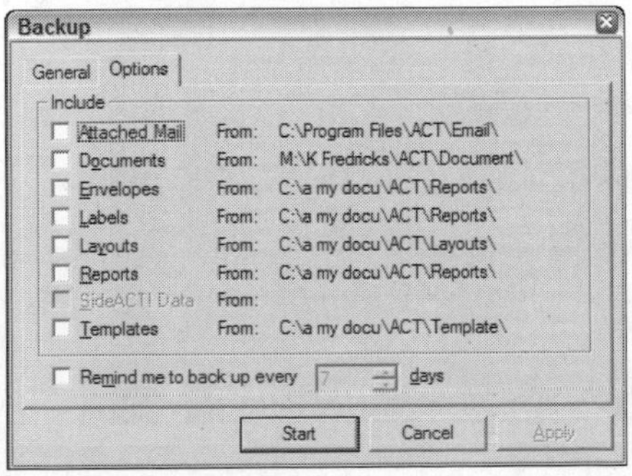

Figure 16-5:
Backup
options.

5. **Click the Start button.**

   An indicator bar appears letting you know that ACT! is creating your backup. The time required to complete your backup varies depending on the size of your database and the options that you've included in your backup. When the backup is complete, a message appears telling you that your backup was completed successfully!

Performing a floppy backup

Unfortunately, because of the size of the typical ACT! database, it generally cannot be backed up to a floppy disk. The ACT! backup file consists of one large file; a single file cannot be divided across several floppy disks. As you try to perform the backup, ACT! will warn you that your file is too big to be backed up on a single floppy. If you attempt to perform a backup in spite of this warning, ACT! will probably prompt you to insert a rather large number of floppy disks. Save your time! There is a very good probability that even after you back up your database on to 210 floppy disks, you will not have created a backup.

Saving your backup to a Zip drive

So far I've used the term *Zip* to indicate the type of backup file created by ACT!. As if life weren't confusing enough, Iomega created a nifty little gizmo known as a Zip drive. Repeat after me: I have zipped my Zip file onto my Zip drive — because that's exactly what you're doing if you use one of the Iomega drives.

Unfortunately, there's a slight compatibility issue between the Iomega Zip drives and the ACT! backup file: The Zip drive can be used as long as you either

✔ Assign a new filename to each new backup

✔ Erase your previous backup file before creating the new one

If you decide to use a Zip drive as your drive of choice when creating a backup file, you must delete any earlier backup files that you might have already created on that disk *using the same filename*. If you don't, ACT! gives you a prompt reminding you that you already have an existing file of the same name. You will be asked very nicely whether you'd like to overwrite that file. After you respond that yes, you'd like to replace that nasty old backup with your new improved version, ACT! will pretend to write to the Zip drive. However, ACT! *isn't* doing this. ACT! *won't* replace the earlier file, and you won't have a new backup.

There is another little peculiarity regarding Zip drives and ACT!. If you try to open a database that was created on a Zip 250 Drive, you'll see the following error message: This database is currently locked by another user. You'll need to copy the ACT! files on to your hard drive and open the database from that location instead.

Restoring a backup copy of your database

A backup is no good if you don't know how to use it to restore your data. Although I hope you never have to use a backup copy, follow these steps to restore a copy of your database:

1. **Choose File⊅Restore.**

   The Restore dialog box opens, as shown in Figure 16-6.

Figure 16-6:
Restoring a
backup.

Restore	☒
Please select the file you want to restore and the folder where you want to restore it.	
File to restore: C:\ACT Databases\Karen_1104223906 ▼ [Browse...]	
To folder: C:\ACT Databases\ ▼ [Browse...]	
[Start] [Cancel]	

2. **Enter the filename of the file that you're restoring in the File to Restore text box.**

   If you need to specify a different location, click the Browse button to navigate to the location of your backup file. Your backup file ends with the .zip extension.

Many of you are familiar with the .zip extension because you have worked with the WinZip software. Do not be tempted to unzip an ACT! backup file using WinZip. The files will not be placed in the correct locations, and the backup file will probably be rendered useless!

3. **In the To Folder text box, enter the location where you want the file restored.**

Don't blindly restore your data to whatever folder ACT! recommends. This might not be the location that you assume it to be. Playing hide-and-seek isn't a good idea when it comes to file management — always click the Browse button so that you can select the location that you're going to restore your file to.

4. **Insert the disk in the appropriate drive (if you're backing up your data to removable media, such as a Zip disk or CD).**

5. **Click the Start button.**

   ACT! warns you that if you continue, the database that's currently open will close and the newly restored database will open.

6. **Click Yes to acknowledge that you'd like to continue.**

   Your computer whirs and hisses for a few moments and soon the new database opens.

Weeding Out Duplicate Contacts

Finding pesky duplicates in your database is tricky but not impossible. Because it is so common to have multiple records for the same person or company, ACT! allows you a way to easily check for duplicate records based on predefined criteria. You can then create a lookup of the duplicate records and delete them. You can also change the criteria used to find these duplicate records.

By default, ACT! looks for duplicate contact records based on the company name, contact name, and phone number. If any *one* of these three fields is identical, ACT! will view it as a duplicate.

As I stress throughout this book, having some semblance of uniformity is very important. Lack of uniformity is a great way to sabotage your database. As I mention in Chapter 4, a search for all your clients in *Ft.* Lauderdale will not include those clients in *Fort* Lauderdale. In the same way, a company or contact might be duplicated if it is entered into your database in two different ways. For example, you might have *John Q. Public* and *John Public,* or *ABC Company* and *ABC Co.* ACT! doesn't recognize any of those examples as duplicates.

You can specify the criteria that ACT! uses to look for duplicate records. By default, ACT! searches through your records looking for duplicates by company, contact, and phone. To find the duplicates that I mention in the preceding paragraph, you need to use a different criterion for your search. Changing your search parameters to search for duplicated phone numbers might just give you the results that you're looking for.

1. **Choose Edit⇨Define Fields from the Contacts view.**

   The Define Fields dialog box appears.

2. **On the Advanced tab, choose Contact from the Record Type drop-down list (see Figure 16-7).**

   You can now specify how ACT! checks for duplicate contact records.

3. **In the Match Duplicates Using box, choose the three fields where you want ACT! to search for duplicate contact data.**

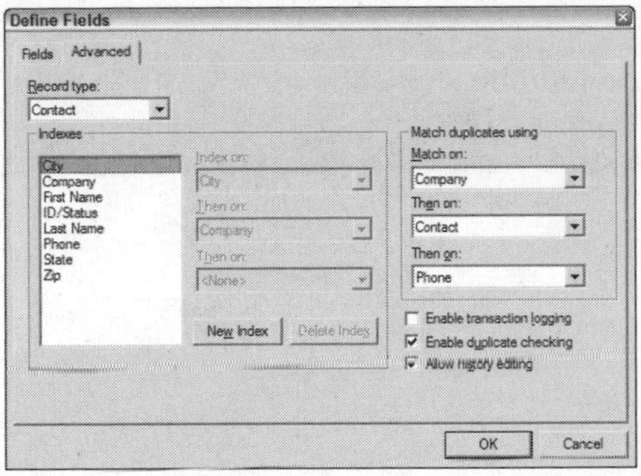

Figure 16-7:
Defining
duplication
criteria.

4. **Select the Enable Duplicate Checking check box if it isn't already selected.**

   When this option is turned on, ACT! notifies you when you're trying to add a contact that's already in your database. (Incidentally, you can ignore the other two options listed with this one.)

   Before you perform any type of maintenance, I recommend that you back up your database — so that you can retrieve any data you accidentally delete.

5. **Go to the Contacts view by clicking the Contacts icon on the View bar.**

   Need a refresher on the View bar? Check out Chapter 2.

6. **Choose Tools⇨Scan for Duplicates.**

   This is one of the few times when ACT! doesn't give — or ask for — more information.

   ACT! scrounges around in your database for a moment or two looking for duplications. If your database does contain duplicate records, ACT! creates a lookup of these records.

7. **Switch to the Contact List view by clicking Contact List in the View bar.**

   Although you can delete contact records from either the Contacts or the Contact List views, you might want to first look at your duplicates in the Contact List so that you can look at a list of the duplicates, as shown in Figure 16-8. You are now ready to begin deleting your duplicate contact records.

8. **Verify that the contacts that ACT! designated as duplicates are actually duplicates.**

   You might want to do a little private investigation into each of the duplicated records. You can hone in on any one of the contacts by double-clicking the Contact button to the left of each record listed in the Contact List.

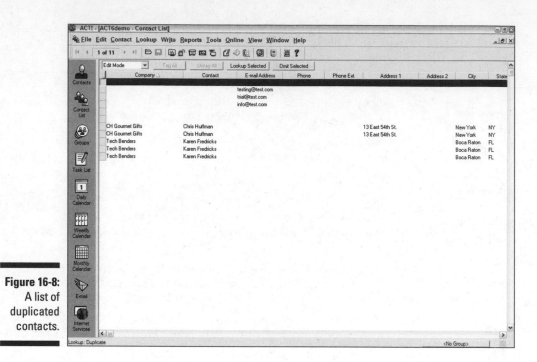

Figure 16-8:
A list of
duplicated
contacts.

9. **If you decide that a contact should remain in your database because it is not a duplicate, click the Contact button one time and then click the Omit Selected button in the Contact List button.**

10. **Decide which one of your duplicate contacts you want to remove.**

In a perfect world, one of your duplicate records would be chock full of correct contact information and notes, and the other evil twin would be missing most of the information. Well, you already know that the world isn't perfect; after all, you did manage to sneak in some duplications along the way. The decision as to which one of the records to delete becomes a little more obscure. Again, this decision requires a bit of detective work on your part.

Following are some points to keep in mind:

Although ACT! does not allow you to merge two duplicate records, the Database Deduplication Wizard does. In Chapter 24, I talk briefly about this neat add-on product.

If you want to save the information in duplicate records, you need to copy and paste the data between fields in different records.

Copying both Notes and Histories and Activities from one contact record to another is possible. Here's what you need to do:

a. Change to the Contacts tab.

b. On the Notes/History tab of the contact you want to delete, highlight all the notes by clicking the first Notes/History item and pressing the Shift key while pressing Ctrl+End.

c. Press Ctrl+C to copy the Notes/History tab items.

d. Place your cursor in the Notes/History tab of the contact that you want to keep and press Ctrl+V.

All the Notes/History items are copied into the second contacts record.

You can repeat this procedure for the Activities tab as well.

11. **Choose Contact⇨Delete Contact.**

The warning that you see in Figure 16-9 appears.

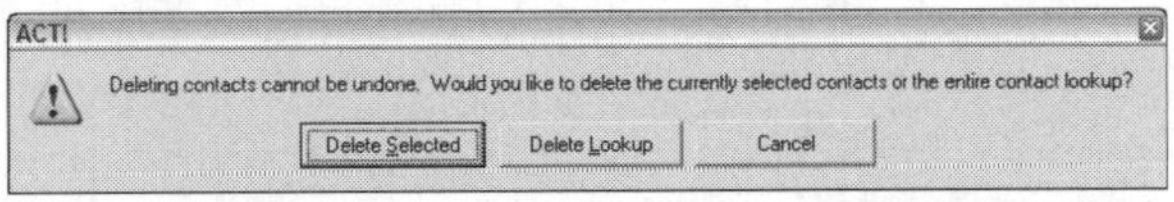

Figure 16-9:
The contact deletion warning.

ACTI
⚠ Deleting contacts cannot be undone. Would you like to delete the currently selected contacts or the entire contact lookup?
[Delete Selected]   Delete Lookup   Cancel

12. **Depending on what you want to delete, click either the Delete Selected or the Delete Lookup button.**

Click the Delete Selected button to eliminate your currently selected contact; click the Delete Lookup button if you want to delete all the contacts that are currently in your lookup.

You can find out the number of contacts in your current lookup by glancing at the record counter conveniently located in the top-left corner of the Contacts window.

If you delete duplicate records, you cannot undo the deletion. If you're not sure how many contacts are in your current lookup — click the Cancel button and start over!

13. **Verify that you truly intend to delete either a contact or the current lookup.**

The warning message shown in Figure 16-10 probably falls under the category of overkill, but wouldn't you rather be safe than sorry?

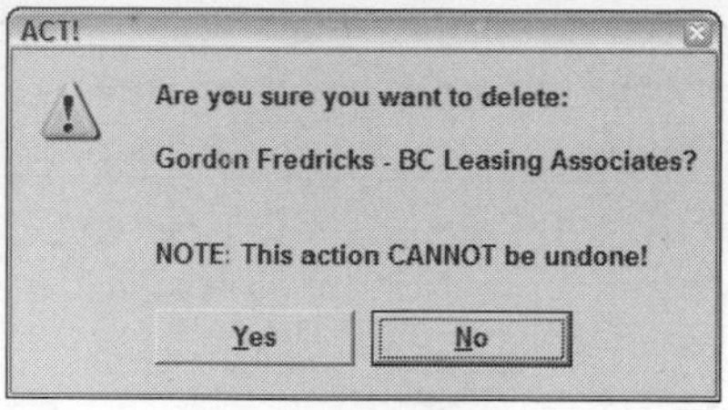

Figure 16-10:
Final
warning
before
deleting a
contact.

ACT!

⚠ Are you sure you want to delete:

Gordon Fredricks - BC Leasing Associates?

NOTE: This action CANNOT be undone!

Yes   No

Editing and Replacing Contact Information

Another way that you can keep your database working well is by ensuring that all fields contain consistent information. You might notice that some of your contacts have the city listed in all capitals while others don't. You might see that some contacts are listed in *Florida,* whereas other contacts reside in *FL* or *Fla.* This lack of consistency makes it extremely difficult to query your database. Like a forgiving mother, ACT! provides you with the ability to correct the error of your ways. After you pinpoint your inconsistencies, you can standardize them in one fell swoop (rather than by correcting each field on an item by item basis); just do this:

1. **Perform your lookup.**

   In the preceding example, you might create a lookup of *FLA* and then add *Florida* to the mix. If you need help, flip to Chapter 6 and review performing lookups.

   Unless you're planning on changing field data for every contact in your database, make sure you perform a lookup *before* proceeding. These changes are irreversible! For example, let's say you notice 27 instances of *Fla* that you'd like to change to *FL*. If you fail to do a lookup first, you'll end up changing the state field for *every* contact in your database to *FL* rather than just for the original 27 that you intended to change. Unfortunately, unless you have a backup handy, you're stuck with the changes because, again, these changes are irreversible.

2. **In the Contacts View, choose Edit⇨Replace.**

   You will now be looking at a totally blank record. Don't be alarmed! This is exactly what you should be seeing!

   The ACT! menus change depending on your currently selected view. You're only able to access the replace command from the Contacts view.

3. **Type your desired change in the appropriate field.**

   In this example, you would type **FL** in the state field.

4. Click the Apply button.

I am not quite sure what the picture on the Apply button is supposed to represent. Personally, I like to call it the *Road Kill button.* Look at Figure 16-11 and you'll see what I mean!

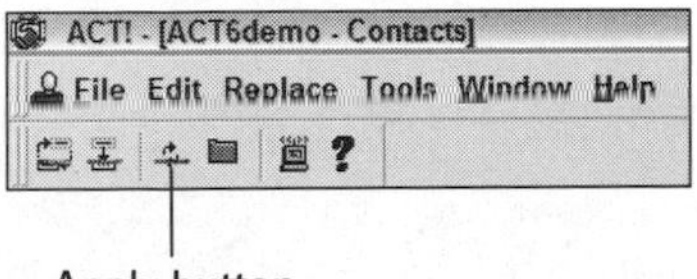

Figure 16-11:
The Apply
button.

ACT! - [ACT6demo - Contacts]

File Edit Replace Tools Window Help

Apply button

5. Read the warning that appears (see Figure 16-12).

ACT! is politely asking you to verify that you intend to change all the contact records in the current lookup. If you're not sure as to the exact number of contacts in the current lookup, click No and read the record counter in the top-left corner of the Contacts view.

Figure 16-12:
One final
check.

ACT!

⚠ This function modifies all records in the lookup. Are you sure you want to continue?

Yes   No

6. Click Yes.

Make sure that you create a backup of your database before proceeding. You can find out how to do that by flipping to the beginning of this chapter.

ACT! might have to think about this for a moment depending on the number of contact records in your lookup. When finished, you'll notice that the field that you indicated in Step 3 has now changed for each of the contact records in your lookup.

If your mission is to empty out all the data in any given field, you can accomplish that by clicking in the chosen field and then pressing Ctrl+F5. This will put the <<BLANK>> operator in the field.

Chapter 17

Calling in the Reinforcements

· ·

In This Chapter

▶ Running ACTDiag

▶ Exploring advanced file options

▶ Performing emergency maintenance

▶ Running advanced database reports

▶ Making emergency changes to your preference settings

· ·

*O*ne of the best-kept secrets of ACT! is the ACT! Data Diagnostic Tool (ACTDiag). This free program is loaded on to your computer when you install ACT!. It can be used to perform emergency maintenance functions and run database reports that can't be generated through ACT! itself.

Maybe you're surprised to learn that such a tool actually exists and wonder why it isn't mentioned in ACT!'s Users Manual. The simplest explanation is that ACTDiag is a very powerful tool: Many of the changes affect your network and operating system. So ACTDiag is geared to more experienced Windows users. The reports generated through ACTDiag will serve as little or no use to the average ACT! user but will prove to be invaluable for experienced ACT! database administrators who are trying to make the database run faster or are trying to add triggers to a database. This is the place you turn when you need to turn off Opportunistic Locking or to do a little research into a synchronization that is not working correctly.

The information that I cover in this chapter is not supported by ACT!'s technical support team. If you feel at all hesitant about following any of the directions that I give you here, I recommend calling in an ACT! Certified Consultant to help repair your database.

Running ACTDiag

So you've decided to take the plunge and run ACTDiag? Okay, here we go. Remember, ACTDiag is automatically loaded onto your computer when you install ACT!, so it's there — you just have to find it and run it. To do so, just follow these steps:

1. **Exit ACT!.**

2. **From the Windows Start menu, choose Run.**

3. **Type** Actdiag **in the Run dialog box and then click OK.**

   The ACT! Data Diagnostic Tool (ACTDiag) window opens, as shown in Figure 17-1.

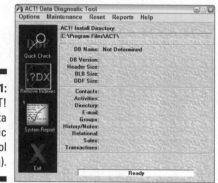

Figure 17-1:
The ACT!
Data
Diagnostic
Tool
(ACTDiag).

You will find three of the most commonly used features of ACTDiag listed in a View bar to the left of the ACTDiag screen. All other features can be accessed from four drop-down menus (Options, Maintenance, Reset, and Reports) at the top of the ACTDiag screen. I spend the rest of this chapter explaining these features in detail. I provide steps to show you how to perform the tasks that you'll most likely need to perform.

Exploring the ACTDiag Options Menu

The Options menu provides access to functions that are used for file management tasks, including

✔ **Database Quick Check:** Displays record counts for all of the files that make up the ACT! database that you specify. If the general structure of the database is correct, the record counts and sizes are displayed. If any item shows a red error message, click the Help menu, and then choose Error Messages for additional information.

✔ **Remove Index Files:** Enables you to quickly delete index files from any database. *Index files* are the files that help ACT! hunt down information in your database quickly and efficiently. Index files are subject to corruption, particularly among ACT! users who don't perform routine maintenance on a regular basis (hint, hint). Removing the index files doesn't result in a loss of data and often removes corruption from your database.

The next time that you attempt to open your ACT! database after you have removed the index files, ACT! will display the very ominous warning shown in Figure 17-2. Click the Yes button, and ACT! rebuilds the index files. (Want a salary increase or to sadistically upset your boss? Show him the scary warning. As he heads off in search of aspirin, call after him and tell him that you might have a way to fix the problem. Then surreptitiously click Yes.)

✔ **Remove Unapplied Sync Packets:** Removes unapplied synchronization packets from the default synchronization, Briefcase, Outbox, and Temp folders.

✔ **Remove Temp Files:** Deletes unnecessary `.tmp` files from the Windows temporary folder.

✔ **Failed Conversion Check:** Helps troubleshoot a failed database conversion when you're attempting to convert a database from a previous version of ACT!. This option creates a temporary folder called `TCAnnnn`. `tmp` where `nnnn` is a random number. If you browse to that folder and open the database, you will see the last contact that ACT! was trying to convert. You can then open the database in the previous version of ACT! and check the contact information for problems.

✔ **Back Up ACT! Registry:** Enables you to back up the ACT!-related keys in the Windows registry. You can back up all the ACT!-related keys or check just the keys that you want to back up. The registry backup makes it possible to transfer your ACT! preferences from one workstation to another. However, only computers using the same Windows version can share the same copy of a registry.

✔ **Opportunistic Locking on NT/2000/XP:** Disables the opportunistic locking features found in some networked versions of Windows. Opportunistic locking is enabled, by default, when Windows NT, 2000, or XP is installed. Opportunistic locking is re-enabled whenever a Service Pack is applied to Windows NT, 2000, or XP. If enabled, Opportunistic Locking will corrupt any database shared over a network from a server running Windows NT, 2000, or XP.

If you're using Windows NT, 2000, or XP and are sharing your ACT! database across a network, be sure to disable Opportunistic Locking.

The Opportunistic Locking on NT/2000/XP function is grayed-out on Windows 95, 98, and Me because opportunistic locking does not exist on those versions of Windows.

✔ **Undelete Records:** You probably felt a rush of power and control when you discovered that ACTDiag contained the Undelete Records feature. First of all, there is no replacement for a good backup to ensure against loss of data. That said, Undelete Records allows you to retrieve accidentally deleted records and their associated activities; just follow the steps.

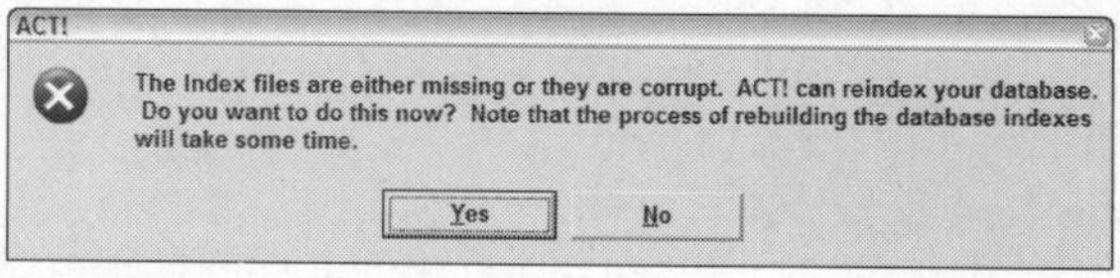

Figure 17-2:
You see
this scary
warning
after
removing
index files.

To recover accidentally deleted records:

1. **Make a backup of your ACT! database (I show you how in Chapter 16).**

2. **Close ACT!.**

3. **Open ACTDiag and then choose Options⊅Undelete Records.**

   The dialog box shown in Figure 17-3 appears, warning you that after you've undeleted the deleted contact records, you can't re-delete them again at the touch of a button. In other words, ACTDiag is hoping that you know what you're doing and won't be changing your mind. Again.

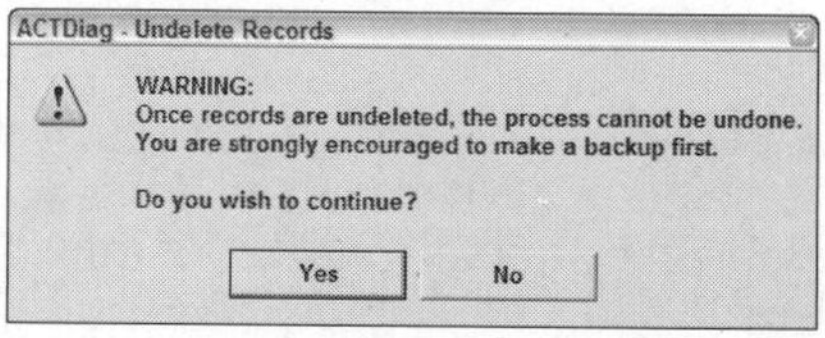

Figure 17-3:
Click Yes to
undelete
records.

4. **Click the Yes button.**

   A dialog box appears that shows the default database location.

5. **Select the database that has records that you want to recover and then click Open.**

   Another dialog box appears telling you that the records have been undeleted and that when you restart ACT! and select that database, the database will reindex itself.

Before the feeling of euphoria rushes to your head, I have two points of caution for you:

- ✔ Records and activities are retrieved; notes, histories, and attachments are not. In other words, you'll be able to retrieve a contact record but not any other information previously stored on the Notes/History tab, including links to documents that you might have attached to a note.

- ✔ If you have performed routine maintenance by compressing and reindexing your database after deleting contact records, you will not be able to get them back using ACTDiag. They are gone. Destroyed. Lost.

Performing Emergency Maintenance

The Maintenance menu provides access to functions that are used to test and, in many cases, to repair internal database problems.

- ✔ **Scan Database Integrity:** Tests the selected database to determine whether problems exist. Because it is only scanning your database and not attempting to repair it, the scan moves pretty quickly. If ACTDiag detects a problem, it will put a red check mark next to the corrupted item.

- ✔ **Scan and Repair Database:** Scans the database for integrity and also corrects or removes any problems that it may find. Depending on the number of contacts, notes, and activities found in your database, the Scan and Repair may take a while to process. Following this bulleted list, I've included the steps necessary to scan and repair your database.

- ✔ **Backup Database:** Makes a backup of your database directly from ACTDiag. This saves you the inconvenience of returning to ACT! to create a backup before performing various maintenance tasks. The backup file is created in the same folder as the database. The filename of the backup will be a combination of the database name and a date/time stamp.

To run scan and repair on your database, just follow these steps:

1. **Close ACT! and open ACTDiag.**

2. **Choose Maintenance⇨Scan and Repair Database.**

   The dialog box shown in Figure 17-4 appears, prompting you to make a copy of your database.

3. **Click the Yes button to continue.**

   You will be prompted to open the database that you want to scan and repair.

4. **Select your database and click Open.**

   If the database is not in the default database directory, you need to navigate to the database first.

   Scan and Repair automatically makes a backup of your database before starting the scan and repair process. You'll find the backup file in the same folder as your database. The filename of the backup will be a combination of the database name and a date/time stamp.

5. **When the backup is complete, click Close.**

   ACTDiag now asks you to choose which user of your database users should become the Record Manager for the ACTDiag repair records. If ACTDiag finds an error, it creates a new contact record in the ACT! database that contains information about the error. This record may contain notes and histories that had previously been attached to a corrupted contact record. You'll be able to spot this record the next time you open your database because the company name will begin with *ACTDiag*. The user whom you choose in this list will become the Record Manager of this new contact record.

6. **Choose the Record Manager and then click OK.**

   ACTDiag now warns you that the scan and repair is about to begin and that you do not want to interrupt the process. I recommend always heeding ACTDiag's warnings!

7. **Click Yes to continue.**

   ACTDiag will start the process of scanning and, if necessary, repairing your database. You may want to cross your fingers at this point and hope that ACTDiag finds nothing but green check marks. *Green* is a good thing; *red* indicates a problem.

When the scan and repair process has completed, you see two further options:

- Clicking the repair log option opens a text document in Windows Notepad. The repair log contains all of the problems that ACTDIAG found, and what, if anything, was done to fix them.

- Clicking the second link takes you to the ACT! Database Services Database Repair Web site.

8. Click OK and exit ACTDiag.

9. Open ACT! and open your database.

You once again see the scary message that appears whenever you remove ACT!'s index files (refer to Figure 17-2).

10. Click the Yes button.

ACT! rebuilds the index files. This may take some time depending on the size of the database.

After the scan and repair has completed and you've reopened the database, I strongly recommend that you compress and reindex the database. As I mention in Chapter 16, it's always a good idea to compress and reindex your database whenever something unusual has affected your database.

Overriding Existing Settings

The Reset menu provides you with the ability to reset various ACT! preferences to their default settings. Suppose, for example, that you've changed ACT!'s startup preference to always open a specific database or layout, but that database or layout becomes corrupted and prevents you from opening ACT! at all. By resetting the default settings, you'll be able to open ACT! and then try to open a different database or layout.

To reset various ACT! preferences to their default values:

1. Open ACTDiag.

2. Choose Reset⇨Options and Window Positions.

ACTDiag responds by opening the dialog box shown in Figure 17-5. You can select (check) items that you want to return to their default settings.

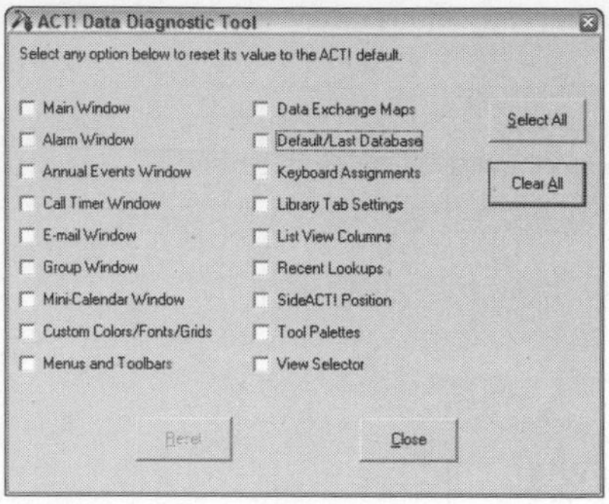

Figure 17-5:
Resetting
options and
window
settings.

3. **Choose the items that you want to reset.**

4. **Click the Reset button (grayed out in Figure 17-5) to return the selected items to their default settings.**

   A few of the settings that you might find to be particularly useful are

   - **Menus and Toolbars:** After you have customized your menus and toolbars, you may decide that you'd like to change them back again.

   - **Default/Last Database:** By default, the database that you were last viewing automatically opens again the next time that you start ACT!. Problems arise if that database becomes corrupt, and you can't open it. Resetting this preference enables you to open ACT! and select another database.

   - **List View Columns:** In Chapter 5, I discuss ways in which you can customize the Contact List in order to create quick reports. This option allows you to view the Contact List in its original state.

Running the ACTDiag Reports

The ACTDiag Reports menu (see Figure 17-6) includes six reports that are useful for system or database troubleshooting. Because the reports don't offer you any fancy reporting options, they are very easy to run. To run any of the ACTDiag reports, simply click the ACTDiag Reports menu and choose the report that you want to run.

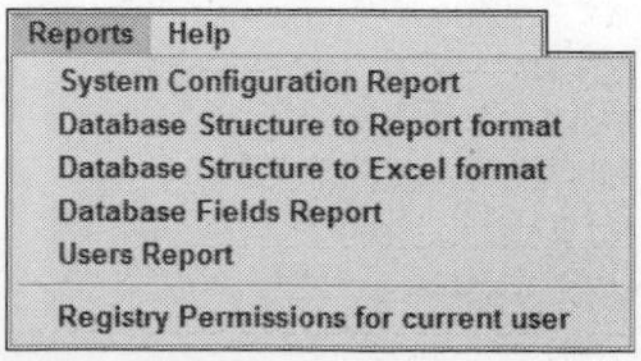

Figure 17-6:
The ACTDiag
Reports
menu.

As you run each report, ACTDiag asks whether you'd like to see the report in Notepad. Click Yes, and you'll see the report displayed in Notepad. After it's opened, you can print the report by choosing File➪Print in Notepad. ACTDiag reports are automatically saved to your desktop. You might want to remove the reports from your desktop when you no longer need them.

The six ACTDiag reports are

- ✓ **System Configuration Report:** Tells you everything that you need to know about your computer — but were afraid to ask. The pearls of wisdom include

  - Your operating system and machine information

  - File information, including your ACT! version and serial number as well as release dates for key ACT! files

  - The free drive space on your computer

  - ACT! startup information

  - Your registry settings

- ✓ **Database Structure to Report Format:** A comprehensive listing of the fields from both the contact and group tables in the selected database. It includes the following information:

  - Record and field counts for both the contact and group tables

  - Name and ID number for all fields

  - The database ID

  - Field size and configuration

  - Any entry or exit triggers

  - Listing of the drop-down entries for the field

The Database Structure report is very lengthy. When asked whether you want to include pop-up information in the report, you'll probably want to answer No. For many diagnostics, the only thing that you need is in the first paragraph: the database Unique ID. I recommend copying this information into a separate document to conserve on paper.

The database ID is essential to the synchronization process; if two databases have the same database ID, they might not synchronize correctly. The field ID numbers are essential for creating entry and exit triggers in your database fields. The field ID number is not the same tab-order number that you see from the Layout Designer.

- ✓ **Database Structure to Excel Format:** Gives the same information as the Database Structure to Report Format report, but this report is generated as an Excel spreadsheet. The benefit to running the field in a spreadsheet format is that you can sort your fields based on the criteria of your choosing.

✔ **Database Fields Report:** Lists the fields from both the contact and group tables in the selected database. It includes the following:

- Record and field counts for both the contact and group tables

- Name and ID number for all fields

✔ **Users Report:** Lists all the users for the selected database. It lists all the defined users along with their security level, logon status, and synchronization status. Most importantly, it lists the unique ID assigned by ACT! to each user of the database. If you want to synchronize data between databases in two separate locations, the unique ID of a user listed in one database must be identical to the ID of the same user listed in another database.

✔ **Registry Permissions for Current User:** Displays the current user's access rights to certain registry keys that are critical to successfully running ACT!.

Part V

Commonly Overlooked ACT! Features

"For 30 years I've put a hat and coat on to make sales calls and I'm not changing now just because I'm doing it on the Web from my living room."

In this part . . .

If you aren't content with relying on the basic ACT! functions to keep your life organized, and you want to squeeze every last drop of functionality out of ACT!, here's the place to find some of the best-kept secrets of ACT!. Want to surf the Net or edit your documents without leaving the comforts of ACT!? Interested in keeping a record of your ongoing sales activities? Want the functionality of a high-priced relational database — without mortgaging the farm? ACT! can help you accomplish these goals, and Part V shows you how.

Chapter 18

ACT!ing on the Internet

The functionality of ACT!'s Internet Services keeps improving with each new release of ACT!. Just like you can merge your contact data into a template, you can merge your data into a Web site to find contact-specific information. ACT! 6 now includes its own browser so that you can surf the Net right from ACT!. And if you find a site with pertinent information, you can attach that Web site to a contact record for future reference.

After you enable the Internet Services feature, you can access various Internet Services from the View bar or the Online menu. You can also customize the ACT! browser's toolbars and menus.

If you want to share real-time information with remote users, check out the ACT! for Web application that enables you to access your ACT! database from the Internet.

Using the Basic Internet Services

To use the ACT! Web browser, you must first enable it as one of the preference settings. Enabling ACT!'s browser means that a new ACT! window appears each time that you access a Web site. If you've created a favorites list in your Web browser, you can also view it directly from the ACT! Online menu. Don't sweat — enabling the ACT! Web browser is a piece of cake.

Although ACT! is so good that it can create certain things as if by magic, an Internet connection is not one of them. In order to connect to the Internet using ACT!, you must first have an Internet service provider (ISP). You'll also need to have Microsoft Internet Explorer 5.5 or later installed.

To enable the ACT! Web browser:

1. **Choose Edit⇨Preferences.**

   The Preferences dialog box appears.

2. **On the General tab, select the Enable ACT! Internet Services check box.**

3. **Click OK.**

Disabling this feature means that you won't have access to the ACT! Web browser. The default Windows Web browser will be used instead. When you attempt to view a Web page, your browser opens as a separate program outside of ACT!. You also won't be able to see your Internet favorites from ACT!'s Online menu or the Internet Services on ACT!'s View bar.

The most basic Internet task that you'll perform is viewing a contact's Web site. Accomplish this feat of daring by following these steps:

1. **Click the Web site address that you entered into the contact record.**

   You've probably already noticed that the Web site appears to be blue, and that when you hover the mouse over the field, your cursor turns into a pointing hand indicating that this is a link. If you click the link, you're hurled into the exciting world of the Internet.

2. **Depending on your preference setting, either ACT!'s or your own default Web browser launches and displays the contact's Web site.**

3. **After you have perused the site and are ready to continue working in ACT!, close the browser.**

Attaching a Web Site to a Contact Record

ACT! comes with a predefined Web site field — a convenient way to access a contact's Web site. But what if you need to reference information on more than one page of the contact's site? Or what if you need to access this information when an Internet connection is unavailable? ACT! allows you to attach as many Web pages as you need right in the Notes/History tab of the contact's record.

To attach a Web page to a contact record:

1. **Click the Internet Services icon on the View bar.**

   The ACT! browser opens, taking you to the Internet.

   If you haven't enabled the ACT! Internet Services preference, the Internet Services icon doesn't appear on your View bar. Before continuing, you must enable the service; see the preceding section.

2. **Navigate to the Web page that you want to attach to your contact.**

3. **In the ACT! browser, click the Attach icon on the toolbar (see Figure 18-1).**

Click to attach Web page to a contact.

Figure 18-1:
The Attach icon on the Internet Services toolbar.

4. **In the Attach Web Page to Contact(s) dialog box that appears (see Figure 18-2), select the contact or contacts that you're attaching this Web site to.**

   You can attach the Web page to more than one contact. In the Select Contacts From area of the dialog box, select the All Contacts, Current Lookup, or Selected Group radio button. If you select Selected Group, you can select the group from the Group drop-down list.

Figure 18-2:
Attach a Web page to a contact record.

5. **Select a contact from the list on the left and click the Add button to add only one contact to the Attach To box.**

6. **Click the Add All button to attach the Web page to every name in your list.**

7. **To remove contacts from the Attach To list, select the contact(s) in the Attach To list and then click the Remove button.**

8. **Click OK.**

   The attachment appears in the contact's Notes/History tab (see Figure 18-3).

Figure 18-3:
Web page
attachment.

9. **To view the Web page, click the attachment in the Notes/History tab.**

Taking Advantage of NetLinks

If you're like me, you like to take advantage of the abundance of information on the Internet. Even more important to me — and probably to you, too — is the ability to find information about contacts. As its name implies, ACT!'s NetLinks link your contact information to a site on the Internet. Among the most frequently used informational sites are the various Yahoo! sites that help you find information on anything from a local weather report to driving directions and maps. By using a NetLink in ACT!, you can access these sites in a new, unique way: Yahoo! searches for your information based on the information in the current contact record.

If one of your contacts is located in Boca Raton, Florida, you can go to that contact's record and click the Yahoo! Weather NetLink to find the local Boca Raton weather report. If your My Record has you listed in the city of Miami, and you're currently on the record of a contact located in Fort Lauderdale, the Yahoo! Driving Directions NetLink supplies you with the driving directions to get there.

Adding a new NetLink is a little complicated but doable. To add a NetLink to ACT!, here's all you need to do:

1. **Open your Web browser and navigate to the Web site that you're adding to ACT!.**

2. **Highlight the entire Web site address and choose Edit⇨Copy.**

3. **Open Notepad, and in the body of a blank text file, type the menu name for your new Internet link, surrounded by square brackets.**

   The square brackets are located to the right of the P key.

4. **Copy and paste the Web site address next to your bracketed menu name (see Figure 18-4).**

   Leave no spaces between the ending bracket that you typed and the Web site address that you pasted.

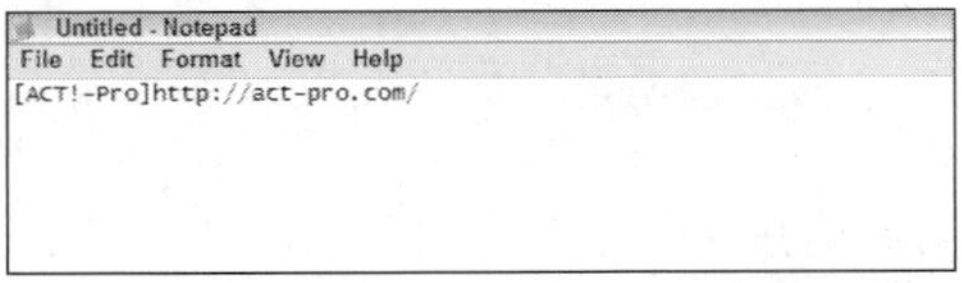

Figure 18-4:
Creating a
new
NetLink.

```
Untitled - Notepad
File  Edit  Format  View  Help
[ACT!-Pro]http://act-pro.com/
```

5. **To save the file, choose File⇨Save As.**

   The Save As dialog box appears (see Figure 18-5).

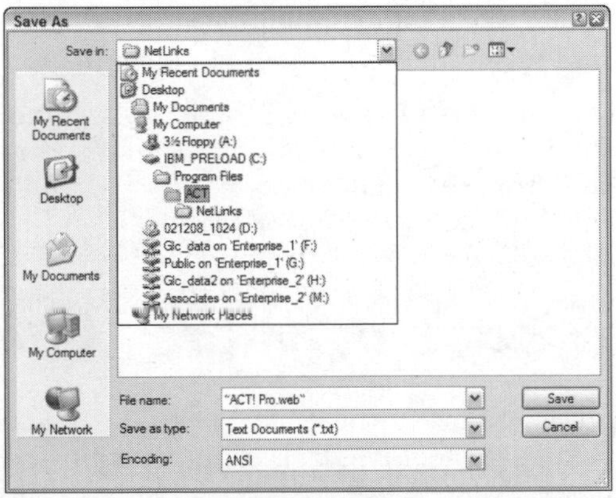

Figure 18-5:
Saving
a new
NetLink.

6. **From the Save In drop-down list, choose the NetLinks folder located at** c:\program files\act\netlinks **(unless you installed ACT! to a different location).**

7. **Name the file using the extension** .web **and be sure to place double quote marks around the entire filename (refer to Figure 18-5).**

8. **Choose Text Documents (*.txt) from the Save as Type drop-down list to save the file as a text file.**

9. **Click the Save button.**

10. **Close Notepad.**

You can program a NetLink between your ACT! information and virtually any site on the Internet. To make life easy for you, visit `http://techbenders.com/act4dummies.htm` and download the NetLink package that includes NetLinks to nine popular Yahoo! sites. The links are also available on the ACT! Web site (`www.act.com`).

To use one of your NetLinks, just follow these steps:

1. **In ACT!, display the contact record containing the information that you want to use.**

2. **Choose Online⇨Internet Links.**

   You see a menu featuring the NetLinks that you've installed on your computer.

3. **Choose the site that you'd like to link to.**

   Depending on the site that you're linking to, you might be asked to confirm the information that you've selected in ACT!. The ACT! Web browser then displays the results; the My Record information appears on the left side of the screen, and the contact's information is on the right.

Internet sites are extremely volatile — here today, gone tomorrow. If a NetLink fails to function, maybe the site has changed its content information or disappeared from the scene altogether.

Sharing Your Database over the Web

For the past 15 years, ACT! users everywhere have been relying on ACT! to take care of their contact management needs. During that same time, reliance on the Internet has increased dramatically. Maybe you've contemplated using an online calendaring system, such as the one that Yahoo! provides, just so that you could access your calendar while away from the office. If you choose that solution, however, you lose some of the functionality that makes ACT! so appealing in the first place. Keeping your calendar in an online program other than ACT! essentially cripples ACT!'s power.

One of the greatest strengths of ACT! is the ease in which you can enter notes and other pertinent data into a database. Better still, if your database is located on a network drive, you can share all that information with the other members of your staff. However, many salespeople find that they are not in the office on a regular basis yet want to share updates with the home office. One way to share information is by using a Web-based product.

Using an online product allows you to access, update, and share ACT! information via the Internet. Best of all, the information is in real time. You can perform lookups, run reports, and work on the Web-based version of ACT! just as if you were working back in the main office.

ACT! for Web is the Web-based version of ACT!. Although not available in retail stores, the product is available for purchase directly from any ACT! Certified Consultant or the official ACT! Web site (www.act.com). Users who want to access their databases remotely need to buy ACT! for Web rather than ACT!.

So why isn't everyone using a Web-based version of ACT!? Well, the service does have its limitations:

- ✔ **You must have access to the Internet.** If you like to work from various client locations or even on an airplane, you likely won't have an Internet connection, limiting when you can use the Web-based version of ACT!.

- ✔ **You can't synch your personal digital assistant (PDA) to a virtual database.** You must have a copy of the ACT! database on your computer's hard drive in order to synchronize that information to your handheld device.

- ✔ **You must purchase the Web-based version of ACT!, which is slightly more expensive than the ACT! program itself.** Each of your remote users also must purchase the Web-based version of ACT! rather than the traditional version.

- ✔ **You need a Web server with IIS installed at the site where your ACT! database resides, a licensed copy of ACT!, and a Web site.** This doesn't mean, however, that you have to host your own Web site. What it does mean is that you must buy a fully licensed copy of ACT! for both your Web server and anyone wanting to access ACT! offline.

One benefit of ACT! for Web is that it offers good security options to limit which users have access to your database and which contacts they're allowed to view and edit.

Figure 18-6 shows you the opening screen in ACT! for Web. When you access your database online with the Web-based version of ACT!, you'll have the same look and feel as if you were actually using ACT!. Note that the View bar icons are slightly different although all the basic ACT! features are virtually identical. One minor difference is the addition of a Reports menu on the View bar. ACT! for Web comes with a full assortment of Online Reports that you can run and print from your remote location.

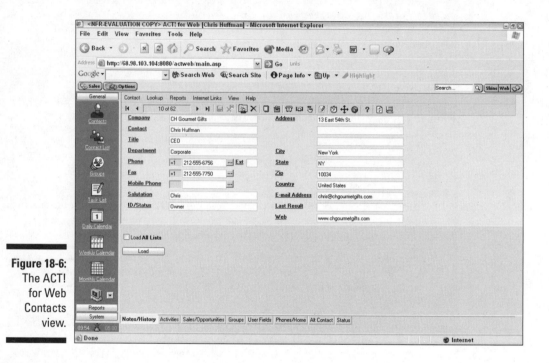

Figure 18-6: The ACT! for Web Contacts view.

ACT! for Web has also made a slight enhancement to the Contact List. If you have thousands of contacts in your database, it can take several seconds to sort through your list — even if you're accessing your database directly from the server. Pulling up a large list is going to take even longer when you're accessing it through your Web browser. As shown in Figure 18-7, ACT! for Web provides you with a toolbar containing the letter of the alphabet. Click a letter to see an abbreviated list. (For example, click H to see all contacts whose last name begins with H.)

Figure 18-7:
The ACT!
for Web
Contact List.

Contact	Company	Phone	Phone Ext.	Title	E-mail Address	Address 1
Colleen McCarthy	Ace Pet Service	+1 541-555-3648		Owner/Operator	12mccarthur@august7.com	925 Cabby St.
Hayleigh Frieda	American Dreams	+1 972-555-1007		Vice President of Product Management	hfrieda0525@americandreams12.com	1113 Greenbrook Dr.
Jackie Jorgensen	Arcadia Ave. Florist	+1 602-555-8169		Proprietor	jackie1@arcadia.netx.com	7201 N. Arcadia Ave
Dylan Nguyen	Bechtel Corp.	+1 602-444-5410		Marketing Director	DNguyen12@bechtel3.com	5550 South West Co
Benny Lender	Best Lender Financing	+1 847-555-9100		Sales Manager	blender1000@lender.com	4500 Payment Way
Kristi Elmendorf	Black Forest Baking	+49 211 9917 0		Manager	Kristi@bforest.netx.com	Grafenburger Allee 1!
Emily Dunn	Boomer's Artworx	+1 602-555-3789		Owner	e.dunn71@boomersartworx1.com	8907 E. Rosebud La
Mackenzie Jensen	Brandee's Bakery	+1 480-555-0405		President	mackjen@bakery.com	41169 Alec Lane
Paul Brushman	Brushy's Golfing World	+61 4-555-30000		Chief Golf Sales Manager	bushy899@brushgolf.com.au	Level 36 989 York St
Ernst Anderson	CH Gourmet Gifts	+1 415-555-2909		Sales Representative	ernst@chgourmetgifts.com	552 Everett Ave.
Cecil Carter	CH Gourmet Gifts	+1 212-555-7323		Public Relations Manager	cecil@chgourmetgifts.com	13 East 54th St.
Jane Chan	CH Gourmet Gifts	+1 212-555-4534		Creative Consultant	jane@chgourmetgifts.com	13 East 54th St.
Chris Huffman	CH Gourmet Gifts	+1 212-555-6756		CEO	chris@chgourmetgifts.com	13 East 54th St.
Allison Mikola	CH Gourmet Gifts	+1 212-555-6743		CFO	allison@chgourmetgifts.com	13 East 54th St.
Melissa Pearce	CH Gourmet Gifts	+1 212-555-7423		Assistant	melissa@chgourmetgifts.com	13 East 54th St.
Juliette Hosseux	CH Gourmet Gifts	+33 (1) 2 31 44 134		Sales Representative	juliette@chgourmetgifts.com	12 Rue La Rouge
Jonathan Sommer	CH Gourmet Gifts	+1 212-555-7345		Marketing Manager	jonathan@chgourmetgifts.com	13 East 54th St.
Sarah Whiting	CH Gourmet Gifts	+1 212-555-7575		Sales Representative	sarah@chgourmetgifts.com	13 East 54th St.
Jonathan Jenkins	Circle Photography	+1 214-555-9577		Owner	jack4@circlephoto6.com	2256 Circle Lane
Herman Better	Continental Energy	+1 919-555-4815		Vice President Operations	herman@continental123.com	54 S. Utica
Morty Manicotti	Corleone's Pasta Company	+1 480-555-3053		Director of Manufacturing	morty.meatball1@pasta.org	8800 Pasta Way
Kristi Cameron	Corporate Forms, Ltd.	+1 480-555-8656		Marketing Director	klvnn@corpfrm.net	515 E. Cameron Way
Dr. Deiter Brock	CPQT	+682 33 021		Cardiothoracic Surgeon	deiterbrock1@cpqt.co.ck	FLC Lane
Michaela J. Zip	Django Consulting	+1 415-555-1940		Vice President	michaela@djangoconsulting8.com	1111 Easy St.
Annette Sharkey	Goldfish Records	+44 555-1483099		New Media Manager	annette.sharkey@goldfish.com.uk	Goldfish House
James Jawson	HAL's Consulting Corp	+1 503-555-4357		Man In Charge	jjawson@jawsonconsulting.com	10 Countdown Loop

Chapter 19

ACT!ing on Your Sales Opportunities

. . . .

In This Chapter

▶ Creating a sales opportunity

▶ Completing the sale

▶ Tracking your opportunities through the various sales stages

. . . .

*I*n this chapter, I lead you through the entire sales process using ACT!. I show you how to create an initial sales opportunity, make changes to it as the sales makes its way through the sales funnel, and view your sales opportunities by using various ACT! sales reports.

Creating Sales Opportunities

In ACT!, a *sales opportunity* is a potential sale to a contact. Each sales opportunity must be created with a contact. All sales information for a contact appears in the Sales/Opportunities tab of the contact record. (Figure 19-1 shows an example of the Sales/Opportunities tab.) When you create a sales opportunity, you can enter the name of your product or service; the type of product, service, or sale; and a main competitor for the sales opportunity. If you have a list of products, sales types, or competitors, you can import the list into ACT! so that you can select it from a drop-down list.

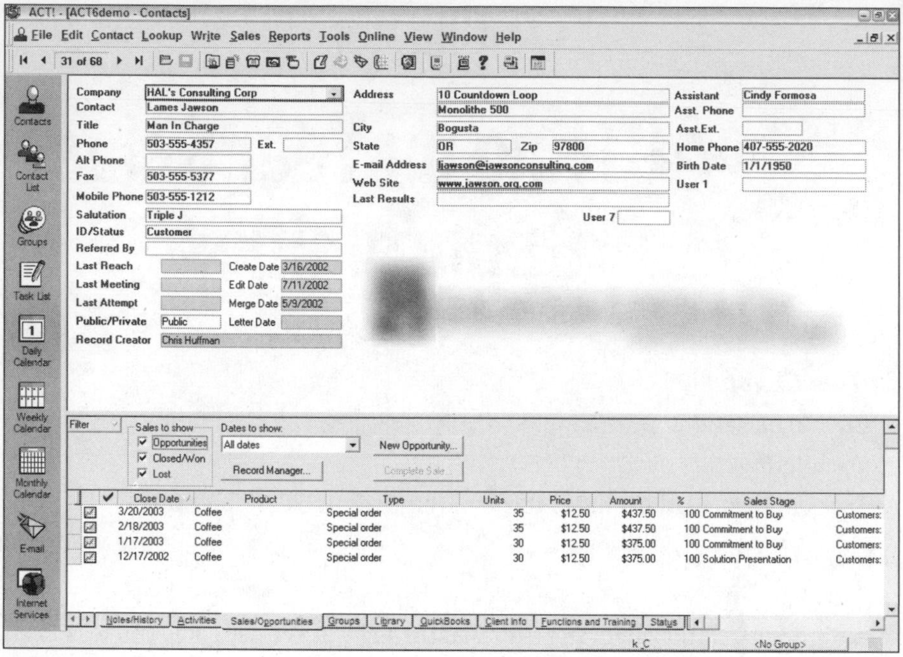

Figure 19-1:
The Sales/
Opportun-
ities tab.

By automating the sales process using ACT!, you'll have a better chance at closing more sales. First of all, if you're following up on your activities as I show you in Chapter 8, you should have significantly fewer contacts falling through the cracks of your database. Secondly, you can adjust your predictions as the opportunity moves through the sales stages. Most importantly, you can generate reports based on your projected sales allowing you to focus on the deals that you think you have the best chance of closing.

Although most of the ACT! program is highly customizable, the Sales Opportunities portion of the program is not. Although you can build drop-down lists, you can't add or modify the fields themselves. I'll point out some of the other limitations of the Sales Opportunities as they come up.

Initiating the sales opportunity

So why are you sitting around reading a book? It's time for you to go out there and make some money. Here's how you're going to make your first million:

1. **Go to the Contacts view by clicking the Contacts icon on the View bar.**

2. **Perform a lookup to find the contact for whom you're creating a sales opportunity.**

What? A little rusty on those lookups? Fear not — and head to Chapter 6 for a quick refresher.

3. **Create a new sales opportunity in one of the following two ways:**

   - Choose Sales⇨New Sales Opportunity.

   - Click the Sales/Opportunities tab and then click the New Opportunity button.

   The Sales Opportunity dialog box opens, as shown in Figure 19-2.

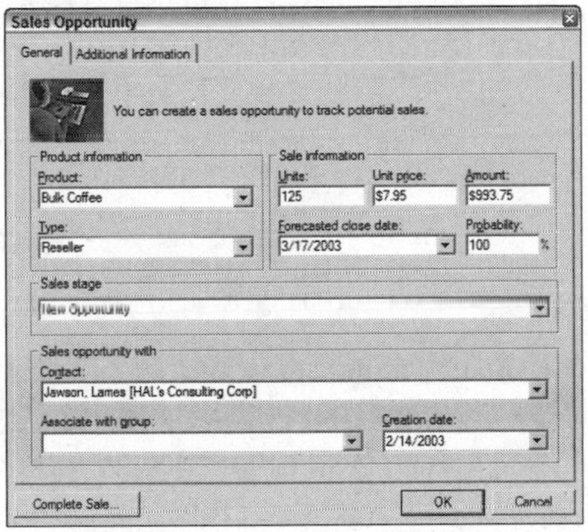

Figure 19-2:
The Sales
Opportunity
dialog box.

4. **In the Product Information area, enter the product name in the Product text box or choose it from the drop-down list.**

   If you or someone else in your organization has been using ACT! to track sales opportunities, you'll be able to select the product from the product drop-down list. New products are automatically added to the list as you enter them. If your product name doesn't appear, simply type it in. You can also import data here; see the sidebar where I discuss this further.

   Unfortunately, one of the limitations of ACT! is that you can enter only one product name in the Product text box. If you're in the business of selling only one product at a time, you're in luck. However, if you normally sell 100 widgets at the same time when you sell 101 gadgets, you'll either have to create two separate sales opportunities or combine your sale into one generic item.

   Lists improve your efficiency in creating sales opportunities and ensure consistency among users of the database.

5. **Select the type of sale or product from the Type drop-down list or type the information in the field.**

   The Type field can contain any information that is useful to you. You might use this field to identify the type of product (such as a model number, size, or color) or to indicate the type of sale (such as a discounted sale). When you enter a new type, it is automatically added to the list.

6. **In the Sales Information area, enter the following information in the appropriate text boxes:**

   • **Units:** Enter the forecasted number of units for this sale. If the sale involves a service rather than a product, you can leave this field blank.

   • **Unit Price:** Type the price of a single unit of the product or the total price for the service.

   • **Amount:** After you make entries in both Units and Unit Price, ACT! automatically calculates the total amount of the sales opportunity and enters it in this field.

   You can also type a total sale amount in this field, but remember that ACT! automatically calculates the value for a field that you leave blank.

I know that many of you will become frustrated with ACT!'s sales opportunities because of your inability to edit or add new fields. Do not, however, attempt to circumvent this limitation by using the sales information fields to house other types of information. First of all, you can only input *numbers* into the sales fields. Secondly, any numbers you enter into these fields will automatically calculate into the Amount field.

7. **Enter a forecasted close date or select a date from the date selector.**

   This date can be used in reports later to track your sales opportunities. Stay tuned to the end of this chapter for further help in creating sales reports.

8. **In the Probability field, enter the probability of closing the sale.**

   Type in a number between 1 and 100; you don't need to type the percent sign. The probability is a pure guesstimate on your part. You can leave this field blank or fill in your best estimate and change it later.

9. **Select the sales stage for this sales opportunity from the Sales Stage list.**

   ACT! comes with 11 predefined sales stages. When you create a sales opportunity in ACT!, you can assign one of these stages in the sales development cycle. You can also add, edit, or delete any of the sales stages. (Want to add sales stages? Check out the nearby sidebar, "Adding sales stages to sales opportunities," where I show you how to do it.)

10. **To associate this sales opportunity with a group, select the group from the Associate with Group list.**

    Any sales opportunities that are directly associated with a group can also be created in the Groups view.

11. **In the Creation Date field, enter the date for the creation of the sales opportunity.**

    ACT! automatically enters today's date in this field, but you can change it.

12. **If you'd like to add additional information about the sales opportunity, click the Additional Information tab.**

    As you can see in Figure 19-3, ACT! doesn't provide you with a whole lot of extra informational fields in the Additional Information area. However, it does provide you with an area to note the record manager's name as well as your competitor's name, if you know it. You'll also see a large Details area in which you can write in more detailed information about the opportunity.

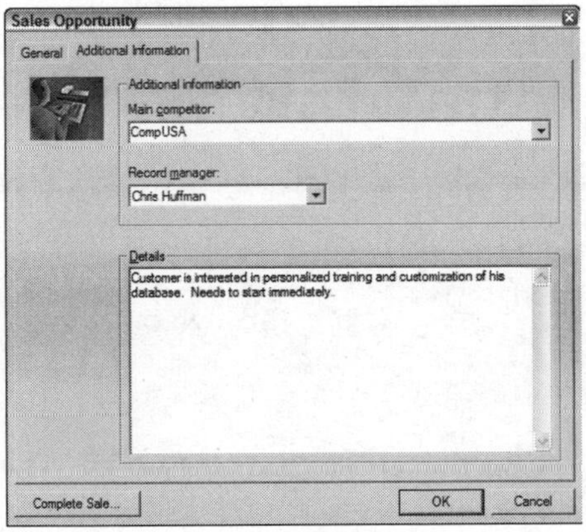

Figure 19-3:
Adding
additional
information
to a sales
opportunity.

If the information that you want to include with the sales opportunity is in a document, such as a word processing file, you can copy the text in the other application and paste it into the Details box in the Additional Information tab.

The information that you use to fill in the Sales Opportunity fields will later appear in any of the Sales Reports that you run. You can find out how to run your sales reports at the end of this chapter.

13. **Click OK.**

    All the information that you input as part of a sales opportunity will appear on the Sales/Opportunities tab for the associated contact.

Importing product data

If you're a new user of ACT!, you might have already developed a rather lengthy product list in another piece of software. For example, you might have created a price list using Word or Excel or created an inventory list in your accounting software. When you're creating sales opportunities, ACT! very considerately gives you the option of importing data into the Product, Type, or Main Competitor fields. (The Main Competitor field appears on the Additional Information tab of the Sales Opportunity dialog box; refer to Figures 19-2 and 19-3.) Just remember that the import files must be text files. To import data, follow these steps:

1. **In the Sales Opportunity dialog box, click in the Product, Type, or Main Competitor field.**

    A drop-down arrow appears in the field.

2. **Click this arrow and scroll down the list to select Edit List.**

3. **In the Edit List dialog box that appears, click Import.**

4. **In the Import dialog box that appears, designate the file to be imported by entering the filename of the text file or by clicking the Browse button to navigate to the file.**

5. **To add the imported items to items already in the drop-down list, select the Append Imported Items option.**

    If you turn off this option, the imported items will overwrite any existing items in the drop-down list.

6. **Click OK.**

At this point, you're essentially done with creating the sales opportunity. What you do after this point involves carrying through on various sales stages and then, finally, closing the sale.

Modifying the sales stage

As your sales opportunity progresses, you'll find it necessary to go back and modify the sales stage. Again, this information appears in your various reports, so updating your sales opportunities is important. This is a painless and short process:

1. **Find the contact for whom you're changing a sales opportunity.**

2. **On the Sales/Opportunities tab, double-click the Selection button (the little square to the left of the Sales Opportunity) to display the Sales Opportunity window.**

3. **Change the information in the Sales Stage field as necessary.**

   The purpose of ACT!'s sales opportunities is to allow you to track a potential sell from its inception to its final outcome. You'll probably find it useful to edit your sales opportunities as they progress through the various sales stages. This will allow you to view any of your sales opportunities to assess exactly where you stand.

4. **Click OK.**

Closing the sale

When you close a sale, you can record the outcome and the closing date. ACT! records a history in the contact's Notes/History tab and, if you associated the sales opportunity with a group, in the Notes/History tab for the group as well. The sales opportunity, now marked as Closed, remains on the Sales/Opportunities tab.

1. **Find the contact for whom you're recording the outcome of a sales opportunity.**

2. **On the Sales/Opportunities tab, select the sales opportunity that you want to complete.**

3. **Click the Complete Sale button.**

4. **In the Complete Sale dialog box that appears, indicate whether the sales was Closed/Won or Lost, as shown in Figure 19-4.**

5. **Click OK.**

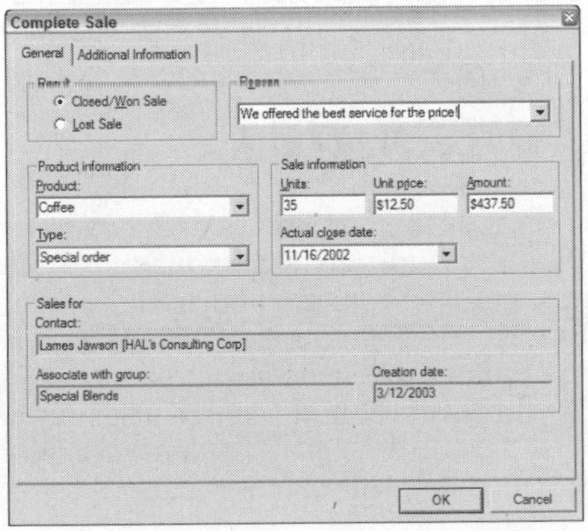

Figure 19-4: Closing a sale.

Adding sales stages to sales opportunities

With 11 pre-defined sales stages already available in ACT!, you might not need to add any of your own. However, you might find that the sales stages don't reflect the steps that you normally follow when selling your products and services. You might not give presentations or negotiate pricing, but you might have your own set of procedures that you follow. For example, you might routinely send out an introductory e-mail, follow it up with a fax, and then call the prospect directly. In case you do need to add sales stages, here's what you do:

1. **Click the Sales Stage drop-down list and choose Edit List.**

   You'll see a numbered list of your sales stages, as shown in the figure.

2. **In the Edit Sales Stages dialog box that appears, click the Add button.**

3. **In the Add Sales Stage dialog box that appears, type the Sales Stage name and an optional description, and then click OK.**

   The new stage will be added under the sales stage that was previously selected.

4. **To change the order of the sales stage, select the stage and then click either the Move Up or the Move Down button.**

5. **Click OK.**

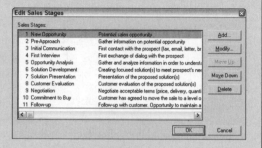

As you modify your sales stage list, keep these two important points in mind:

✔ When you add or delete a sales stage, the other sales stages are automatically renumbered.

✔ Changes to sales stages are not sent to your remote users as part of the synchronization process. Your remote users will need to duplicate the list of sales stages on their own individual databases.

Tracking Sales Opportunities

Okay, do you want the good news or the bad news? Well, I can't hear your response — and don't you feel silly responding to an inanimate object — so I'll give you the bad news first. The ACT! Sales Opportunities feature is not one of the better aspects of ACT!. The good news is that if you are one of the lucky readers whose business follows the same structure as the Sales Opportunities, ACT! rewards you with an abundance of sales reports and charts. Whether you need to report on a single customer or all your current opportunities, ACT! has a way of giving you the information.

You can monitor the sales opportunities that you have at each stage of the sales development cycle and display this information in a report or graphically in a sales funnel or sales graph.

Reporting on a single contact

The Sales/Opportunities tab provides you with the sales information on any given contact. The columns in the Sales/Opportunities tab work just like the columns in other ACT! areas, such as Notes/History and the Contact List. You can make them wider, change their order, sort by any column, and add new columns. You can filter the list so that it shows only the information that you need by using the Filter dialog box.

You can use the information contained in the Sales/Opportunities tab to create a quick-and-dirty report in the exact way that you would create a report based on the Contact List. ACT! prints the report in the same exact order as it appears onscreen — that is, what you see onscreen is what you'll see on paper. To print a report on a single sales opportunity, follow these steps:

1. **Go to the contact record of the person for whom you'd like to track sales opportunities.**

2. **On the Sales/Opportunity tab, modify any or all the fields that you find there.**

   There are 15 informational fields that you can use when you enter a new sales opportunity. All 15 of these fields can be portrayed as a column on the Sales/Opportunities tab. You can customize the tab in any one of the following ways:

   - **Add a column:** Right-click the Sales/Opportunities tab, choose Add Columns, select the column you'd like to add, and then click Add.

   - **Change the order of the columns:** Drag a column to your desired location.

   - **Remove a column:** Drag it straight up the screen until your cursor turns into a garbage can.

   - **Change the width of a column:** Place your cursor on the line to the right of the column heading, hold down your left mouse button, and drag it to the left or right, depending on how large or small you'd like to make the column.

3. **When you've made all your modifications, choose File⇨Print Sales/Opportunities.**

Reporting on all your sales opportunities

If you feel an overwhelming desire to chop down a few more trees in the rain forest, ACT! can help. ACT! comes equipped with a half-dozen sales reports to suit most of your sales reporting needs. If, for some reason, you don't find a report that suits you, at least you'll look busy when the boss walks by! ACT! sales reports provide details and summaries of sales opportunities, closed sales, and lost sales.

Throughout this book, I keep trying to knock one idea into your poor, over-worked brain: Perform a lookup before printing anything! Well, now you know one of the few times when you get to forget that little pearl of wisdom. ACT! offers you six sales report from which to choose, and five of them don't even let you specify whether to run the report for a Current Lookup or All Contacts. In fact, when you go to run the sales report, you'll notice that the General and Activities/Notes/Histories tabs that you've grown accustomed to using with other ACT! reports have been grayed out. You haven't been bad — the choices just aren't available.

In Chapter 24, I discuss the Crystal Clear Reports product that provides you with 15 additional sales reports giving you much more flexibility when report-ing on your sales.

The six ACT! sales reports are

- ✔ **Sales Totals by Status:** Lists all your sales opportunities subtotaled by Closed/Won and Lost sales.

- ✔ **Sales Adjusted for Probability:** Lists all your sales opportunities by con-tact, sorted by sales stage. I'm not sure what love — or probabilities — got to do with it; they don't affect the report.

- ✔ **Sales List:** Lists all information for your sales opportunities sorted by company.

- ✔ **Sales by Record Manager:** Lists information on your sales opportunities, subtotaled by the Record Manager.

- ✔ **Sales by Contact:** Lists information on sales opportunities subtotaled by contact. This is the only report that gives you the option of basing your report on the current lookup.

- ✔ **Sales Pipeline:** Lists information subtotaled by sales stage; this is a great accompaniment to the Sales Pipeline graphic.

Creating a sales opportunities graph

The sales graph can show your sales forecast or your closed sales for a month, a quarter, or any period of time you choose. Many sales organizations prefer to see their sales information in the form of a graph. As usual, ACT! is up to the task and can create one for you in the blink of an eye — or at least in the click of the mouse.

Here's all you need to do to see all your sales opportunities translated through the wonder of modern technology into a graph:

1. **Create a lookup of contacts to include in the graph.**

   Need a warm-up on performing lookups? Head to Chapter 6.

2. **Choose Reports⇨Sales Reports⇨Sales Graph.**

   The Graph Options dialog box appears, as shown in Figure 19-5.

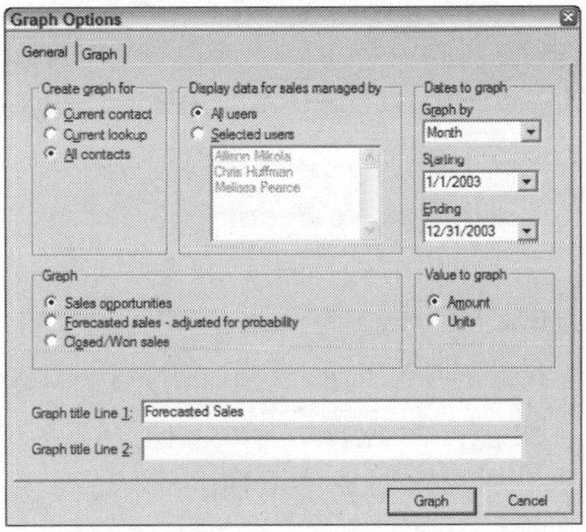

Figure 19-5:
The Graph
Options
dialog box.

3. **On the General tab, indicate the information that you want included in your graph:**

   a. In the Create Graph For area, select the Current Contact, Current Lookup, or All Contacts radio button.

   b. Choose the Record Managers of the contacts you're including in your graph from the Display Data for Sales Managed By window.

   c. Enter a title and subtitle for your graph in the Graph title areas.

   d. Fill in the date range (Dates to Graph) and increments (Value to Graph) to be used in your graph.

4. **On the Graph tab, make a few more graph-specific choices, including adding grid lines, changing the colors used in the graph, indicating whether you want a bar or line graph, or changing the scaling used in your graph (Figure 19-6).**

5. **Click the Graph button.**

   Voilà! Your graph appears before your eyes. Try not to look too surprised. If the boss walks by, you might want to make little grunting noises indicating how studiously you're working on your graph. You can see a sample graph in Figure 19-7.

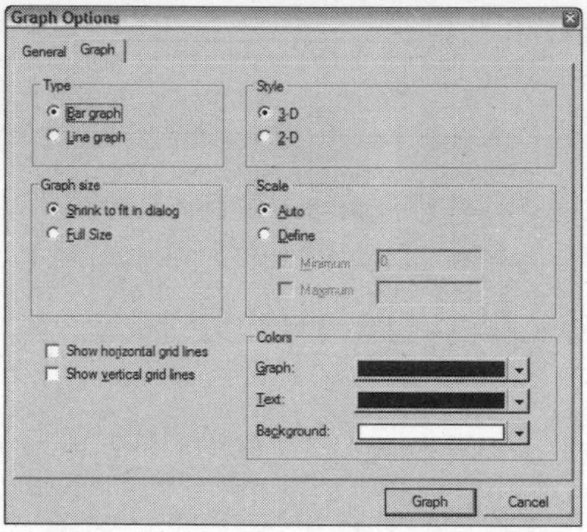

Figure 19-6:
More graph
options.

6. **In the Sales Forecast Graph window, you can**

- Click the Close button to exit the graph without printing or saving it.

- Click the Options button if you'd like to modify the graph.

- Click the Save Graph button to save it as a bitmap (.bmp) file to preserve your artwork for future generations.

- Click the Copy Graph button to save it to the Windows Clipboard in case you want to perform a little cosmetic surgery on it. After you've copied the graph to the Clipboard, you can paste it into your favorite graphics program and change any of its elements.

- Click the Print Graph button to do just that.

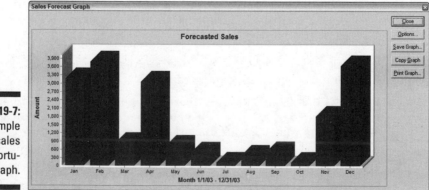

Figure 19-7:
A sample
sales
opportu-
nity graph.

Viewing the sales pipeline

A picture is worth a thousand words — or in this case, it might be worth thousands of dollars! Most large sales organizations are already familiar with the concept of a sales pipeline. The ACT! Pipeline graphic represents the number of sales opportunities at each stage of the sales development process. Each section of a sales pipeline represents one of your pre-determined sales stages. Sales opportunities that are marked as closed, or those that are missing a sales stage, are excluded.

1. **Perform a lookup to find the contacts that you want to include in the sales pipeline.**

   Although you don't have to assign a sales stage to a sales opportunity, only sales opportunities with assigned stages are included in the sales funnel.

2. **Choose Reports➪Sales Reports➪Sales Pipeline.**

   The Sales Pipeline Options dialog box opens, as shown in Figure 19-8. The sales stages that you assigned when creating your sales opportunities appear in the Assign Colors area. If you'd like to change a color, click the ellipsis button to the right of the color and select another color.

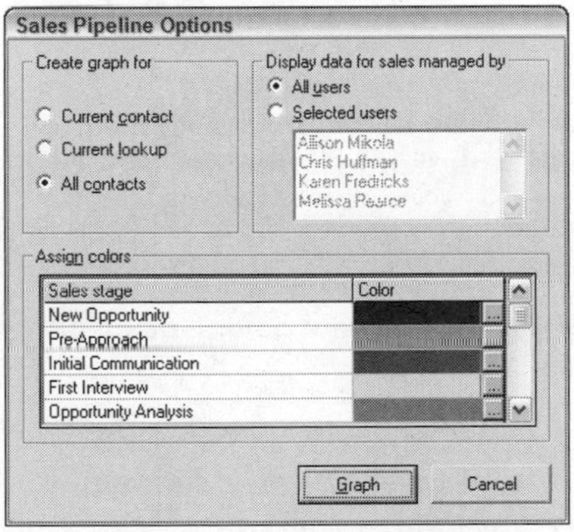

Figure 19-8:
The Sales
Pipeline
Options
dialog box.

3. **Select the Current Contact, Current Lookup, or All Contacts radio button in the Create Graph For area of the Sales Pipeline Options window.**

4. **In the Display Data for Contacts Managed By box, select the All Users or Selected Users radio button.**

5. **Click the Graph button.**

You will now be the proud owner of a beautiful sales pipeline (similar to what's shown in Figure 19-9), guaranteed to impress the heck out of your boss and other members of your sales team.

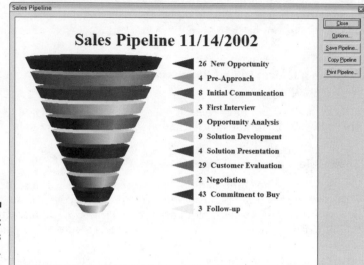

Figure 19-9:
A sales
pipeline.

6. **In the Sales Pipeline window, you have options similar to those available in the Sales Forecast Graph window (see the preceding section).**

The size of each section is fixed and does not scale based on the number of sales opportunities at each stage:

- Click the Close button to exit without saving or printing the pipeline.

- Click the Options button if you'd like to modify the pipeline.

- Click the Save Pipeline button to save it as a bitmap (`.bmp`) file to preserve your artwork for future generations.

- Click the Copy Pipeline button to save it to the Windows Clipboard and later paste it into a graphics program for modifications.

- Click the Print Pipeline button. It doesn't get any more self explanatory than this!

Chapter 20

Grouping Your Contacts

*I*n this chapter, I focus on a very commonly overlooked ACT! feature: the ACT! Group. What exactly is a *group*? Generally speaking, a group is a collection of something. In ACT!, a *group* is a collection of *contacts*. More specifically, a group is a semi-permanent lookup whose contact records can be assigned to the group by any criteria that you want.

The contact record helps you to keep track of all activities as they relate to an individual; the group allows you to track activities as they relate to an entire group of contacts. So when used correctly, ACT! groups provide you with the potential to increase the overall power and efficiency of the ACT! program.

Throughout this chapter, after explaining all the ins and outs of groups, I show you how to create a group. I then move to showing you how to put groups to work so that you can enjoy all the benefits that groups have to offer. After reading this chapter, you'll become a real group pro — knowing when to use them (and when not to) and how to use them to their greatest potential.

A Few Good Reasons to Create a Group

You can't just create groups willy-nilly without putting any thought into them. If you do that, you're liable to end up with bad groups, which consume your time without offering any real benefits. (See the nearby sidebar "Don't create bad groups!" to see what I mean.) So what exactly makes a *good* group, you ask? Here are a few examples of when groups can really make life easy for you:

✔ **Tracking members of a large company or account:** If you work with very large organizations, you might end up speaking to numerous members of the same company in order to get your job done. Those contacts may be located in separate locations. Without using groups, you might forget which particular person you discussed vital details with and be forced to search through all your contacts looking for the information. Using groups enables you to see all the related notes in one place.

✔ **Managing large projects:** Groups are particularly well suited for those who work on large projects. For example, if you're building a home, you'll be involved with any number of people from building inspectors and city officials to subcontractors, your own personnel, and the new homeowner. Assigning all these contacts to a group makes it easy for you to zero in on only those contacts involved in the project.

✔ **Improving on sales opportunities:** In Chapter 19, I show you everything there is to know about sales opportunities. One thing that the ACT! Sales Opportunities feature does not provide you with, unfortunately, is the level of detail that you need to track your potential sales. If your business generally involves one sale per contact, you can create user fields (see Chapter 14) to create your own sales fields. However, if you sell to the same clients over and over again, the information about your previous sale is replaced with newer information when you change the content in the sales fields you created. By using groups, you're able to track numerous sales back to the same contact.

✔ **Tracking real estate listings:** If you're a real estate agent or broker, setting up a group for each listing allows you to track all clients that see a particular property and to list all properties that you show to a particular client.

✔ **Organizing your classes and seminars:** If you teach classes and seminars, you can set up groups to track all attendees. Then, when the time comes, you can print out class lists to ensure that you contact all class members.

✔ **Determining which contacts to synchronize:** Perhaps you've set up a synchronization to send and receive contact updates between the home office and remote users, or perhaps you synchronize to a handheld device such as a Palm Pilot. You might have thousands of contacts in your ACT! database but want only a portion of them to reside in your handheld. Setting up a group provides you with the option of just exchanging data for a specific group.

✔ **Saving a lookup:** The preceding examples all represent fairly creative uses of the ACT! Groups feature. But what if you aren't a builder or a real estate agent, and you don't run seminars or synchronize your contacts? Another simple but popular reason to use the Groups feature is that a group is actually a saved lookup that allows you to keep targeting the same bevy of contacts. You probably wouldn't want to create a group for everyone in your database from the state of Florida; you could just as easily accomplish that by creating a simple lookup. However, you might want to create a group for all your *customers* in Florida to save yourself from running a more complicated lookup.

Don't create bad groups!

Here's an example of a *bad* group: I once worked with an ACT! user who had exactly 50 groups — one for each state. He had then subdivided each group into subgroups representing each Zip code within the state. This user had overlooked the obvious — his database already contained fields for both state and Zip code. His groups provided him with no more information than he already had — and after he had put all that time and effort into creating them.

What All Groups Have in Common

In the preceding section, I provide examples of using groups that surely give you an idea of how you can use groups for a wide range of tasks. Despite the flexibility of groups, however, all groups share a few common elements:

✔ **Volatility:** In general, groups and the contacts within them do not have to be permanent. A contractor, for example, will replace subcontractors he works with if they do a poor job. And, after that contractor completes a house, he might no longer need to use the group that he created for the project and may choose to delete it. Also, removing a contact from a group doesn't in turn remove the contact from the database.

✔ **No limit to the number of groups:** You're allowed to create as many groups as you want; your only limitation is self imposed. Working with thousands of groups, however, is probably rather cumbersome.

✔ **No limit to the number of contacts that belong to a group:** However, if your database appears as though it has taken a tranquilizer every time you try to go to the Group view, look at the number of contacts in the first of your groups. If the number is quite large, I recommend creating a fake group that appears alphabetically at the top of your group list. This little trick should improve the performance dramatically.

✔ **No limit to the number of groups a contact can belong to:** Depending on the type of groups that you set up, you might find that a contact needs to belong to more than one group. For example, if you use groups to help with project management, you might need to include the same subcontractor in several groups.

✔ **Relational cross-referencing:** By creating a group, you can easily move between the group as a whole and the individual members within the group. From the Group view, you can see a list of all the contacts that belong to that group; from the Contacts view, you can see all the groups that a contact belongs to.

Creating a Group

Like most of the other ACT! commands, creating groups is as easy as pie. Just remember that planning is always the first step: If you work in a shared database, all users should agree on how groups will be used *before* creating groups and adding contact records to them.

A group is not meant to be a replacement for the ID/Status field (or any other existing field for that matter; see the sidebar "Don't create bad groups!"). The ID/Status field serves to categorize each contact. For example, you might categorize each contact as a vendor, customer, or prospect using the ID/Status field. Limit your groups to help you accomplish something that *can't* be done through the use of fields.

To create a group, simply follow these steps:

1. **Display the Groups window by clicking the Groups icon in the View bar.**

   The Groups window should look vaguely familiar — in fact, it's nearly identical to the Contacts view window. Just like the Contacts view, the Groups view features tabs along the bottom of the screen. And, just like the Contacts view, the Groups view allows you to choose the layout of your choice. As shown in Figure 20-1, the only difference between the Groups and the Contacts views is the list of Groups running down the left side. If you're creating your very first group, an Untitled group appears.

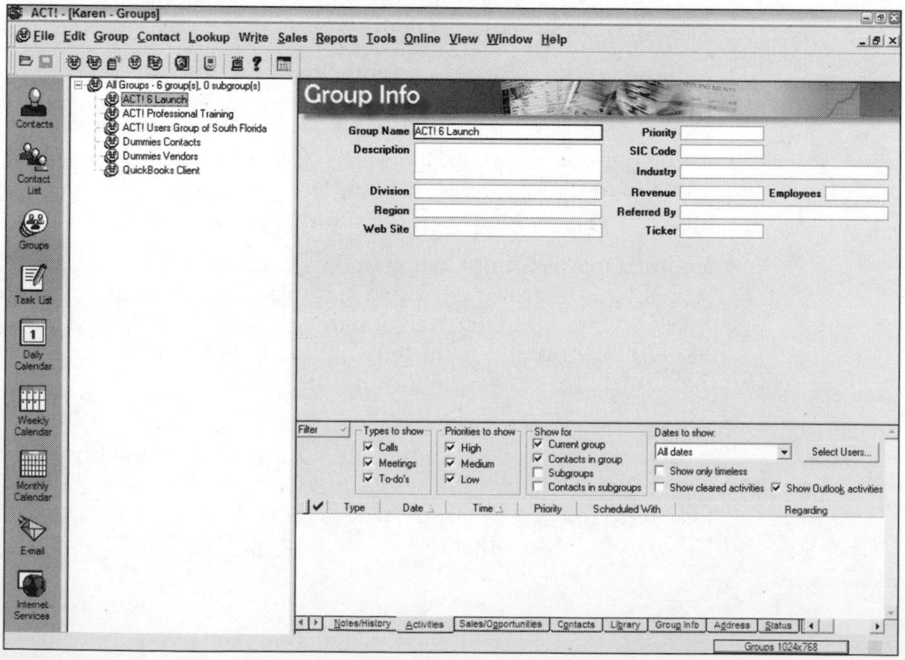

Figure 20-1: The Groups view.

2. **Choose Group⇨New Group.**

   If you prefer, you can right-click the list of Groups and choose New Group. Or, feel free to click the New Group icon on the toolbar (the third icon on the left). We aim to please!

   A new Group appears with the name Untitled.

3. **In the Group Name field, enter a name for the new group.**

   When you move to another field, the group list is automatically updated and your group is saved.

4. **(Optional) Create a subgroup by selecting the primary group, choosing Group⇨New Subgroup, and then filling in the name of the subgroup.**

   You can have as many subgroups per group as you'd like. However, you can have only one level of subgroups; in other words, you aren't able to further divide your subgroups into sub-subgroups. But after you create a group, you can go back to the scene of the crime and add a subgroup at any time.

5. **Add some contact records to your group.**

   Generally, you have two ways of adding contact records to your groups:

   Create a Lookup of selected contacts and dump them en masse into a group: Typically, you've created a group for a purpose, so you probably know what contacts you'll add to that group. Working on that assumption, here's how you go about adding those contacts to a group:

   a. Create a lookup of the contacts that you're adding to your group.

      Need a little help in creating a lookup? Skip back to Chapter 6.

   b. Click the Group icon on the View bar.

   c. Choose Group⇨Group Membership⇨Add/Remove Contacts.

      The Add/Remove Contacts dialog box appears (Figure 20-2).

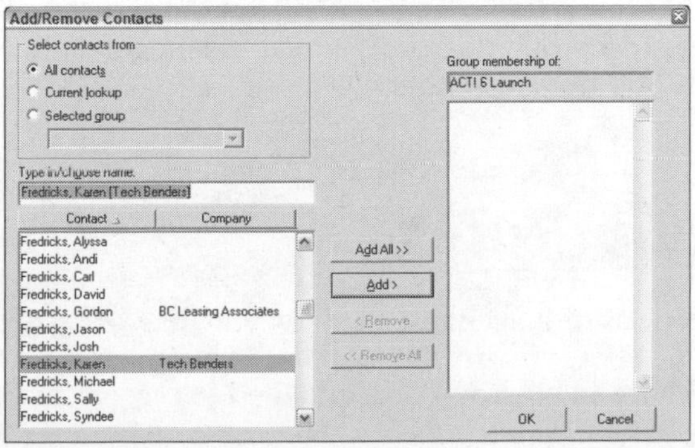

Figure 20-2:
The Add/
Remove
Contacts
dialog box.

d. Select the Current Lookup radio button if you want to add all the contacts in your current lookup to the Group.

e. Click the Add All button and then click OK.

Add contacts to your group one at a time while you create the contact: You often might need to add a contact to a group as you create that contact. The procedure for this is as follows:

a. Create a new contact (see Chapter 4).

b. Click the Groups tab, conveniently located at the bottom of the Contacts view.

c. Right-click anywhere on the Groups tab and then choose Group Membership.

A list of your current groups appears (Figure 20-3).

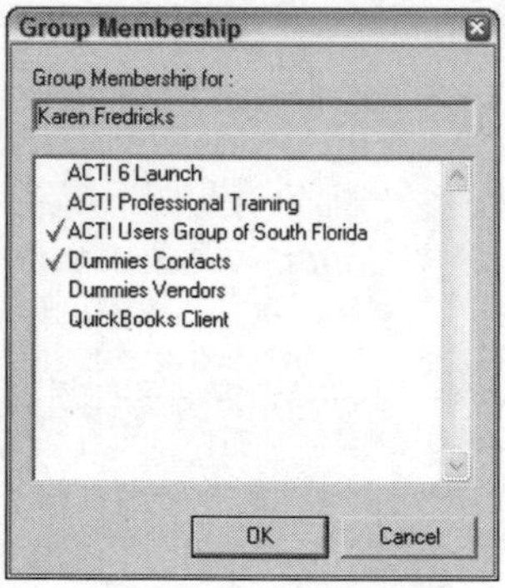

Figure 20-3:
Adding a single contact to a group.

> **Group Membership**
>
> Group Membership for :
>
> Karen Fredricks
>
> ACT! 6 Launch
> ACT! Professional Training
> √ ACT! Users Group of South Florida
> √ Dummies Contacts
> Dummies Vendors
> QuickBooks Client
>
> OK   Cancel

d. Select all the groups in which you want to include the current contact.

This is the same procedure you'd follow to disassociate a contact from a group — except that you'd clear the check mark!

Adding new contacts to a group does not *remove* existing members of the group — it just adds additional members.

Setting Up Group Rules

In the preceding sections of this chapter, I show you how using groups in ACT! is a good thing. I show you how to add and remove contacts to groups. By now, you're probably an ol' group pro, qualified to receive an Official ACT!

Groupee certificate. But, like the best-laid plans of mice and keyboards, there is one small hitch to your otherwise perfect world. What happens if you forget to add a contact to a group?

For some of you, forgetting to add a contact to a group isn't a life-threatening event; someone might not receive a newsletter or receive a holiday card. Not a huge deal. In other circumstances, however, it might be absolutely crucial that all appropriate contacts be added to the proper group. For example, what if you send a notification to all members of a group about an important meeting, but the CEO isn't included in the group?

Step away from the aspirin — this problem is easily licked with the simple creation of a *group rule*. Contrary to popular belief, a group rule has nothing to do with your political persuasion. A group rule is ACT!'s way of automatically adding contacts to a group based on information in specific fields. Your group rules can be as simple as adding all contacts created by Joe Blow to the Joe Blow Group, or they can be based on much more complex criteria, such as "All customers in the Southwest region managed by Joe, Sue, or Steve belong in the Widgets Group."

You can create a group rule based on a particular field value or on a saved query. For example, you might set up a group rule to find all the *prospects* in *New York* for whom *Mike* is the sales rep.

A *query* is an advanced form of a lookup, which you can save for reuse. Chapter 6 talks about creating and saving advanced queries through the use of Boolean logic. Unless you have a little bit of programming skills in your bag of tricks, you'll probably do best by sticking to the simpler field value rules.

To set up a group membership rule:

1. **Click the Groups icon on the View bar.**

2. **Select the group to which you want to add a membership rule and then choose Group⇨Group Membership⇨Define Rules.**

   The opening screen of the Group Membership Rules Wizard opens, as shown in Figure 20-4.

3. **Select the Field Values radio button and then click Next.**

   The wizard's Rule 1 screen appears, as shown in Figure 20-5.

4. **Select the contact field that you want ACT! to check when following the rule.**

   You'll notice that all the fields that you have added to your database are included in The Contact Field drop-down list. Select the field that will determine the membership into your group.

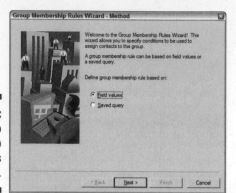

Figure 20-4:
The Group
Membership
Rules
Wizard.

5. **Click the Add Value button.**

   ACT! opens the list of drop-down choices based on the field you selected. If the field doesn't contain the information that you want in the drop-down list, type in the value that you want.

Figure 20-5:
Group
Membership
Rules
Wizard -
Rule 1.

6. **Click OK.**

   The value is added.

7. **Repeat the process until all values are selected and then click Next.**

8. **(Optional) Add a second condition to your group membership rule.**

   For example, if you want the contact record to be in one of a series of states and have an *ID/Status* of *customer*, you can add a second condition.

   If you add a second condition, the contact must match both conditions, not one or the other. For example, if you specified values for both the city and ID/Status fields, all members of the group would reside in the same city and have identical ID/Statuses.

9. **Click Next.**

The Group Membership Wizard Finish page appears.

10. **Click Finish.**

ACT! records the new rule and then prompts you with a dialog box asking whether you want to run the new rule.

11. **If you have more rules to add, click No; otherwise, run the new rule to make sure that your group now contains all the correct contact records.**

If a contact record was already a member of the group, it is not added again.

If you have a large database and a complex rule, you might want to run your membership rule before going out to buy a double latte. It could take a while!

For those of you having trouble with your short-term memory, ACT! is ready to jump in and help you remember to run a group rule. I cover setting reminders in Chapter 3. How often you run the group membership rules is directly proportional to how often you add new contacts to your database. You can run your group rules once a day if you'd like.

You can customize groups in the same exact way that you can customize the Contact screen. You can add new fields, change the layout, and add tabs. While in the Groups view, you can even do a special group lookup to search for a group based on the information in any one of the group fields that you created. For a crash course in adding new fields, scurry back to Chapter 14. For a refresher course in customizing layouts, scamper over to Chapter 15.

Working with Groups

Now that you've created a group and stuck a few unsuspecting contacts into it, things really get exciting. I love to use the phrase "unleash the power of ACT!" — I have this vision of Mr. Clean roaring out of my monitor. Okay, maybe I need to get a life, but I feel that by correctly using groups, you can really get a lot of bang for your buck with the ACT! program. This is how you can fool ACT! into believing it's a relational database. Try not to let too many people in on the secret — it might just raise the price of the software.

Think of your groups as a program within a program. You have nearly the same functionality that you do with the contact portion of ACT! — with one big difference: The activities you create while in the Groups view affect the entire group. After you've set up a group, you can add group notes, activities, and sales opportunities for the *group* in exactly the same way you set them up for a *contact*. This is a great timesaver because information that you input belongs to the group and doesn't have to be duplicated on the contact level.

Viewing the contacts in a group

I mention earlier that using groups is a quick way to save a lookup. By creating a group, you can create a lookup of those contacts faster than a speeding bullet. In fact, you can create the lookup with two measly clicks. Here's all you have to do:

1. **Click the Contacts icon in the View bar.**

   In the lower-right corner is a <No Group> button, indicating that you haven't yet decided on the group you'd like to work with.

2. **Click the <No Group> button.**

   You'll now see a lovely list of all your groups (Figure 20-6).

Figure 20-6:
A listing of groups.

| <No Group> |
| ACT! 6 Launch |
| ACT! Professional Training |
| ACT! Users Group of South Flori |
| Dummies Contacts |
| Dummies Vendors |
| QuickBooks Client |

<No Group>

3. **Select the group of your choice.**

   ACT! filters out all other contacts except the ones in the group that you select. If you look at the record counter, you'll notice that your number of contacts has dropped.

4. **When you're finished working with the group, either choose Lookup⇨All Contacts or click the Group button (bottom-right corner of the Contacts view) and then choose <No Group>.**

   You'll now be looking at your entire database once again.

Using groups to schedule activities

One of the most powerful aspects of ACT! is its ability to associate a *contact* with an *activity*. (See Chapter 8 to read more about activities in ACT!.) Many scheduling programs allow you to design beautiful calendars; the problem is that these calendars aren't tied in to a particular contact record. For example, if you schedule an appointment to visit Jane Smith and forget the date of the appointment, your only recourse is to flip through your calendar until you find the appointment. After you met with Jane, you'd have no history of the appointment unless you once again searched through your previous appointments.

To take this analogy one step further, suppose that you chair a special committee for your local Chamber of Commerce and need to schedule a meeting. Scheduling the same appointment with each of the twenty-odd participants would be very time consuming. Trying to fit each committee member's name on your calendar isn't very practical either. By scheduling the meeting with the group, however, you achieve your goal without the hassle.

Here's how it works:

1. **Create a lookup by clicking the <No Group> button at the bottom-right corner of the Contacts view.**

2. **Select the group with which you'd like to schedule a meeting and then create a new meeting, call, or to-do (as outlined in Chapter 8).**

   The Schedule Activity dialog box pops open (Figure 20-7). The name of the group that you select magically appears in the Associate with Group field.

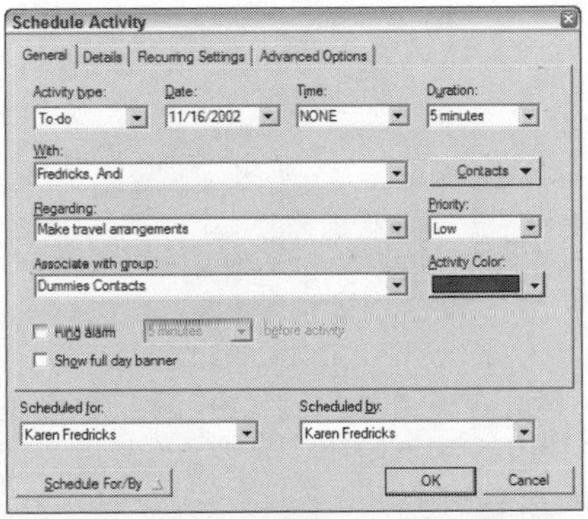

Figure 20-7. Scheduling a group activity.

3. **Click the Contacts button to the right of the With field and then select My Record.**

   Theoretically, you could schedule this appointment with each and every member of your group. Associating the appointment with yourself alleviates the need to select multiple contacts, keeping things simple. Besides, you've already associated the appointment with your group.

4. **Flip over to the Groups view by clicking the Groups icon on your View bar.**

5. **On the Activities tab, remove all check marks in the Show For area except for the check mark next to Current Group.**

You probably have several contacts in your group, and chances are that you've probably scheduled activities with many of these contacts that have nothing whatsoever to do with the current group. As I explain further in Chapters 7 and 8, never underestimate the power of a filter! Your filters determine the information that you actually see in any ACT! list. Notice that the only check mark that appears in the Show For area on the Activities tab in Figure 20-8 is next to Current Group.

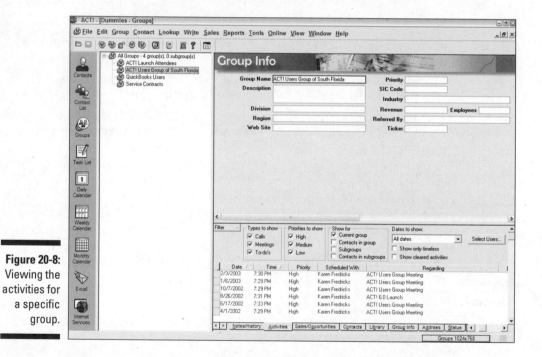

Figure 20-8:
Viewing the
activities for
a specific
group.

That one lonely check mark accomplished a very important task: It filtered out all those pesky activities that had nothing to do with the group as a whole. When you click the Contacts in Group filter, you're treated to a display of *every single activity* that you ever created for *every member* of your group.

Using notes with groups

There are three different ways that you can create a note and assign it to a specific group. I describe each of these ways in the following subsections.

Entering a note directly from the Groups view

This is by far the easiest way to enter a Group note. All you need to do is:

1. **Click the Groups icon on the View bar.**

2. **Select the name of the group for which you want to enter a note.**

3. **On the Notes/History tab, click Insert Note.**

Creating a group lookup and then creating the note in the Contacts view

If you've already created a group lookup, any notes that you enter into any contact record are automatically considered part of the current group. Here's all you need to do:

1. **Create a group lookup by clicking the <No Group> button (bottom-right of the Contacts view).**

2. **Enter a note as usual. (See Chapter 7 for more on creating notes.)**

Entering a note from the Contacts view and designating it as belonging to the group

The third method of adding a group note is more complicated than the first two methods. So why, you might be wondering, am I including this in a *For Dummies* book? The reason is that you might find yourself in a situation where you need to designate a note as belonging to a group *after* the note was created. Although complex, this is certainly possible; here's how you do it:

1. **From the Contacts view, go to the contact record of the member of the Group for whom you want to create a new — or edit an existing — note.**

2. **On the Notes/History tab, right-click the Notes Column headings.**

   You're treated to a little menu of choices, as shown in Figure 20-9.

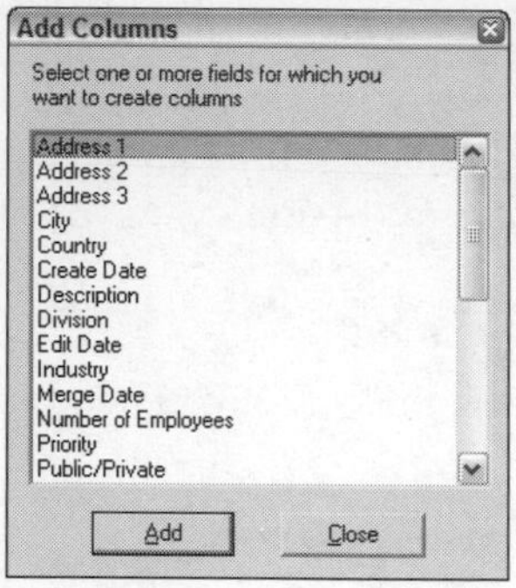

Add Columns

Select one or more fields for which you
want to create columns

Address 1
Address 2
Address 3
City
Country
Create Date
Description
Division
Edit Date
Industry
Merge Date
Number of Employees
Priority
Public/Private

[Add] [Close]

Figure 20-9:
Adding
columns
to the
Group tab.

If the Add button doesn't appear, you probably goofed! Try right-clicking again. Remember, your right hand is the opposite of the left hand. You also need to watch your aim. You're aiming for the Notes/History column headings, not the target out in the backyard.

3. **Click Add.**

4. **Click-and-drag Group to where you'd like it to appear on the Notes/History tab.**

5. **Resize the columns if necessary.**

Chapter 7 is where I provide you with all the details of resizing your Notes/History columns.

6. **To edit an existing note, give it a click.**

7. **Click in the Group column of the note.**

You'll see a drop-down of all your groups.

8. **Click the appropriate Group name.**

After you create a note, you can view it just like an activity. It's all in the filters:

- If you want to see *all* the notes created for *all* the members of your Group, just click the Contacts in Group filter.

- If you want to view only those notes and histories that you have specifically associated with a group, click only the Current Group filter. These choices are shown in Figure 20-10.

When you clear the Group activity from your calendar, a notation will be entered into the Groups Notes/History tab in the same way that a history is recorded for all your other activities.

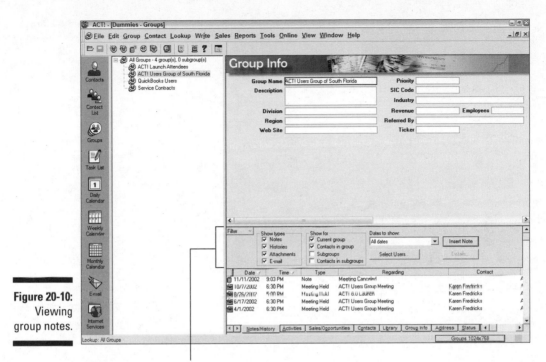

Figure 20-10:
Viewing
group notes.

Use filters to control what you see on-screen.

Chapter 21

I'm Going to the Library Tab

*T*he Library tab is one of the cool new features in ACT! 6. You'll find the Library tab button at the bottom of the Contacts view, nestled between the Groups tab and the first of your own user-defined tabs. The Library tab allows you to add documents created in other programs right to ACT! and then review and/or edit them without ever having to leave ACT!. If you use Excel, you can even import contact information from ACT! directly to Excel.

Exploring the Library Tab

You have always been able to attach a file to a note in previous ACT! versions, and that ability still exists in ACT! 6. What makes the Library tab special is the ability to actually edit the document right from ACT! — without having to open another program. If you want to review a Microsoft Word document, for instance, you can do so from within ACT! without having to open the Word program.

Before you get too excited about this new feature, you do need to know that only the following files can be included on the Library tab:

- ✔ Microsoft Word documents
- ✔ Microsoft Excel spreadsheets
- ✔ Microsoft PowerPoint presentations
- ✔ Microsoft MapPoint documents

✔ Adobe Acrobat documents

✔ Bitmap and JPEG images

You need to have the appropriate program installed on your computer. The documents will still be created using the other program. However, after you place a document on the Library tab, you can open the file using either ACT! or the original program. When you save the document, the file location remains the same; the file location is also recorded in the contact's Notes/History tab. You can edit the file using ACT! or the original program.

The overall procedure for using the Library tab is as follows:

1. **Create a document in one of the programs listed previously.**

2. **Add the document to the Document list.**

3. **Open the document in view or edit mode.**

4. **Close and save the document.**

If you look and look and don't see the Library tab residing happily to the right of the Groups tab, you have to tell ACT! that you want to use the Library tab. To see the Library tab, follow these steps:

1. **Choose Edit⇨Preferences in the Contacts view.**

2. **On the General tab, click Enable Library Tab.**

   A check mark indicates that the feature is enabled.

Adding Documents to the Library Tab

The Library tab isn't where you create new documents but rather where you can add existing ones to ACT!. The Library tab comes fully equipped with its own set of icons to help you to work with your documents.

Here's how you go about adding documents to the Library tab:

1. **Select the contact record for which you want to add a document.**

   If you'd like the same document to appear for all your contact records, you can be on any contact record.

2. **On the Library tab, click the Add Document tool on the Library toolbar.**

3. **Indicate the type of file that you want to add in the Files of Type text box (Figure 21-1).**

   Your choices are limited to the programs that I list previously. ACT! identifies these documents by extension. If you named an Excel file with something other than the usual .xls extension, ACT! won't recognize it as an Excel spreadsheet. So be sure to use the correct extension.

Figure 21-1: Choosing a document to add to the Library tab.

4. **Browse to the document of your choice and then click Open.**

   The document name appears in the document list.

5. **If you want this document to be displayed when moving to another contact record, select the Display for All Contacts option.**

Editing Documents in the Library Tab

If, after adding one or more documents to the Library tab, you decide to go back and make changes to them, you can easily do so either by using ACT! or the original program. Using the Library tab, however, might be slightly more advantageous:

✔ If you're already in ACT!, you don't have to open the other program.

✔ If you need to review a document because you're talking to a contact or reviewing a contact's information, opening a document in ACT! provides one-stop shopping.

✔ ACT! gives you a shortcut to the path of a document so that you can pull up the document quickly and easily without having to remember the path to the document.

You can't view a document in ACT! if the original program is open. For example, if you want to view an Excel spreadsheet, be sure to close Microsoft Excel, even if you're working on a different spreadsheet. If you try to open a document with the other program running, ACT! gives you an unfriendly warning (Figure 21-2) and won't let you proceed until the other program is closed.

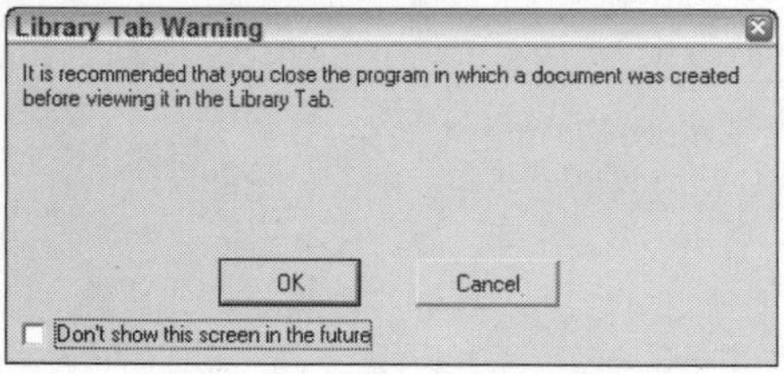

Figure 21-2:
Close other programs before editing a document.

> **Library Tab Warning**
>
> It is recommended that you close the program in which a document was created before viewing it in the Library Tab.
>
> [OK]   [Cancel]
>
> ☐ Don't show this screen in the future

To edit a document using ACT!'s Library tab:

1. **Close the program in which the document was created.**

2. **Click the Library tab from the Contacts view.**

   The Library tab comes equipped with its very own icon bar sporting the icons that you'll use when working with documents in the Library tab.

3. **Select a document from the document list.**

   If you've only attached one document, that document appears in the document list; otherwise, you'll need to choose from the drop-down list. Figure 21-3 shows an example of the document list.

4. **Click the View Document icon, which is located to the immediate right of the document list.**

   ACT! will whirl and hiss for a moment before displaying the first page of your document in read-only mode. If you prefer, select the Auto View check box on the Library tab icon bar to specify that documents will always load automatically in the View Mode.

5. **Click the Edit Document tool (to the right of the View Document icon).**

The document opens in edit mode and holy cow! Something magical has happened: The toolbars and menus from the creator program are displayed above the Library tab toolbar. You have nearly all of the comforts of the original program, as shown in Figure 21-4.

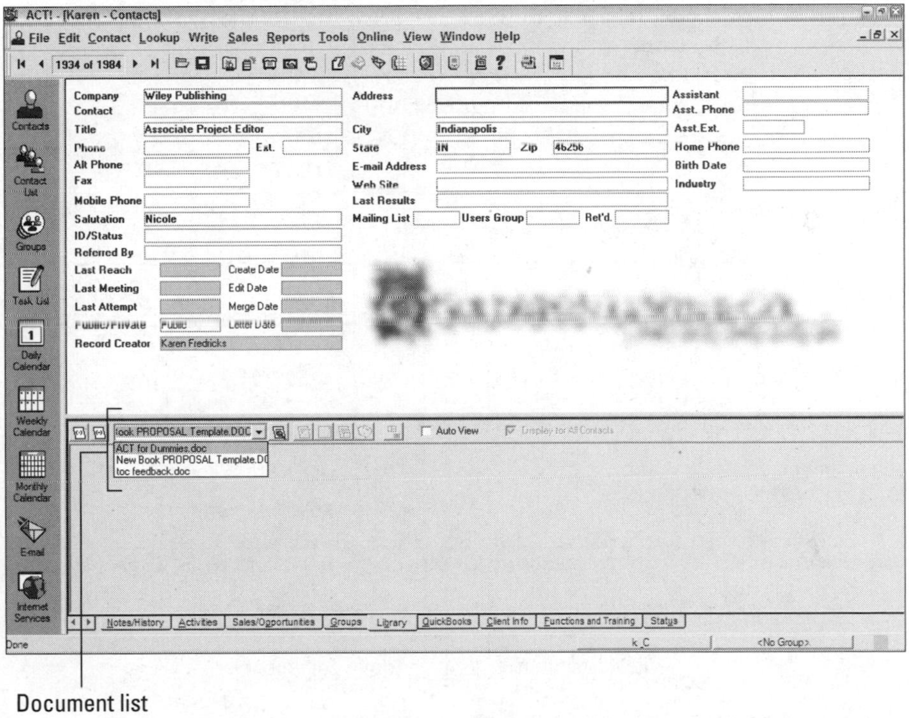

Figure 21-3:
Choosing the document to edit in ACT!'s Library tab.

Document list

If you'd like to increase the space devoted to the document, simply drag the separator bar that divides your basic contact information from the tab information.

6. **Edit the document by typing text or use the tools from the document's toolbar.**

7. **When finished editing, click the Save tool (on the Library toolbar).**

The document is saved, and the file location is recorded in the contact's Notes/History tab.

Remove
document

Current
document

Edit
document

Print
document

Word toolbars

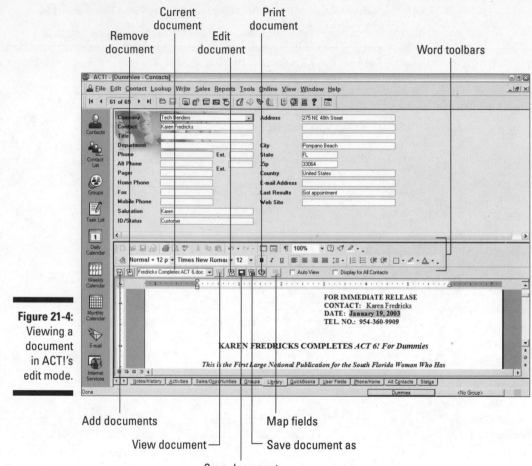

Figure 21-4:
Viewing a
document
in ACT!'s
edit mode.

Add documents

View document

Save document

Map fields

Save document as

Merging ACT! and Excel Fields

When you add an Excel spreadsheet to the Library tab, you have the option of merging ACT! fields into the spreadsheet's cells. ACT! refers to this as *field mapping*, which is the ability to merge a value or piece of information from a specific ACT! field into a corresponding cell in your Excel spreadsheet. You do this by creating a spreadsheet like you would create a template for your mail merge documents (Chapter 12) and then updating the spreadsheet with your ACT! information.

If you're currently using Excel to create estimates or other contact-driven spreadsheets, this is a great feature. You can merge ACT! contact information, such as company, name, and address, directly into your estimating spreadsheet. You can also choose to automatically update cells in your spreadsheet when you update a value in the corresponding field in ACT!.

To map ACT! fields to Excel spreadsheet fields, here's what you need to do:

1. **Create the Excel document.**

   While you design the spreadsheet template, keep the following two things in mind:

   • You can't incorporate information from ACT! into a blank cell.

   Your Excel spreadsheet can be as complex or simple as you need, but the cells to which you're mapping must contain some data, such as a space or other character, in order to map to it. In Figure 21-5, I created a sample spreadsheet. I placed either the name of a field or an X in the fields that will eventually contain ACT! data.

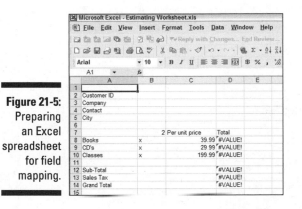

Figure 21-5:
Preparing
an Excel
spreadsheet
for field
mapping.

   • You can't incorporate information from ACT! into the first row of a spreadsheet.

2. **On the Library tab toolbar, click the Add Document icon to add the Excel spreadsheet to the Library tab.**

3. **Click the Edit Document icon to open the spreadsheet in edit mode.**

4. **Click the Map Fields icon on the Library tab toolbar.**

   You're rewarded with the ACT/Excel Field Mapping dialog box that's shown in Figure 21-6. The left side of the screen shows the fields from your ACT! database; the right side shows your Excel fields.

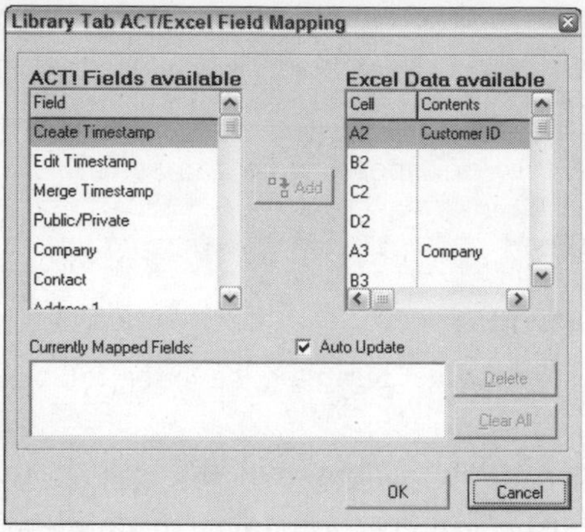

Library Tab ACT/Excel Field Mapping

ACT! Fields available

Field
Create Timestamp
Edit Timestamp
Merge Timestamp
Public/Private
Company
Contact
Address 1

Add

Excel Data available

Cell	Contents
A2	Customer ID
B2	
C2	
D2	
A3	Company
B3	

Currently Mapped Fields: ☑ Auto Update

Delete

Clear All

OK   Cancel

Figure 21-6:
The ACT/
Excel Field
Mapping
dialog box.

5. **Select a field from the ACT! Fields Available list, and then select the corresponding Excel cell to map it; then click Add to map fields.**

6. **Continue mapping fields as necessary.**

   While you map the ACT! fields to the Excel cells, you'll see a list of the mapped fields (Figure 21-7).

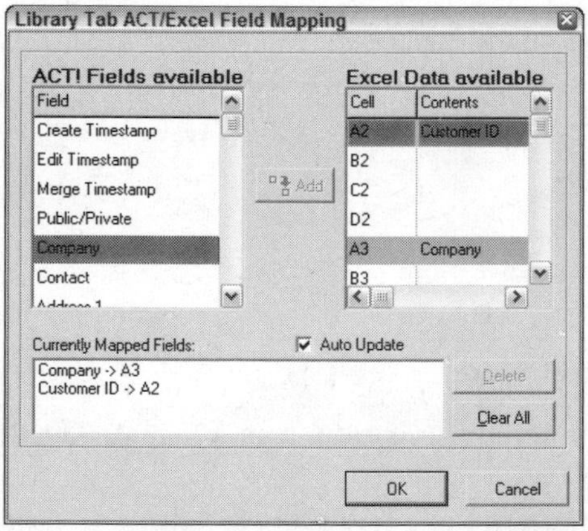

Library Tab ACT/Excel Field Mapping

ACT! Fields available

Field
Create Timestamp
Edit Timestamp
Merge Timestamp
Public/Private
Company
Contact
Address 1

Add

Excel Data available

Cell	Contents
A2	Customer ID
B2	
C2	
D2	
A3	Company
B3	

Currently Mapped Fields: ☑ Auto Update

Company -> A3
Customer ID -> A2

Delete

Clear All

OK   Cancel

Figure 21-7:
The cur-
rently
mapped
ACT! and
Excel fields.

If you make a mistake and need to delete a field's mapping, select a field name from the Currently Mapped Fields list and then click the Delete button. You can also click the Clear All button if you need to remove all the field mappings and start over again.

7. **(Optional) Select the Auto Update check box to automatically update a cell when you change data in an ACT! field and then click OK.**

8. **Save your document.**

   - Click the Save Document icon if you'd like to keep a blank template that reflects each contact's information.

   - Click the Save Document As icon and rename the file if you'd like to preserve the current information in the spreadsheet.

   Refer to Figure 21-4 to see where these icons are located on the Library tab toolbar.

   Your final result is shown in Figure 21-8. If you selected the Auto Update check box (Step 7), the information in your spreadsheet changes when you make changes to the contact record information.

Figure 21-8: A merged spreadsheet.

After you save it, you can modify the Excel spreadsheet just like you would modify any of the other documents that you've stored on the Library tab.

Part VI
The Part of Tens

The 5th Wave — By Rich Tennant

"Why, of course. I'd be very interested in seeing this new milestone in the project."

In this part . . .

Every *For Dummies* book has a Part of Tens. By golly, this book is no exception to that rule. Think of this as the icing on your ACT! cake. Here's where I've put some ways to make a good program like ACT! work even better:

- ✔ First I give you a rundown of the coolest new features that ACT! 6 offers.

- ✔ Next, I offer you some hints for improving and beautifying your ACT! layouts.

- ✔ Finally, I show you some nifty add-on products that can improve ACT!'s functionality.

Chapter 22

Ten Cool New Features in ACT! 6

*T*here's always room for improvement and ACT! is no exception. The new enhanced features of ACT! 6 have been so carefully placed into the existing framework of ACT! that many of you maybe haven't even noticed the changes — but the changes are there, quietly making life a little easier for you. For the benefit of you loyal fanACTics out there who upgraded to ACT! 6 from a previous version — and for the new fanACTics, too — I use this chapter to highlight a few changes that I find particularly useful.

New and Very Much Improved E-mail

In prior versions, you had to be content with plain black and white text messages if you wanted to send e-mail through ACT!. Color and formatting features just weren't available; graphical or HyperText Markup Language (HTML) formatting just didn't exist. ACT! 6 now includes the ability to incorporate color and formatting in your daily e-mails. And, with the incorporation of graphical e-mail templates (see Chapter 13), designing e-mail templates that include hyperlinks, graphics, and attachments in addition to any of your contact fields is amazingly easy.

What's that mean to you? It means that you can

✔ Compose your message in blue text, bold and italicize the key points, and include a link to your Web page — all within the body of your e-mail. But that's just for starters.

✔ Send out an e-mail blast personalized with your contacts' names appearing in the body of your message. Wait — there's more!

✔ Make your message look and feel like a Web page (that's what I mean by HTML): Add graphics, borders, backgrounds, or whatever it takes to make your message stand out of the crowd.

Some new enhancements regarding your incoming e-mail include

✔ A right-click menu that's loaded with several cool features. One of these features is the ability to create a new contact from a piece of e-mail.

✔ The ability to attach the e-mail to a current contact to create a history of the incoming correspondence.

Better Integration with Outlook

Outlook is a great program for e-mail; ACT! is a great program for contact management. If you need to use both programs for whatever reason, you'll be happy to know that ACT! 6 has thoughtfully included Outlook users in its new list of features. Previously, you could view your Outlook e-mail addresses from within ACT! but not see your ACT! e-mail addresses from within Outlook. ACT! 6 allows you to view as many as three of your ACT! address books directly within Outlook.

In addition, if you send your e-mail via Outlook, you can still create a history of your correspondence in ACT!. This eliminates the need to keep two different e-mail address books, which means you won't need to update two address books, which means that you won't forget to remember which address book is the most accurate, which means there's less work for you to do, which means you have more time for the beach, which means . . . okay, you get the drift. This feature comes in handy!

Improved Internet Services

ACT! 6 now allows you to surf the Web without ever leaving ACT!. When you install ACT!, your Internet favorites are copied over to ACT!'s Online Favorites menu. When you click one of your favorites, ACT!'s browser opens and allows you to surf the Net without leaving ACT!. Any new link that you add to your browser is automatically added to ACT!'s Online Favorites menu. Chapter 18 has the full scoop on ACT!'s Internet services.

Another timesaving Internet feature is the ability to attach a Web page to a contact. The Web page is attached to a note on the Notes/History tab. Double-clicking the attachment pulls up the Web page even if you aren't connected to the Internet. For example, a vendor might post its latest specials on his Web site; you can refer back to that page as you fly across the country even if you don't have Internet access. Just be careful not to spill your drink on your laptop if you encounter turbulence.

New Contact Lookups by Activity

The larger number of contacts that you're working with, the more likely some will fall through the cracks. The typical ACT! database contains thousands of contacts. That's a lot of cracks to fall through! If you'd like to know which contacts you've reached or touched during a given time period and which contacts have remained untouched — or if you'd simply like to clean up your database by removing the dead wood — the new Contact Activity lookup feature is your friend. Read all about it in Chapter 6. This feature allows you to filter your search to find changes to contact fields, notes, histories, e-mail addresses, sales opportunity information, and activities within any given date range. It also enables you to use those same criteria to isolate those contacts with which you haven't had contact. Figure 22-1 gives you a look at this feature.

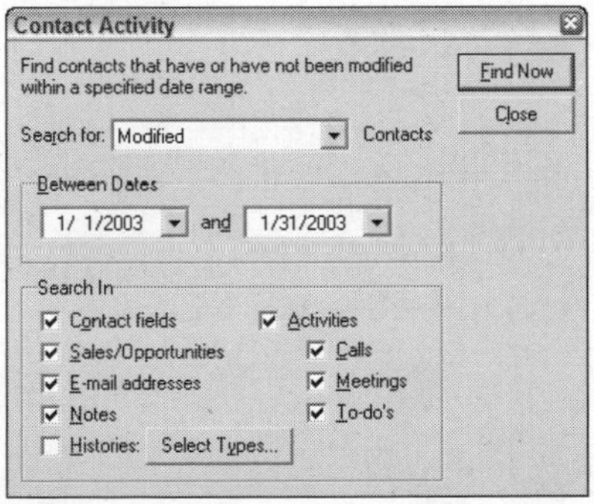

Figure 22-1:
The lookup
by contact
activity.

New Calendar Pop-Ups and Totals

If you're like me, you have days when your calendar becomes so full that deciphering what's happening when becomes very difficult. Calendar Pop-Ups give you all the details that you need about any event without having to click a single calendar item. If you *mouse-over* (that is, hover your mouse over without clicking) any item on your calendar, a pop-up note instantly provides you with pertinent information regarding that activity, including the type of activity, the associated contact, the regarding information, the date, the time, and the first three lines of detail for each activity. Take a peek at Figure 22-2 to see what I mean.

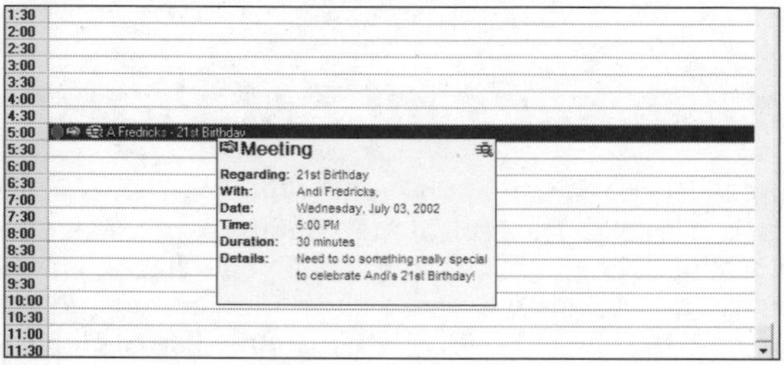

Figure 22-2:
Calendar
pop-ups.

The new Activity Totals gives you an accurate count of the day's activities, including the number of meetings, calls, and to-dos that you have scheduled. You're able to view this information from any of the ACT! calendars as well as from the Task List.

New Annual Event Tracking

One of the reasons why you're probably using a Contact Manager is that you want to be able to keep in touch with your contacts. Sometimes you may want to run a direct mail campaign of some sort, but other times you may want to take a more subtle approach. Many business and professionals like to send birthday and anniversary cards as a way to stay in touch with their contacts. The Annual Event Search fields (see Figure 22-3) make it a snap to look up birthdays, anniversaries, expiration dates, and other annual events.

After you define a field as an Annual Event, you can choose Annual Event from the Lookup menu and retrieve all your contacts with birthdays, anniversaries, or contract expirations within a given date range. You can print a list of all your contacts with birthdays in August; remind yourself to call everyone with an anniversary in October; or create a lookup and send all the contacts in it a renewal notice. In Chapter 6, I give you all the information you need to perform an Annual Event lookup, and I show you how to add an Annual Event field into your database in Chapter 14.

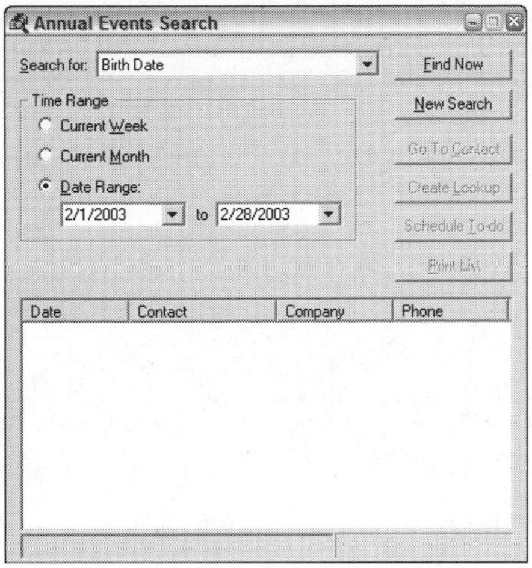

Figure 22-3:
Annual
event
tracking.

The All New Library Tab

There's a new tab in town, and it's called the Library tab because it lets you keep a library of important files. After attaching a file to a contact, you can view or edit that file from within ACT!. Files that can be attached to the library tab include Microsoft Word documents, Excel spreadsheets, or PowerPoint presentations. MapPoint, Adobe Acrobat, and bitmap and JPEG images can also be viewed and edited right from the Library tab.

If you'd like, you can attach the same file to each of your contacts. For example, you might have an Excel spreadsheet that you use for calculating all your quotes. Adding it to the Library tab enables you to generate the appropriate spreadsheet information while you talk to your prospect. One nice feature about linking a spreadsheet to the Library tab is the ability to merge ACT! Contact field information directly into your spreadsheet. In Chapter 21, I give you the full skinny on the Library tab.

Mail Merge Wizard

In Ancient Times prior to the advent of the Personal Computer, we had very little junk mail. In the early days of computing, we still had very little junk mail because performing a mail merge just wasn't that easy. The WordPerfect program achieved great success in the mid-1980s because it revolutionized the way in which we created a mail merge. Even so, the process wasn't what you'd call easy. If you're familiar with WordPerfect, you remember all too well the myriad of functions that you had to memorize to perform even the simplest of tasks; creating a mail merge was pretty much an all-day affair.

The new Mail Merge Wizard that comes with ACT! 6 makes broadcast e-mailing simple even for beginners. The wizard walks you through four input screens, allows you to analyze your responses, and then create your mail merge in seconds. If you think that this sounds good, head to Chapter 12, where you'll find all the pertinent details.

Several Great New Reports

ACT! 6 comes equipped with four brand new reports for you to test drive:

- `CountGroupMem.rep` is a report that displays group information. This particular report shows you the number of primary and subgroups, the name of each primary and subgroup, and the number of contacts in each primary and subgroup.

- `EmailList.rep` is a report that prints out the company name, contact name, and e-mail address of the contacts in either your current lookup or in your entire database.

- `FaxList.rep` works exactly like `EmailList.rep` except that it displays the fax number of each of the contacts in either your current lookup or in your entire database.

- `CallMtgSum.rep` is a report that counts your attempted calls, completed calls, meetings held, and messages left. The report can be filtered by date and/or record manager and can be run for either your entire database or for the current lookup.

These reports won't appear with the other reports listed on the Report Menu; you can access them only by choosing Reports⇨Other Report, and then choosing the Other Reports folder, as shown in Figure 22-4. If you want to modify your Reports Menu so that these reports are more readily accessible, check out Chapter 3, where I show you how.

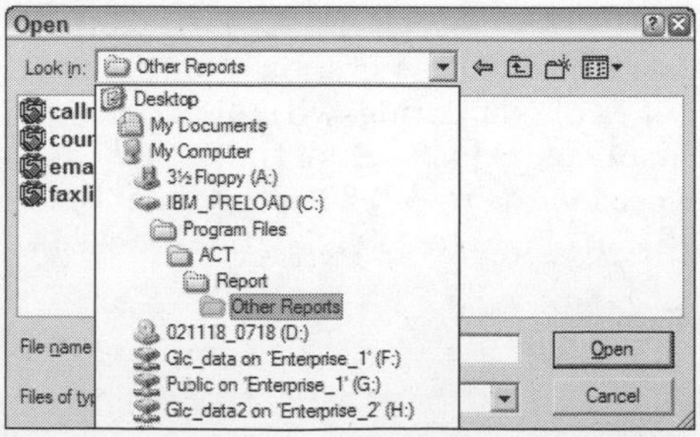

Figure 22-4:
Finding
ACT!'s new
reports.

Cool New Icons and Layouts!

All right, I know it's not one of the more crucial new features, but ACT! underwent a nice facelift with the advent of 6. Although the icons are still located exactly where you would expect them to be, they were updated to give them a slightly more modern look.

The Essentials and Contact Layout layouts were added to ACT! 6. The Essentials layout features a subtle graphic background that's easy on the eyes. The layout also arranges all phone numbers together and all the user fields together on one tab. ACT! 6 also comes with three versions of the Contact Layout layout, each numbered to correspond with your video settings. The 1024 x 768 Contact Layout, which is designed for higher resolution settings, features three columns of information on the Contacts view instead of the traditional two.

Chapter 23

Ten Cool Ways to Customize Your ACT! Layout

*I*n Chapter 15, I show you how to customize your layout. Here I focus on giving you a few additional tips to really personalize your ACT! database and layout. Your goal is to make entering a contact as easy — and fun — as possible.

Some of my suggestions require the use of third-party add-on programs. If you'd like to check out all the suggestions in this section, visit http://techbenders.com/act4dummies.htm.

Figure 23-1 presents you with an illustration for a totally redesigned layout that includes several of the design features that you can use to give your own layout a complete makeover.

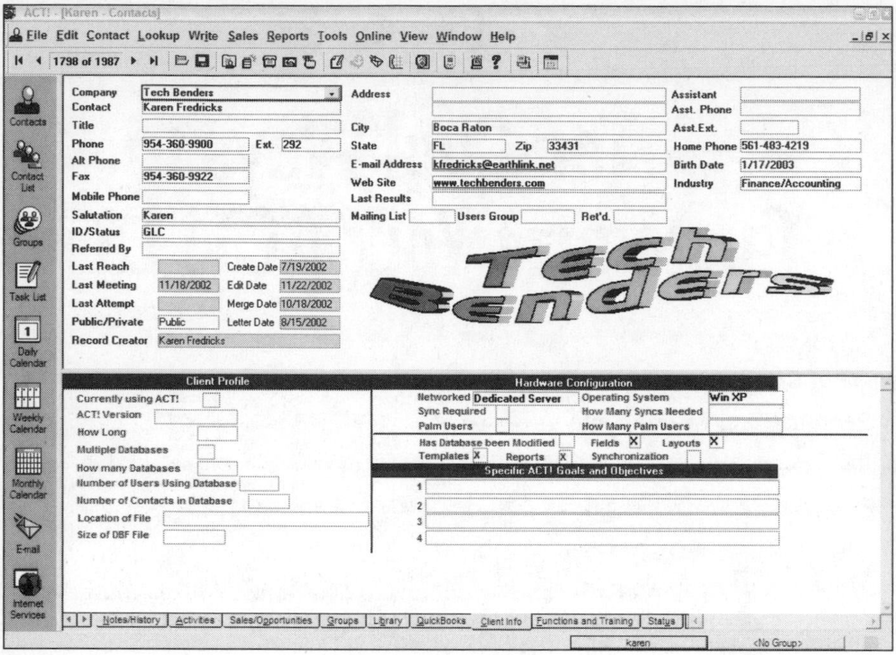

Figure 23-1:
A totally
customized
layout.

Arrange Fields the Way <u>You</u> Want Them

This hint may sound like a no-brainer, but many ACT! users never realize the importance of changing the locations of fields in their layouts. For example, you might choose a layout that has the main business phone number on the top portion of your layout, the home phone number on a different tab along the bottom, and the mobile phone number in a third location. If you're constantly flipping between tabs to find phone numbers, move them together into one strategic place on your layout. Chapter 15 gives you complete instructions for moving the fields on your layout.

Add Color

ACT! comes with a palette of 19 background colors that you can add to your layouts. Many of you may find that these colors tend to be a little too bright, or perhaps they just don't match the décor of your home or office. If you'd like to add your own custom blended color to your layout, you can easily do so by using the Paint program that comes with Windows.

To create your own custom color:

1. **Open Paint by choosing Start⇨Programs⇨Accessories⇨Paint.**

2. **In Paint, choose Colors⇨Edit Colors⇨Define Custom Colors.**

3. **Click one of the basic colors.**

4. **Click the color palette on the right side of the screen if you'd like to refine your color choice.**

5. **Click Add to Custom Colors and then click OK.**

   You will have now landed safely in the main Paint screen.

6. **Click the Fill with Color icon.**

   This icon looks like a miniature paint can.

7. **Click in the middle of the main Paint screen.**

   You should now have a large square filled with the color you chose in Step 5.

8. **Choose File⇨Save to save your artwork as a** `.bmp` **file.**

   If you suffer from short-term memory loss, you may want to jot down the location of this file — it just might come in handy when you insert your color into your layout.

9. **Add your newly created graphic file to your layout as I describe in Chapter 15.**

Add a Logo or a Graphic

There are two ways to add logos and graphics to your layout. The simplest method involves pasting the graphic of your choice on to the body of your layout. You do this by following these easy steps:

1. **Open the graphic file of your choice and copy the graphic by pressing Ctrl+C.**

2. **Open the ACT! Layout Designer as I describe in Chapter 15.**

3. **Paste in the graphic by pressing Ctrl+V.**

4. **Move the graphic by placing your cursor in the middle of the graphic and dragging it to the desired location.**

   You can resize a graphic by placing your mouse on any one of the little squares located along the edges of your graphic, holding down the left mouse button, and then dragging.

5. **Save the layout.**

   You can also add graphics as a background to your layout. This method requires that your graphic be saved as a bitmap (`.bmp`) and that you know the location of the graphic.

The other way to add a graphic to your layout is to use it as the background of your layout (rather than cutting and pasting):

1. **From the Layout Designer window, place your cursor anywhere in the background of the layout.**

2. **Right-click an empty space in your layout and then click Properties.**

3. **Click the Browse button to the right of the Bitmap field area, navigate to your graphic file, and then click Open.**

4. **If you'd like to have the graphic repeat throughout the background, click the Tile option.**

   If you don't select this option, the graphic appears only in the upper-left corner of the layout.

Add Text Boxes

If a picture is worth a thousand words, a text box might just be worth a million. As I mention in Chapter 4, inconsistent data input is a sure-fire way to decrease the productivity of your database. This lack of uniformity is often caused not by lack of knowledge but rather by lack of communication. Adding a text box to your layout is a great way to help users input key pieces of information in the right place and to help organize the groups of data on the layout.

Add Calculation Triggers

Your ACT! layout can be further customized through the use of math triggers. When added to a field definition, a *trigger* can perform a series of calculations based on the contents of several fields and insert the mathematical result into another field. For example, you might input the price, quantity, and sales tax rate into each of three separate fields and have the total purchase amount appear in a fourth field.

In Chapter 24, you can read about the ACT!PAK! program that includes several fairly sophisticated math triggers. If you're like me, your math requirements are limited to "My Dear Aunt Sally" — that is, multiply, divide, add, and subtract — which means that you need ACT! Trigger, a free utility from Practical Sales that performs basic math functions. Both of these programs are available for download from www.act-pro.com.

An example of a relatively simple math calculation using ACT! Trigger is shown in Figure 23-2.

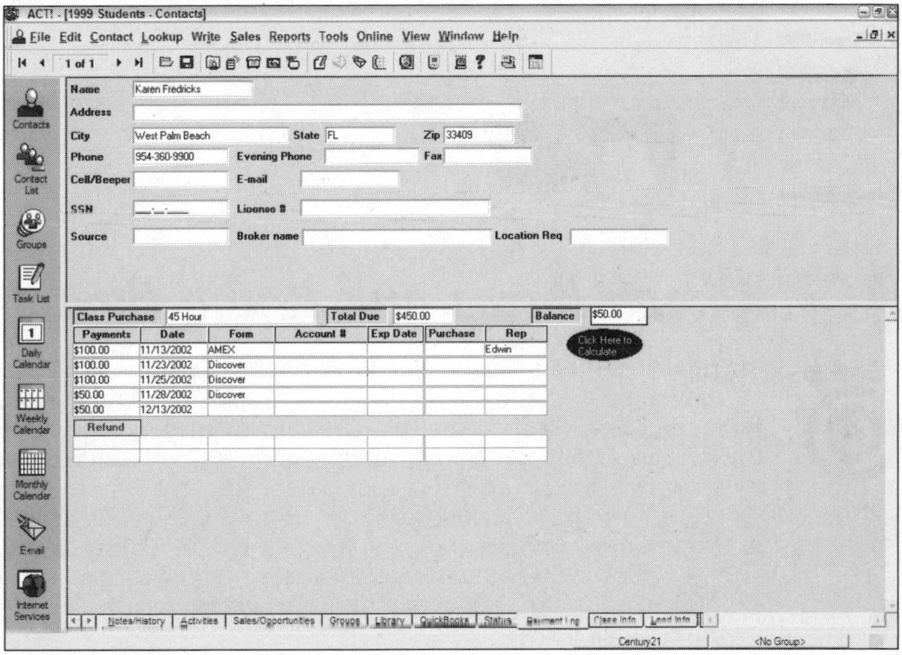

Figure 23-2: Use ACT! Trigger to perform automatic math calculations.

Build a Table

Some of you may find yourselves running out of room on your layouts because you needed to add so many customized fields. As an alternative to the traditional concept of listing all your field labels next to your actual fields, you might consider arranging your fields in table format, as shown in Figure 23-3. The idea here is to save room and make it easier for you to fill in vital information. Chapter 15 tells you how to move your fields to a new location on your layout and to remove field labels.

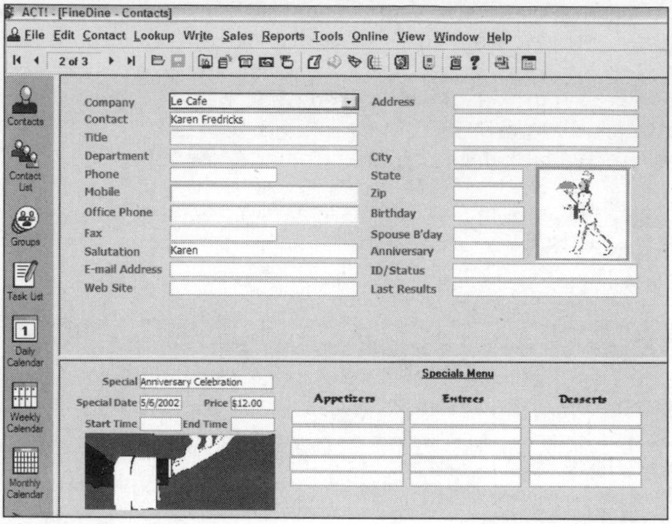

Figure 23-3:
A layout
formatted
as a table.

ACT! Check Boxes and Radio Buttons

The four items that I describe in the remaining sections of the chapter were all created by ACT! add-on developer extraordinaire, Geoff Blood of The New Hampton Group. Geoff very nicely agreed to bundle four of his great programs together especially for the readers of *ACT! 6 For Dummies*. You can find them by going to `http://techbenders.com/act4dummies.htm`.

In Chapter 4, you can see how easy it is to get your contact information into ACT!. Sometimes, you may find yourself needing a lot of fields requiring simple yes or no answers; in this case, it would be even easier to just check off the relevant items.

As their name indicates, check boxes allow you to indicate your preference with a single click on a field. When you add check boxes to your layout, clicking on a field will add an X to the field. If you click on the field a second time, the X will disappear. Think of a very good Chinese restaurant; you can pick as many items as you want from Column A. For example, you may want to track whether a contact is to receive your monthly newsletter via snail mail, e-mail, or fax. Some contacts may wish to be contacted by all three methods. If this is the case, you might want to consider using check boxes.

Another nice addition to your contact layout is the addition of radio buttons. When using radio buttons, you create a set of fields; you may then click one, *and only one,* choice among the selected items. When you click an item, the other fields in the set become blank. This is the less expensive Chinese restaurant; you only get one choice from Column A! In this scenario, your contact could receive your newsletter only by his one preferred method of delivery.

Many of you may be used to thinking of radio buttons as round. However, because ACT!'s Layout Designer only allows for square fields, the radio buttons are actually square.

Auto Fill Fields

Auto Fill Fields automatically loads any number of ACT! fields with values determined by the contents of another field. You simply tell Auto Fill which field holds the independent value (such as the Territory) and which fields depend on that value (such as Sales Rep, Sales Office, and Region). Then provide the series of dependent values (such as CA/Sally Seller/SF/West). Set the exit trigger on each of the determining fields, and you'll never have to fill in the dependent fields again.

A *relational database* is a type of database that stores data in the form of related *tables:* that is, in rows and columns. An important feature of relational databases is the ability to call up information based on data input; I like to think of it as a database within a database. If you entered ABC Company in the referral field, a relational database would automatically generate the company's pertinent information into other fields. But ACT! is not a relational database.

You can set up Auto Fill Fields to work on any number of fields in a database. You can include Group field specifications as well as Contact Field specifications. Specifications are database specific, so you can vary them from database to database, or you can easily copy them from one database to another.

Copy Fields Contents

One of the nicest things about ACT! is its ability to save you time by achieving your goals with less effort. Most of you have discovered various tricks to help speed up the process of data entry. But you may find that you need both a billing and a shipping address, a business and a home address, or a business and a mailing address. And, for most of your contacts, these addresses are identical. ACT! only allows you to copy and paste information from one field to another on an individual basis; this means that if you needed to duplicate the business name, address, city, state and Zip code to another set of fields, you'd have to copy and paste five times!

Copy Fields Contents duplicates the contents of one or more sets of ACT! fields into other sets of fields on the same ACT! record. This can be done through the use of a trigger or as a custom command so that it happens either automatically or at the touch of a button. You can even set up more than one set of fields to be duplicated so that the business information is copied to the home address and the billing address is copied to the shipping address.

Layout Manager

Some of you who have graduated from Dummies 101 may have moved on to creating a second database. And, if you've read Chapter 15, maybe you've even created a layout especially designed to accompany that database. Herein lies the frustration: As you open each database, you must remember to change to the corresponding layout.

Others of you have two or more distinctive types of contacts in your database, each requiring a distinctive layout or set of fields. You may be looking for certain key points of information for your customers, yet this information may be totally inapplicable for your vendors. Again, you may have created separate layouts or tabs, but you must remember to change to the corresponding tab or layout each time that you encounter a different contact type.

ACT! does not provide a link between an ACT! database or contact and an ACT! layout. But ACT! does give you Layout Manager, a nifty little utility that automatically switches the ACT! contact layout based on the name of the database or on a field value on the contact record. After you start the ACT! Layout Manager, every time you open an ACT! database, the layout changes to the layout with the same name as the database. In addition, every time that you move to a new contact, the layout changes to the layout that you specified for that contact.

Now you can clearly and graphically distinguish between your various databases; between prospects and clients, or business and personal contacts; or between any number of different types of contacts.

Chapter 24

Ten Cool Tools to Make ACT! Work Better

*B*ecause we're all different, we use ACT! differently. Although most folks are able to use ACT! straight out of the box, some of you will want to invest in a few ACT! add-on products to increase your productivity. Literally hundreds of add-on products are available for use with ACT!. In this chapter, I focus on ten commercially available products that I think you'll find particularly useful. You can find links to all these products at http://techbenders. com/act4dummics.htm.

Software for Handheld Devices

Who doesn't use a handheld these days? They're great for people on the go — and ACT! lets you take part of your database with you. In this section, I ever so briefly describe three of the most popular pieces of software that link your ACT! data to your handheld.

ACT! Link 2.0

ACT! Link 2.0 is a free download available from www.act.com. The link allows you to sync your ACT! information (including Notes and History) with your

Palm operating system (OS) handheld in just seconds. PDAs using the Palm OS include those manufactured by Palm, Handspring, and Sony. Your ACT! information will be synchronized to the basic fields that are included with the Palm OS.

ACT! Link 2.0 allows you to

- Map basic ACT! and Palm contact fields including phone numbers, snail mail and e-mail addresses, up to four custom ACT! fields, and the ID/Status field

- Synchronize up to ten ACT! contact notes and histories for each ACT! contact with the Palm

- Synchronize by group if you are using the Group feature in ACT!

ACT! for the Palm OS

ACT! for Palm OS is a miniature version of ACT!, which you install on your handheld device that uses the Palm OS. The great features of ACT! for Palm OS include

- Synchronizing over 60 pre-defined fields and 15 custom fields

- Keeping date- and time-stamped notes on each contact

- Searching by company, first name, last name, phone, ID/status, or other fields, including e-mail, city, state, and Zip or use the Palm search

- Customizing the Contact List display just like you do in ACT!

- Scheduling calls, meetings, and to-do items; viewing daily, weekly, or monthly calendars; and clearing completed activities

- Entering new sales opportunities

Trans/ACT! for the Pocket PC

Trans/ACT! for Pocket PC is actually a mini version of ACT! that you install on a Pocket PC device running with Windows CE. Trans/ACT! for the Pocket PC enables you to

- Synchronize all types of ACT! data, including contacts, groups and group fields, notes, histories, sales/opportunities, and calendars.

- ✔ Synchronize all your fields. The customized contact and group fields that you created in ACT! are automatically created on the Pocket PC and downloaded from ACT!.

- ✔ Create your own custom screen layouts for the Pocket PC.

- ✔ Control how much data you download to your Pocket PC. You can synchronize a single group and/or set the number of notes, histories, sales, and activities to download.

- ✔ Use similar menus, buttons, and terminology that you use in ACT!. You don't need to learn a separate system or how to map your ACT! data.

ACT! Link for QuickBooks Pro or Premier

Any of you business owners out there need at least two pieces of software to run your business: database software to keep track of customers and to market to potential customers, and accounting software to help you keep an eye on your bottom line! Unfortunately, a piece of software that does it all often comes with a whopping price tag and a very large learning curve. As a result, maybe you've chosen to use ACT! for your contact management and QuickBooks for your accounting.

If you use both ACT! and QuickBooks, ACT! Link for QuickBooks eliminates the need to enter your contact information into both applications. You can enter the contact information into either ACT! or QuickBooks and then synchronize the information between the two. The ACT! Link inserts a new QuickBooks tab into ACT!, showing all the pertinent Accounts Receivable information for any linked contact in ACT!. This will allow your sales team access to invoice and payment history without sharing the rest of your confidential accounting information.

AutoAdmin II

In Chapter 16, I show you how to properly maintain your database by compressing and reindexing, and I also explain the importance of backing up your database. When you perform these tasks, you must lock your database so that other users can't use it while you're maintaining it — a problematic scenario at best: You either have to kick off users during peak work hours or put off maintenance duties until a better time. AutoAdmin II to the rescue!

ASDS Computer designed AutoAdmin II to be installed on your server and run when your database is not in use. AutoAdmin compresses and reindexes your database, performs backups, and applies all your sync packets while you're off doing your own thing. You can set to run group rules and even to run the required maintenance on multiple databases during various time slots. Best of all, these procedures can all run automatically in the middle of the night when no one is using the database.

AutoAdmin II is available in either a single version designed for users with a single database or a multiple time slot version for those who administer multiple databases.

Corex CardScan

I promised to tell you about ten add-on software products that would help to make ACT! work better, but the card scanner by Corex is actually a piece of hardware. It's such a cool little gizmo, however, that it really deserves mention here. If you have a mountain of business cards waiting for you to input into ACT!, the CardScan 600c color business card scanner is for you!

This miniature scanner can easily fit on a corner of your desk. As you feed in each business card, the software copies the information from the business card into the correct fields of ACT! — with *no* typing on your part.

Crystal Clear Reports

As I mention in Chapter 11, ACT!'s Report Writer isn't the user-friendliest of the ACT! features. In fact, it has several limitations that often prove to be most frustrating when you start to work on more complex reports.

Crystal Clear Reports allows you to run over 35 additional reports and graphs on your ACT! database right from the ACT! Report menu; that breaks down to only a couple of bucks per report. Figure 24-1 shows you ACT!'s report menu after the addition of Crystal Clear Reports.

Crystal Clear Reports offers the following features (not an exhaustive list):

- ✔ You don't have to perform a lookup before running a report. Most of the reports allow you to select your criteria as you're running the report.
- ✔ After you've created a report, you can export it to different formats, including .xlt, .doc, .pdf, and .xml.

✔ You can sort and select many of the reports by Record Manger, which is not always available with the ACT! Report Writer.

✔ You can report on Groups, Activities, Notes/History, and Sales all from within the same report.

✔ If you've customized your reports using Crystal Reports, you can add them to the Crystal Clear Reports menu.

✔ You're able to run reports that aren't available in ACT!, including

- **History Summary Classic by Record Manager:** Sorts calls, meetings, and letters sent by Record Manager (something that ACT! can't do).

- **What Is Missing?:** Finds contacts that have missing information.

- **Contacts Deleted by Record Manager:** Running this report on a shared database shows you which Record Manager deleted which contact records.

- **Task List:** Prints your Task List, sorted by date! Each day includes a summary count of activities.

- **Time Spent:** Prints the time spent (based on duration) for each activity sorted by contact so that you can see how much time you spend with each.

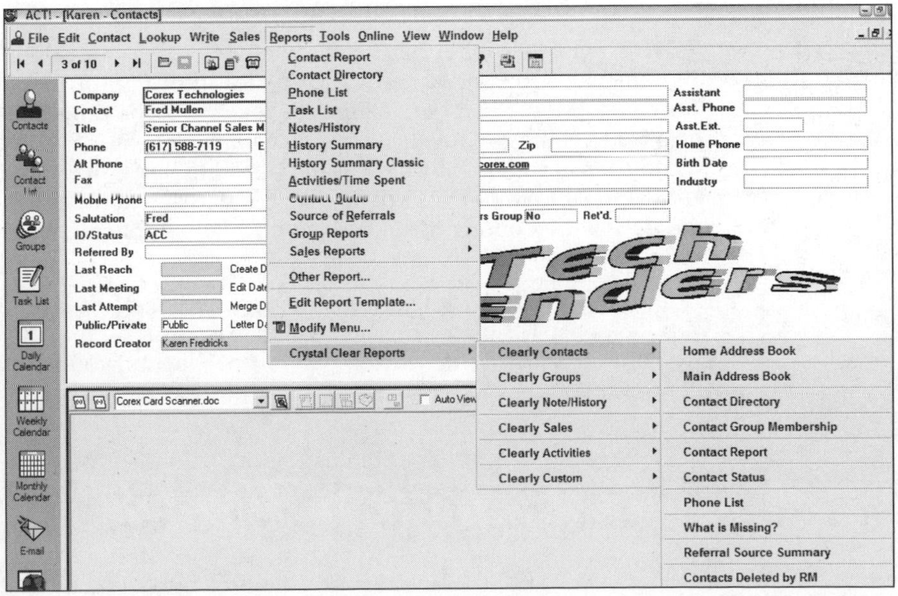

Figure 24-1:
The Crystal
Clear
Reports
menu.

eGrabber Products

Although extremely easy, ACT! data entry is time consuming and very tedious. If you're starting a brand new ACT! database, you probably have hundreds of contacts to add in a hurry — but unfortunately you don't have the time to spend. And after you've created your initial database, you'll continuously enter new information into it. The eGrabber Products can save you tons of time whether you're just building your database or trying to get information from a Web site into it.

- **AddressGrabber:** If you want to get information from an e-mail or a Web site into ACT!, AddressGrabber is what you need. With AddressGrabber, you simply select the contact information, click an icon, and watch as the information is automatically transferred to ACT!. AddressGrabber actually places all the new information into the correct ACT! fields based on clues from the signature block so that name, address, phone, and e-mail information all magically appear in the correct fields.

- **ListGrabber:** Have you searched online directories like the yellow and white pages, club members' lists, or alumni directories and wished that you could get that information into your ACT! database? With ListGrabber, you can. ListGrabber can detect any list format in either documents or online directories (including InfoSpace.com, SmartPages.com, Yahoo! Yellow Pages, and Realtor.com) and enter the appropriate information into ACT! with the click of a button.

- **Web Response Grabber Standard:** Imagine a perfect world in which someone goes to your Web site looking for information. This potential source of revenue likes what she sees and takes the time to fill out the form that you have provided as part of your Web site. The information would then automatically appear in your database. And, if the contact were already found in your database, the existing contact would be updated; if the contact turned out to be a true duplicate, you would be issued a warning.

  Sound too good to be true? Then you probably haven't investigated the Web Response Grabber program, which does exactly that. If your Web site contains a form that is used by your prospects, you need to have this program!

Database Deduplication Wizard

You've been going along your merry way, happily entering contacts into ACT!. Unfortunately, other members of your staff have also been entering some of the same contacts into ACT!. At first glance, you might want to simply look up the duplicate contacts as I demonstrate in Chapter 6 and then delete them as shown in Chapter 4. However, what if one of the duplicate contacts has seven notes and a fax number while the other has eight notes and the correct telephone number? ACT! itself offers no way of merging two contact records. Manually copying and pasting the information between the two contact records is hardly a viable option, especially when this still leaves the possibility of lost data. That's a frightening thought.

Fret no more, for the ACT! Database Deduplication Wizard (see Figure 24-2) merges your duplicate contact records. All your contact data can be merged together on a field-by-field basis. For example, if one of the duplicate contacts has a phone number, and the other a fax number, the resulting contact will have both a phone and a fax number. If both contacts have data in a field, the data from the most recently edited contact will remain. In addition, the notes, activities, sales, and group membership information of duplicate contacts will be combined into a single contact.

Figure 24-2: The ACT! Database Deduplication Wizard.

> **ACT! Database Deduplication Wizard**
>
> **Merge Options**
> What do you what to do with the data on
> duplicate contacts that are going to be deleted.
>
> The ACT! Database Deduplication Wizard keeps the duplicate contact record with the most recent edit date and deletes the other duplicate contact records. The data that is on the contact records that are going to be deleted can either be merged on to the contact record that is going to be kept, or it can be discarded.
>
> The items below that ARE checked WILL be merged to the duplicate record with the most recent edit date (the record that will be kept.)
>
> The items below that ARE NOT checked WILL NOT be merged to the duplicate record with the most recent edit date. These items will be discarded.
>
> ☑ Contact Data (names, addresses, user fields, user defined fields, ...)
> ☑ Notes, Histories, Attachments
> ☑ Activities (calls, meetings, to-dos)
> ☑ Sales Opportunities
> ☑ Email Addresses
>
> < Back   Next >   Cancel

The ACT! Database Deduplication Wizard uses the duplicate matching criteria in ACT! to determine whether records are really duplicates. Chapter 16 shows you how to change the criteria that ACT! uses to identify duplicates.

The Data Cleanup Wizard

If you've been using ACT! for a number of years, have you ever stopped to wonder about the number of notes and histories that reside in your database? Plenty, let me tell you. Obviously, many of these past notes remain crucial to you, but several are likely unnecessary histories that may be negatively affecting your database's performance. I've often seen 5-year-old databases with approximately 5,000 records that have more than 30,000 history items. These historical culprits include

✔ Meetings, calls, and to-do's that you actually deleted from your database

✔ Records of synchronizations that you both sent and received

✔ Lists of contacts that you've deleted

✔ Automatically generated field histories

The ACT! Data Cleanup Wizard (see Figure 24-3) allows you to choose the specific types of notes and histories that you want cleared out of your database, according to the data range that you specify. Before the items are actually deleted, the Data Cleanup Wizard determines exactly how many items will be deleted if you proceed. And (probably because this product was developed by people who spend their time trying to recover lost databases), your database is backed up before any changes are made.

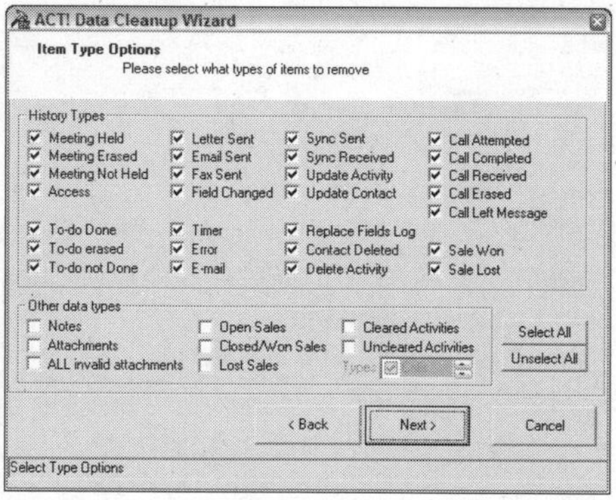

Figure 24-3: ACT!'s Data Cleanup Wizard options.

GoodContacts

"How cool is that?" is the only way I can describe this very impressive program. Building your contact list in ACT! is the easy part; maintaining the quality of the data can be a real pain in the neck. GoodContacts software provides you with an effortless way to obtain the latest information directly from your contacts and automatically updates your ACT! contact database. Here's how GoodContacts works:

1. You select the individuals or groups within your ACT! contact database that you want to verify.

2. The GoodContacts application creates a business card impression for each of your contacts and inserts it into an e-mail template; you personalize the e-mail to your taste and then send out the e-mails.

   Here's the text that I use:

   I am verifying my contact information about you.

   Please take a moment and update inaccurate or missing details by clicking the No - modify link. Clicking Yes - confirm sends me a message indicating that what I have is accurate and complete.

   My contact information is attached to assist you in updating your records; this update is automatic for people who use the GoodContacts service.

   Regards,

   Karen Fredricks

3. Your contact receives the e-mail and clicks the <u>Yes - confirm</u> link if the contact information is correct or the <u>No - modify</u> link if the information is incorrect or something's missing.

   When a recipient clicks the <u>No - modify link</u>, he/she is sent a form to input the new information.

4. Changes made by the recipient are packaged into an e-mail and sent back to you.

5. The GoodContacts software processes the e-mail responses as they arrive in your inbox and automatically updates your contact records with the new information.

The GoodContacts software can also help you to build your database. As new e-mail arrives in your inbox, the GoodContacts application automatically checks whether you already have the sender's e-mail address stored in ACT!. The GoodContacts software then flags any e-mail addressees that are not already in your database. You can then choose to add the e-mail address to an existing contact record or create a new contact record and, at your discretion, send out an e-mail requesting additional information.

Oakhurst Products

I admit it. I am a sucker for late night infomercials and often buy something when enticed by the offer of a freebie. Such is the case with the Oakhurst line of products. These reasonably priced add-ons are like Swiss Army knives — they do a lot of things and come in darn handy!

ACT!PAK!

ACT!PAK! is a set of utilities designed to automate various tasks that you might want to perform from within ACT!. It might just be easier to explain what ACT!PAK! *doesn't* do rather than to list all the neat things that it does do. ACT!PAK! is organized into a series of *deputies*; those that might be of interest include

- **Scheduling Deputy:** Schedules an activity series that includes assignments to more than one member of your staff.

- **Spreadsheet Deputy:** Exports ACT! Contact, Group, Activity, E-mail, or Notes/History data to Excel, Lotus, or Quattro Pro for one or more of your contacts or groups. You can merge specific ACT! fields from a contact record to specific cells in a spreadsheet template.

- **Trigger Deputy:** Allows you to create an automatic trigger to help reduce data entry steps. For example, you can perform math calculations, update a field if certain conditions are met, copy data from one field to another, and assign a unique number to each new record.

OAK!Check!

In Chapter 4, I discuss the importance of entering data in a consistent manner. Unfortunately, this is the real world, and you're dealing with real people. Area codes are constantly changing, and if you allow for a little human error, pretty soon you'll find that your database is a mess. OAK!Check! was designed to be used with less than perfect databases. Think of it as a deep cleaning system for your database.

Here are some cool things that OAK!Check! can do:

- **Automatically compare field entries with drop-downs:** Erroneous contact records are flagged for your attention. You can even build drop-downs (to speed data entry in an existing database) from existing field data.

- **Automatically update out-of-date phone and fax numbers in minutes with a few mouse clicks:** Manually updating area codes is eliminated because OAK!Check! comes complete with an official phone company database of area code changes for North America that's updated every three months.

- **Remove or replace characters from a field:** ACT!'s replace feature lets you replace only the entire contents of a field; OAK!Check! allows you to replace a part of a field.

✔ **Verify that contact record attachments still exist or edit the attachment path to reflect a new location:** If you've been attaching documents to contact records, OAK!Check! ensures that the links to those documents are still working correctly.

✔ **Selectively undelete deleted contacts and their activities:** OAK!Check! restores deleted contacts and the associated activities on a contact-by-contact basis if a compress and reindex hasn't been performed on the database since the records were deleted.

✔ **Update/refresh salutation field to formal, informal, first name/last name:** This feature reads the database contact name field to update the "Dear" field.

Index

• *N* •

Notes

Notes

Notes

Notes

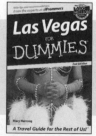

FOR DUMMIES®

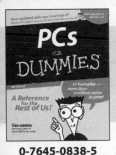

FOR DUMMIES®

Helping you expand your horizons and realize your potential

INTERNET

0-7645-0894-6

0-7645-1659-0

0-7645-1642-6

Also available:

America Online 7.0 For Dummies
(0-7645-1624-8)

Genealogy Online For Dummies
(0-7645-0807-5)

The Internet All-in-One Desk Reference For Dummies
(0-7645-1659-0)

Internet Explorer 6 For Dummies
(0-7645-1344-3)

The Internet For Dummies Quick Reference
(0-7645-1645-0)

Internet Privacy For Dummies
(0-7645-0846-6)

Researching Online For Dummies
(0-7645-0546-7)

Starting an Online Business For Dummies
(0-7645-1655-8)

DIGITAL MEDIA

0-7645-1664-7   **0-7645-1675-2**   **0-7645-0806-7**

Also available:

CD and DVD Recording For Dummies
(0-7645-1627-2)

Digital Photography All-in-One Desk Reference For Dummies
(0-7645-1800-3)

Digital Photography For Dummies Quick Reference
(0-7645-0750-8)

Home Recording For Musicians For Dummies
(0-7645-1634-5)

MP3 For Dummies
(0-7645-0858-X)

Paint Shop Pro "X" For Dummies
(0-7645-2440-2)

Photo Retouching & Restoration For Dummies
(0-7645-1662-0)

Scanners For Dummies
(0-7645-0783-4)

GRAPHICS

0-7645-0817-2

0-7645-1651-5

0-7645-0895-4

Also available:

Adobe Acrobat 5 PDF For Dummies
(0-7645-1652-3)

Fireworks 4 For Dummies
(0-7645-0804-0)

Illustrator 10 For Dummies
(0-7645-3636-2)

QuarkXPress 5 For Dummies
(0-7645-0643-9)

Visio 2000 For Dummies
(0-7645-0635-8)

Available wherever books are sold. Go to www.dummies.com or call 1-877-762-2974 to order direct.

FOR DUMMIES

The advice and explanations you need to succeed

SELF-HELP, SPIRITUALITY & RELIGION

Sex FOR DUMMIES
0-7645-5302-X

Parenting FOR DUMMIES
0-7645-5418-2

Religion FOR DUMMIES
0-7645-5264-3

Also available:

The Bible For Dummies
(0-7645-5296-1)

Buddhism For Dummies
(0-7645-5359-3)

Christian Prayer For Dummies
(0-7645-5500-6)

Dating For Dummies
(0-7645-5072-1)

Judaism For Dummies
(0-7645-5299-6)

Potty Training For Dummies
(0-7645-5417-4)

Pregnancy For Dummies
(0-7645-5074-8)

Rekindling Romance For Dummies
(0-7645-5303-8)

Spirituality For Dummies
(0-7645-5298-8)

Weddings For Dummies
(0-7645-5055-1)

PETS

Puppies FOR DUMMIES
0-7645-5255-4

Dog Training FOR DUMMIES
0-7645-5286-4

Cats FOR DUMMIES
0-7645-5275-9

Also available:

Labrador Retrievers For Dummies
(0-7645-5281-3)

Aquariums For Dummies
(0-7645-5156-6)

Birds For Dummies
(0-7645-5139-6)

Dogs For Dummies
(0-7645-5274-0)

Ferrets For Dummies
(0-7645-5259-7)

German Shepherds For Dummies
(0-7645-5280-5)

Golden Retrievers For Dummies
(0-7645-5267-8)

Horses For Dummies
(0-7645-5138-8)

Jack Russell Terriers For Dummies
(0-7645-5268-6)

Puppies Raising & Training Diary For Dummies
(0-7645-0876-8)

EDUCATION & TEST PREPARATION

Spanish FOR DUMMIES
0-7645-5194-9

Algebra FOR DUMMIES
0-7645-5325-9

The ACT FOR DUMMIES
0-7645-5210-4

Also available:

Chemistry For Dummies
(0-7645-5430-1)

English Grammar For Dummies
(0-7645-5322-4)

French For Dummies
(0-7645-5193-0)

The GMAT For Dummies
(0-7645-5251-1)

Inglés Para Dummies
(0-7645-5427-1)

Italian For Dummies
(0-7645-5196-5)

Research Papers For Dummies
(0-7645-5426-3)

The SAT I For Dummies
(0-7645-5472-7)

U.S. History For Dummies
(0-7645-5249-X)

World History For Dummies
(0-7645-5242-2)

Available wherever books are sold. Go to www.dummies.com or call 1-877-762-2974 to order direct.